THE ENFORCERS

THE ENFORCERS

INSIDE CAPE TOWN'S
DEADLY NIGHTCLUB BATTLES

Caryn Dolley

Jonathan Ball Publishers
Johannesburg & Cape Town

All rights reserved.
No part of this publication may be reproduced or transmitted, in any form or by any means, without prior permission from the publisher or copyright holder.

© Text 2019 Caryn Dolley
© Published edition 2019 Jonathan Ball Publishers

Originally published in South Africa in 2019 by
JONATHAN BALL PUBLISHERS
A division of Media24 (Pty) Ltd
PO Box 33977
Jeppestown 2043

ISBN 978-1-86842-920-2
ebook ISBN 978-1-86842-921-9

Every effort has been made to trace the copyright holders and to obtain their permission for the use of copyright material. The publishers apologise for any errors or omissions and would be grateful to be notified of any corrections that should be incorporated in future editions of this book.

Twitter: www.twitter.com/JonathanBallPub
Facebook: www.facebook.com/JonathanBallPublishers
Blog: http://jonathanball.bookslive.co.za/

Editing by Tracey Hawthorne
Design and typesetting by Catherine Coetzer
Cover by publicide
Proofreading by Paul Wise
Index by Sanet le Roux
Set in Crimson Text

To my family, by both relation and sheer care.

And to those finding their way to good.

Contents

Abbreviations	viii
Map of Cape Town and surrounds	ix
Foreword	xi
Prologue	1
Introduction: When worlds collide	5
1 Apartheid's bouncer blueprint	10
2 Cyril Beeka's rise to bouncer-racket domination	32
3 Enter by blood, exit by death	54
4 Where the dog lies buried	69
5 Strength in numbers: amalgamation	95
6 Money, murder, plots and politics	112
7 Modack makes his move	127
8 Dodging bullets in the City of Gold	151
9 The Eastern European connection	167
10 Friends in high places	181
12 Legacy does not die	192
Notes	198
Acknowledgements	255
Index	258

Abbreviations

ANC	African National Congress
CBD	central business district
CCB	Civil Cooperation Bureau
Core	Community Outreach
DA	Democratic Alliance
IMSI	international mobile subscriber identity
Ipid	Independent Police Investigative Directorate
MK	umKhonto weSizwe
MKs	members of umKhonto weSizwe
NPA	National Prosecuting Authority
Pagad	People Against Gangsterism and Drugs
PSIRA	Private Security Industry Regulatory Authority
SAPS	South African Police Service
SARS	South African Revenue Service
SPS	Specialised Protection Services
TRC	Truth and Reconciliation Commission
TSG	The Security Group
Wecco	Western Cape Community Outreach

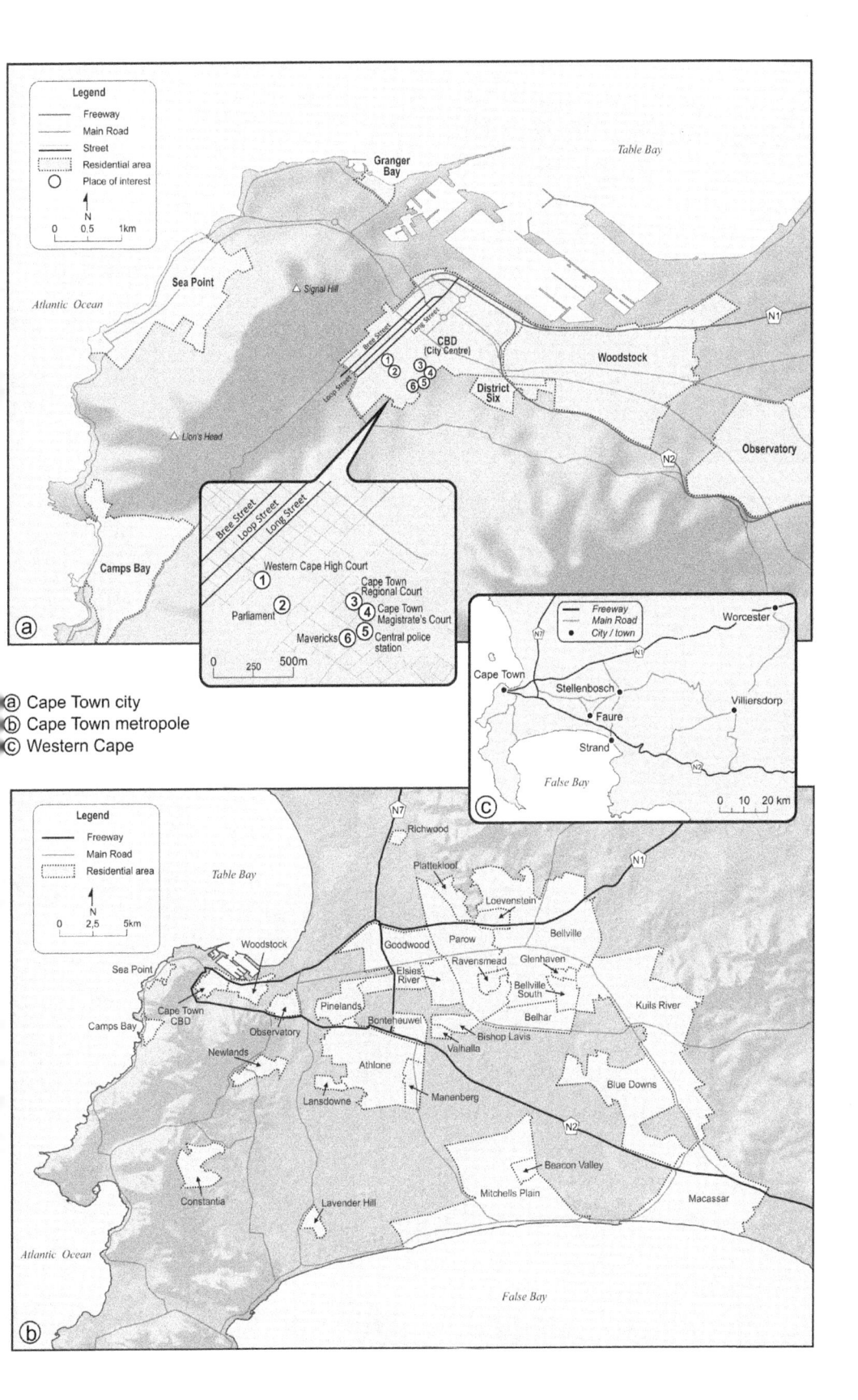

ⓐ Cape Town city
ⓑ Cape Town metropole
ⓒ Western Cape

Foreword

The roots of this extraordinary book go back to 2011, when Caryn Dolley was a reporter on the *Cape Times*.

Caryn was a journalist who could take on any story. But it was the stories about the underworld that drew her from the start and which were to become her main focus as a reporter, first at the *Cape Times* and later at the *Sunday Times*, the *Weekend Argus*, News24 and amaBhungane.

Ours was a newsroom with many talented reporters but Caryn stood out. More than anyone, she could get people to talk to her. People who thought they had decided not to talk to anyone, talked to Caryn. She would go out on a story and bring back to the news editors the interview no-one else had been able to get, with the gang boss, the international mobster, the crooked cop – or the mother who had lost a child.

She would win people over with her quiet manners, her willingness to listen and her integrity. Somehow, people knew they could trust her, that she would respect the anonymity of a source or a promise to keep something off the record, and, most of all, that she would do her best to report accurately. Gang bosses confided in her; whistleblowers trusted her with their lives.

She navigated the peculiar shifting moralities of the underworld without compromising her own ethics as a journalist and a storyteller. She was fearless, as the big powerful men who mistook her diminutive size and gentle manner for weakness soon learned. And she did her research meticulously. Over the years she has doggedly poked and prodded at the underworld, accumulating the wealth of knowledge and the network of contacts which have made this book possible.

Using the 'bouncer wars' in Cape Town's nightclubs as her starting point, Caryn has opened a window onto the world of organised crime. She has stuck her nose into the affairs of some of the most dangerous men in the country, at considerable risk to herself. She has been threatened several times, and for a while had to have personal protection.

To write this book, Caryn has sat through long bail hearings and criminal trials, read interminable court documents, and interviewed gangsters, drug lords, police officers and politicians, to reveal the intricate links between them, and the way the turf battles on the streets of the Cape Flats are mirrored in the turf battles in the carpeted corridors of political power.

Caryn takes the reader from the pumping nightclubs of Long Street in Cape Town's city centre to Johannesburg, which has the reputation of being South Africa's most notorious underworld hub; and beyond, to Serbia in Eastern Europe. Her story ranges from the quiet formality of courtrooms to the luxury hotels where the corrupt meet; and from the bloodstained streets where the gangs rule to government offices and police stations.

It's a story of stolen guns and crooked cops, of lethal games played by politicians, of gangs and gangbusters, of bouncers and drugs and very large sums of money.

It's also the story of what Caryn calls 'the street-level people': the families torn apart by gang violence, the passersby mown down in crossfire, the partygoers caught in a nightclub war – and all the other victims of the crime bosses, the corrupt police officers and the corrupt politicians.

Alide Dasnois
Editor, *Cape Times* (2009-2013)
Winner, Nat Nakasa Award for Media Integrity (2014)
Cape Town, March 2019

'Since the turf war started, patrons are very nervous and the public order in the CBD is under attack. ... [I]t is clear that the safety of the public is at risk and the public order is being disturbed... The problem with these club takeovers and war is that innocent bystanders have been shot.'

– Lieutenant Colonel Peter Janse Viljoen, 31 January 2018, Bellville, Cape Town.[1]

Prologue

It's a Wednesday in March 2017, around lunchtime, in the northern suburb of Parow in Cape Town. Although nearing autumn, it's unseasonably warm, and the sun beats down out of a clear blue sky.

Near-identical townhouses line a wide, treed street. The occasional bark of a dog is the only sound that breaks the midweek suburban peace and quiet – the hum of cars passing on the nearby highway and the gentle rustling of leaves pleasantly combine in this neighbourhood where children can ride their bikes in relative safety.

Suddenly a large, dark vehicle pulls up outside one of the houses – the one with the 'Property for Auction' poster tied to its front gate. Eight burly men emerge, looking suspiciously up and down the street.

Within seconds, four minibus taxis arrive too, and an additional motley assortment of men, some armed with shotguns, pile out. They position themselves along the road in front of the property.

It's immediately clear who's in charge. He's not the biggest man present but there's something about the way he carries himself – nonchalant yet confident, his arms hanging loosely at his sides with his chest puffed out ever so slightly – that sets him apart. He wears a faint goatee and thin moustache, and his fingers are studded with chunky diamond rings.

He walks with a proprietor's air through the gate of the property advertised for auction – for this house does actually belong to him, at least until the auctioneer bangs his gavel.

Some of his men follow him; others remain on the street, watching.

Inside are at least another thirty people, and the goateed man scans the small crowd. He notes that several of them are armed.

His characteristically cocked eyebrows lower and his posture tenses as he spots who he's looking for. It's a strapping, chisel-faced blond man, his expression one of cocky self-assurance. He's laughing at something another man has just said.

The goateed man grits his teeth in anger and resentment: the humiliation of his recent sequestration has been made a thousand times worse by this man, who just this morning bid on and bought another property of his that had gone under the hammer. And here he is again, apparently intent on securing a second bargain at his expense.

The goateed man strides towards the blond man, his men on his heels and fanning out on either side of him. The strapping blond glances up, seems to assess the situation in a second, and without visibly making any move, somehow alerts a posse of men, who quickly whip into place behind and on either side of him.

As the two groups face off, there's a long moment of tense silence. Then one of the blond's henchmen, out on the flank, pulls out a gun and points it menacingly at his counterpart. There's a feeling of electricity in the air.

The goateed man's sidekick doesn't bother to pull his weapon, although it's clearly visible at his waist. Instead, fuelled by bravado and steadfastly refusing to cower in front of a rival, he cocks his head and grins hideously at the gun-wielding heavy. 'Go on, do it,' he goads, his voice barely above a whisper. 'Shoot me.'

The storm breaks, the suburban back yard igniting into a battlefield as the two groups clash.

Jostling, shoving men, throwing punches and kicks, spew into the street. Shouts and thuds fill the air as punches are thrown and blades are drawn; skin is ripped open, flesh is bruised, blood is shed.

The realisation that the longer the melee goes on, the more probable death is, seems to dawn on all simultaneously, and men begin fleeing, some nursing swollen faces, some limping, some awkwardly clutching arms battered by gun butts and barrels. The exodus takes only a few moments, and the leaders of the two groupings are last to leave.

As the blond makes for a waiting vehicle, the goateed man shouts his name and he turns back.

The goateed man points a finger at the blond and says, 'You take what's mine and I'll take what's yours.'

INTRODUCTION
When worlds collide

At night, from a distant and elevated viewpoint, Cape Town sprawls resplendent at the foot of Table Mountain, its lights shimmering and flickering, a conglomeration of tiny twinkling gems.

Zoom in on this mesmerising scene and a raw slice of nightlife emerges. On any weekend evening in Long Street, the city's famous party hub, throngs of bright- or bleary-eyed revellers pack the pavements, young men and women dressed up for a night out, laughing and chatting, pub-hopping, dashing across the roads and meandering down the sidewalks, popping into and out of the restaurants and clubs on this renowned stretch of inner-city one-way road.

Black-clad muscle-bound bouncers stand stoically beneath glowing lights at establishment entrances, alternately frowning and smiling. Informal car guards, some wearing grubby yellow vests, noisily direct metered taxis and private cars moving sluggishly along the street's length, pointing out rare vacant parking bays between bumper-to-bumper stationary vehicles. A few homeless men and women in worn-out clothes weave wearily between the clubgoers.

This lit-up and blaring version of Long Street can ignite a sense of thrill and adventure. But more often than not, the blinking blue light of a police van slices through the merrymaking: a niggling reminder of what's on the other side of this fun façade. For Cape Town has a parallel reality, where nightclub fluorescents and police lights can merge, and the sound of party beats can cover the crack of bullets. It's where the frivolous can meet the fatal.

Beneath the glittering and gritty veneer – a dazzlement of erratically flashing lights, grubby bar surfaces, and sticky dance floors mottled with scuff marks – secrets both decades old and tantalisingly fresh float around Cape Town's nightclubs. What is obviously visible may not be what it seems, and looks really can be deceiving – a fellow clubgoer may be not just another reveller but a state informant, a plainclothes police officer or even a contract killer hired to carry out an assassination.

The city's mostly concealed underbelly crawls with characters from all walks of life, from within the country and from across South Africa's borders, and who all share a lust: for power, for money, for political influence and dominance, for access to intelligence circles. Some harbour dangerous secrets that feed long-held grudges that have grown over the years, continuously sprouting, blooming and producing seeds of mistrust and vengeance.

The Mother City's security turf battles have their roots in pre-democratic South Africa, and branch into the Cape Flats gang wars that have ebbed and flowed since the 1990s. Dotting this landscape are colourful and contentious figures – Yuri 'the Russian' Ulianitski, nightclub-security kingpin and apartheid-state operative (or so it's rumoured) Cyril Beeka, convicted drug dealer Radovan Krejčíř, alleged gangsters Jerome 'Donkie' Booysen and Ralph Stanfield, controversial businessmen Nafiz Modack and Mark Lifman – many of whom have come to a bad end. And constantly making surprise appearances in what are often questionable circumstances are high-ranking members of the South African police as well as prominent people in the ANC and the government.

Cyril Beeka, who had suspected links to all these spheres – politicians, police officers and at least one gang – was gunned down in March 2011. By 2017 Nafiz Modack, a close friend of Beeka's, had become the latest figure identified by police to allegedly be heading up a group hell-bent on taking over control of the lucrative nightclub-security operations in the Western Cape. By September that year Modack and a few others – including convicted cop killer Colin Booysen and an elusive United Kingdom businessman known as Choudhry – were, according to Modack himself, providing security to more than 95 percent of nightclubs in and around Cape Town.

Just five years earlier, however, the situation had looked somewhat different, with a man named Andre Naude, who'd been in the bouncer business since the early 1990s, together with Colin Booysen, Colin's brother Jerome 'Donkie' Booysen, and Mark Lifman running the majority of security operations at nightclubs in Cape Town.

These switches of allegiance and power shifts are common ingredients in an internationally recognised and lethal recipe that has repeatedly been followed in South Africa to brew up intense and reverberating batches of violence. Cape Town's central business district (CBD), the 'city bowl', in particular, has provided the perfect oven for this phenomenon, resulting in the frequent bubbling-over of extreme and often deadly tensions.

The battles to guard Cape Town's nightclub doors centre around bouncers. These strong men are at the literal forefront of nightclub security – but they aren't just visual deterrents to those with untoward intentions. Bouncers represent muscle in underworld circles, which in turn represents power – a critical criminal currency. If you have control of the door of an establishment, you have control of who or what passes through it.

This is where a one-dimensional power struggle to dominate a doorway expands into much broader and more complicated battles.

Money acquired through both legal and illicit activities, including the taking over or hijacking of businesses, drug-trafficking operations, and money made indirectly from the forging of ties between gangs (and illegal trades), can be used to influence or buy off officials in legitimate businesses or within the state – police officers and politicians aren't immune to this, and the greedier an individual, the softer a target they pose. So, for example, cash can be slipped to a cop who in exchange turns a blind eye to illegal dealings. And this is where the murkiness starts – when the legal becomes entangled with the illegal.

The dinginess goes even deeper when state officials start working alongside underworld figures and when top state officials meddle in underworld activities or mingle in underworld circles. It's been happening for many years, and it's made it consistently difficult to unravel whether elements within the state are aiding and abetting underworld figures, or are infiltrating them as part of a greater intelligence-driven plan to ultimately cripple their activities.

Further fuelling confusion is when underworld figures become state informants, thereby 'legitimising' their activities in that they're leaking information to authorities and are thus, in a warped but crucial manner, playing a role in fighting crime.

And sometimes this plays out in reverse, when an initially upstanding state informant or police investigator, rich in highly sensitive and even classified information, becomes an underworld figure. Secret information at their disposal could present itself as a master key able to unlock doors of their choice or as an invisible weapon to force individuals to act on their command.

Duplicitous individuals feed the underworld monster, encouraging it to grow and enabling it to rampantly spread. Key investigating police officers have admitted that for every tentacle chopped off, several more rapidly grow back. This is because these battles aren't simply street fights; they're an integral part of South Africa's invisible, historic and ongoing proxy wars, with individuals and groups secretly acting on behalf of state intelligence agencies. It's this that makes poking or prodding the underworld especially perilous: you could disturb an ever-mutating species from which there is no set form of protection.

Trying to wrangle it from the point of view of law enforcement has profoundly affected the career paths of many cops. Among them are Major General Andre Lincoln, who was ejected from the police and had to fight his way back in; Major General Jeremy Vearey, who helped incarcerate an array of gangsters and headed up several probes into suspected crime kingpins, yet who himself has been the subject of countless claims that he's involved in organised crime; and Lieutenant General Peter Jacobs, who has worked in the intelligence sector, and who was effectively demoted while co-leading South Africa's biggest-ever firearms-smuggling investigation that was closing in on both gangsters and corrupt cops.

These three officers operate in a grimy reality muddied by decades of claims of dirty police officers partnering with underworld figures in order to, among other things, tarnish the reputations of their colleagues to sink their critical investigations.

Combine all these characters who repeatedly crop up in and around Cape Town's clubbing arena for various reasons – gangsters (suspected or otherwise), underworld figures and cops – and season with the inevitable pinch of politics, and you've got a war. It's a war with very high stakes, no parameters, and invisible crosshairs in which anyone can get caught.

CHAPTER 1

Apartheid's bouncer blueprint

Like Cape Town, Johannesburg has a nightclub-security industry that has been gripped by controversy and tainted by violence over the years. The seeds that sprouted bouncer operations in South Africa's city of gold were men from white working-class sports and boxing clubs who were based in Hillbrow, as well as south and east Johannesburg.

'Sharing a background of apartheid-era military service, the bouncers evolved from independent "heavies" into a set of registered private security companies competing for turf and control of the illicit drug trade,' say researchers Mark Shaw and Simone Haysom in a 2016 article on organised crime towards the end of apartheid and Johannesburg's 'bouncer mafia'.[1] 'Changes in the prevailing political and socioeconomic environment of the country during the transition to democracy were reflected in structural changes in the city's night-time economy; this led to the consolidation of the bouncer mafia.'[2]

Elements of this article were nothing new. Back in 1997 the African National Congress (ANC), in its third year of governing democratic South Africa, noted that the National Key Points Act of 1980 had 'created another network of collaboration between the apartheid security forces and the private sector'. 'The militarisation of South African security companies is evident to this day,' the party stated. 'Many senior personnel from the state's security establishment joined private companies on retirement.'[3]

Under the terms of the Act, which enabled the Minister of Police to declare a location critical and in need of special security, hundreds of locations, including mines and factories, had been deemed national key points. 'Owners [of these places] were required to provide and pay for security as well as set up security committees jointly with the South African Defence Force which included recommended private security consultants,' the ANC said. The effects of the legislation, according to the ANC, had included shifting some of the responsibility for so-called national security onto the private sector, and this had resulted in a thriving private-security industry which incorporated aspects of the state.[4]

The situation in Cape Town geographically reflects what the ANC said, in that the proximity of places of law to places where underworld tensions have boiled over is sometimes quite striking – as if dubious private security-related matters have actually spilled over onto state structures. For instance, Cape Town's central police station is situated alongside a strip club, Mavericks; nearby are the Cape Town Magistrate's Court and the Cape Town Regional Court.

Within walking distance is the Western Cape High Court; if you sit on the steps leading up to its entrance and look straight ahead, you can see a portion of the well-known and popular Long Street in the CBD. Two roads running parallel to Long – Loop and Bree streets – are also home to many establishments that make use of private security.

Finally, Parliament is sandwiched between the Cape Town central police station and the Western Cape High Court.

While the reignited nightclub-security takeover of 2017 was by no means limited to the centre of Cape Town, several violent incidents played out there, unfolding right under the nose of the police, practically on the doorsteps of three courts of law and literally around Parliament – South Africa's legislative core.

But this has been happening for decades.

In their article, Shaw and Haysom linked the Johannesburg bouncers to crimes including extortion and drug trafficking, as well as to politics – and to two individuals in particular. 'There was a political imprint to their operation, both to the security services of the apartheid state and later to the security institutions of the new democracy,' the researchers noted. 'Figures in the bouncer mafia were connected to Ferdi Barnard and the Civil Cooperation Bureau (CCB) and later involved in the notorious assassination of Johannesburg mining magnate and ANC funder Brett Kebble.'[5]

On 27 September 2000, Ferdinand 'Ferdi' Barnard, the apartheid-era murderer of anti-apartheid activist David Webster, testified in a Truth and Reconciliation Commission[6] amnesty hearing. He had joined the South African Police Force in 1976, he said, and had worked in various units, including narcotics, until 1984, when he was sentenced to twenty years 'due to murder and other offences'.[7] His effective jail time, due to some sentences running concurrently, was six years, and he was released on parole after only three years behind bars.

Around 1987 he joined the notorious CCB, a government-sponsored death squad during the apartheid era that operated under the authority of Defence Minister General Magnus Malan. His next employment, eighteen months later, was with the Directorate of Covert Collection, which involved the gathering of intelligence.

Barnard testified that what both the CCB and the Directorate of Covert Collection 'wanted, and were intensely interested in from the very beginning ... were ... my criminal contacts, my contacts in the criminal underworld, the networks that I had due to my contacts as a policeman, the informers that I had handled'.[8]

Barnard detailed what he needed to do to worm and connive his way into the heart of underworld operations. 'To effectively penetrate criminal networks in places where it would matter – and I'm not talking about your average mandrax merchant because they're a dime a dozen – to infiltrate persons who had actual access, firstly to establish yourself in a convincing manner, you would have to do illegal things necessarily, there would be no way in which such persons would trust you if you just told them a story or tried to con them. That is not the way it worked. Secondly, unfortunately it is the case that when one is with such persons ... one would be tested... so you would have to be prepared to go the extra mile.'[9]

Barnard, who admitted to using cocaine – a drug that's still closely associated with the underworld – testified about being involved in private security and further acknowledged entering into corrupt transactions with police and being involved in brothels. His testimony was eerily prophetic about what unfolded in Cape Town's underworld decades later; these aspects – claims involving drugs, private security, corruption and cops – and others, including violence, were nearly all the same components causing ructions in Cape Town's underworld in 2017 and 2018.

'At the same time of my involvement with ... the brothels and the porn palaces and the escort agencies, and the nightclub life that I led, I also established private systems by which I was the head of security of eight or nine nightclubs, brothels and perhaps five or six casinos as well,' Barnard continued. 'I placed the bouncers there, I visited the places daily, I addressed security problems, conducted sensitive investigations, I paid off the police who had to be paid off to prevent police raids. I identified the crooked cops, I gave them their monthly pay.'[10]

Barnard seemed to have drawn up a blueprint of how bouncer operations in South Africa were to be conducted, and his activities and those he mingled with became part of an enduring formula consisting of three key factors: security of nightclubs being headed up by an individual, bouncers being placed at doorways, and corrupt cops. Indeed, this bouncer-operation blueprint crafted under apartheid by a criminal cop working for that regime was still being followed years later under a democratic government. This implies that certain elements of corruption segued seamlessly from one government to the next and were still at play decades into democracy.

Through his testimony, Barnard revealed a startling fact: that he'd started committing crimes only after joining the police; that state service had transformed him from cop into criminal. For Barnard, the lines at some point blurred, then disappeared: 'I led two lives, one was the life of a criminal, the other was the actual life that I had, and at a certain point there was no more distinction for me,' he said. 'I will admit readily today that I committed crimes which had absolutely nothing to do with politics.'[11] Trying to explain how and why he led 'a life of violence', Barnard said, 'I live in the nightclub life, I am a night person. I went through the bouncer wars; since I left matric, I cannot stay out of a nightclub. I have been stabbed, I have stabbed people. I have ended up in hospital after assaults on me, attacks that you cannot believe. My whole body full of stitches, and in the process, I have also injured people in a violent way, yes, sometimes in self-defence and sometimes in fighting.'[12]

Nearly two decades later, what Barnard described was to become history repeating itself, but with new characters filling the roles left vacant by those murdered or ousted in power shoves.

Barnard also provided deep insight into still-festering politically rooted tensions among cops. When he'd been in the police, the ANC was a banned party, as was its armed wing umKhonto weSizwe (members of which were referred to as 'MKs'), so these groupings operated underground.

Barnard admitted that he'd used his drug-fuelled nights in clubs and escort agencies as a front to conceal military-intelligence activities. 'I tasked people within the criminal underworld to move in on MK members who had been identified, to establish contact with them, to make friends with them. I established a prostitution network where prostitutes were tasked with long-term and short-term plans,' Barnard testified.[13]

For example, prostitutes would lure MKs to stay in a flat where they would be plied with alcohol and drugs, their conversations would sometimes be recorded and drugs would be planted on them.

Another plan would be for a woman to tell a targeted MK she needed to fetch something, like drugs, in a certain place, and would ask the MK to drive around the block while she did this. 'The man wouldn't know that he would be driving a stolen car, and perhaps there would be a gun that was planted in the vehicle. The police would pick him up ... He would be directly incriminated in an offence without even being political, his bail would be refused or opposed and, in that way, we would disrupt MK activities,' Barnard explained.[14]

This aspect of Barnard's testimony is important because MKs and ANC intelligence operatives would later, after apartheid was abolished, be absorbed into the police, and some of them would head up investigations into the very underworld realms in which Barnard had been involved. These tenuous dynamics between former MKs, ex-ANC intelligence operatives, apartheid-era cops and suspected underworld operatives still exist, and Barnard's testimony therefore provides critical context for later investigations into figures associated with the nightclub-security industry.

And, of course, his words hint at some of the reasons for enduring tensions involving police officers who were former MKs, who headed these probes after the fall of apartheid.

Parts of Ferdi Barnard's testimony echoed and wove into the experiences of a Western Cape police officer, Major General Andre Lincoln. While Barnard and Lincoln worked as police officers under very different regimes – Barnard operating under apartheid and Lincoln under democracy – both worked undercover in the same dank realm of the underworld. But while Barnard got lost in it, Lincoln insists that his life was nearly ruined by those meant to be serving democratic South Africa alongside him – his own colleagues.

Lincoln is one of three high-ranking police officers from the Western Cape involved in deep underworld investigations who have felt unfairly treated by their senior colleagues, because of what they believe they were uncovering and therefore could potentially expose, as well as because of political perceptions about them. The other two are Major General Jeremy Vearey and Lieutenant General Peter Jacobs; all three have resorted to legal action against some of their bosses and co-workers because of how they've been treated.

Their similar backgrounds provide critical context in trying to understand shifts and tensions in policing in the Western Cape and nationally and, because the underworld involves so many claims against cops, it helps in understanding how internal police friction may affect underworld happenings and vice versa.

The Lincoln saga spans decades and is a case, if he is to be believed, of the absolute betrayal within policing that fertilised some of the first roots of state capture[15] in this country as a democracy, and it involves the names of an iconic president, an Italian crime kingpin and several government officials.

Lincoln comes across as a kempt, courteous man with a steady demeanour and an old-school air, but some who've associated with him in the past claim that this is put on. This could be sour grapes due to investigations he's conducted or dissatisfaction stemming from a belief that Lincoln has never been held properly accountable for crimes or deceitful deeds he allegedly committed.

Before 1994 and under apartheid, Andre Lincoln was involved in underground umKhonto weSizwe activities as an operative for the ANC. His official role was later that of deputy head of the party's Department of Intelligence and Security in the Western Cape, and one of his clandestine duties was to infiltrate the structures of the then-South African Police's Security Branch (also known as the Special Branch),[16] a notorious unit known for torturing those who opposed apartheid.

The full impact of Lincoln covertly keeping tabs on Security Branch members would only later manifest fully, because spies and their targets all went on to become part of South Africa's shiny new police service in the democratic era after 1994.[17] While this should have meant that any clandestine cat-and-mouse operations officially ended, these seem to have unofficially continued.

In 1995 Lincoln became a member of the National Intelligence Coordinating Committee tasked with identifying and neutralising threats to the South African public, and was also involved in the integration of umKhonto weSizwe members into the police. This is where the friction went from rubbing to grating – the amalgamation wasn't a smooth process, given the radically differing political beliefs and allegiances of the people involved, and this created lasting divisions within the police. 'On both sides there was mistrust, and in certain instances hostility ... we came from opposing backgrounds and we just didn't trust each other when it came to the way forward within the new service,' was how Lincoln put it.[18]

During this tumultuous time within the cop service, in 1995, a police inspector approached Lincoln with a document containing classified and explosive claims, including that a head of the police's organised crime unit, Neels Venter, and a cabinet minister, Pallo Jordan, were on the payroll of high-flying Italian businessman Vito Roberto Palazzolo, then believed to be the sixth-highest-ranking member of the organised-crime group Cosa Nostra.[19]

Granted a South African permanent-residence permit in 1993 (despite Italy wanting his extradition at the time – Mafia association is not a crime in South Africa), Palazzolo had settled in Cape Town.[20] He and his wife owned Hemingways, a city-centre club that was popular with Cyril Beeka and former Hard Livings gang boss Rashied Staggie.[21]

Major General Andre Lincoln outside the Western Cape High Court on 24 April 2017. Lincoln launched a R15-million civil claim against the Police Minister because he believed colleagues had orchestrated criminal charges against him in the 1990s. Picture: Caryn Dolley, News24

These ties to nightclub-related matters linked Palazzolo to several other controversial characters, one of them reportedly a Serbian criminal wanted by Interpol and also based in Cape Town, and who may have been involved in a number of murders that played out in the 1990s.[22] (Connections between Serbian criminals secretly staying in South Africa and local underworld suspects endured and years later culminated in a spate of shootings.)

On 11 June 1996 President Mandela appointed Major General Lincoln to head what became known as the Special Presidential Investigative Task Unit, intended to look into the striking claims about Palazzolo's relationships with state officials. The task force was set up, according to Lincoln, so that it could basically operate separately from the police, with members reporting directly to Mandela, Deputy President Thabo Mbeki, or newly appointed national police commissioner George Fivaz.

Lincoln faced the daunting task of leading a unit consisting of members whom he could trust implicitly and who were to investigate highly sensitive and dubious dealings during a tense time in the police and in the country – and at a time when the Western Cape was a National Party-controlled province[23] and 'the hierarchy of the South African Police in the province consisted mainly of white Afrikaner males of the old order'.[24]

Aside from investigating Palazzolo, members of Lincoln's investigative unit were tasked with infiltrating the Cape Town underworld. Operation Intrigue was a secret project 'functioning in a covert manner gathering secretive or confidential information on its main targets through surveillance and infiltration of the criminal underworld operating around the nightlife of Cape Town, most of whom were connected to police officers operating on the ground.'[25] Lincoln was, therefore, in a fresh democracy, probably investigating gang-boss informants who'd been handled, or were still being handled, by apartheid-era cops. (Handlers are effective and invisible puppetmasters, secretly guiding their informants on how to operate, and exchanging information with them.)

To get close to those he was probing, Lincoln said he concealed his true motive, creating a 'legend', or guise, and went to the nightclubs frequented by the subjects of his clandestine investigations. For those who didn't know him or what he was up to, Lincoln would have come across as a club trawler (which is how some sources still view him). In this way Lincoln probed, among others, Palazzolo, Beeka, Ulianitski, Rashied Staggie and Moroccan national Houssain Taleb, better known in bouncer circles as 'Houssain Moroccan'. 'All of them [whom I was tasked with probing] were connected to the criminal underworld, to the nightlife in Cape Town, and to police in Cape Town,' Lincoln claimed.[26]

Rumour had it that Andy Miller, a former key figure and negotiator in the South African Police Union, was Beeka's handler

Italian businessman and alleged Mafia member Vito Roberto Palazzolo. Picture: *Sunday Times*

for some time in the 1990s. Beeka's possible link to Miller is intriguing and hints at why Beeka is widely suspected of having been an informant for the Security Branch – a 1995 article in the *Mail&Guardian* said that a well-placed source alleged that the South African Police Union was actually created by apartheid-era police generals with ties to the Security Branch, which was vehemently denied by the union's spokesperson at the time.[27] (The union, a non-profit organisation, was created in 1993 to protect the rights of police and other law-enforcement officers, and its membership consists largely of cops.[28])

In a 1995 radio interview that same year Miller's mindset about South Africa's fresh police service under democracy was revealed. He stated that 'people with no education, no formal qualifications, and with no police history in the police force have come out of the bush, and the government says, "Thank you. You are a major or a colonel."... These are political appointments. This is not affirmative action. We are going to take a strong stand, and if we have to take action on this point, then that is what we are going to do.'[29]

Heading an elite team of investigators who were looking into high-profile indivuals was no easy task for Andre Lincoln. In a 1996 letter to his bosses outlining the stumbling blocks he faced, he expressed 'great concern' about 'the fact that it would seem as if there is a concerted effort by certain members to harass and sabotage the efforts of this investigation'.[30]

Then, in 1997, Lincoln's investigative team was dealt a severe blow when the *Mail&Guardian* ran an article saying that the Mandela-mandated unit was effectively a rogue unit which was under investigation on the instruction of George Fivaz.[31] The details of the article mirror more recent claims of rogue units operating in South Africa's police and revenue services – claims widely believed to have been concocted to protect high-flying politicians, including former president Jacob Zuma, involved in overwhelmingly suspected corruption.

'[The article] clearly indicates that certain members of the South African Police Service [SAPS] with very devious intentions have passed on information to the press with the intention of discrediting the unit and its members. This newspaper report and the continuous radio reports over the weekend have blown a considerable part of our investigation as well as putting the lives of the unit members, our agents and sources in danger,' Lincoln noted in a letter to Fivaz two days later. 'One of this unit's best sources was attacked ... at a nightclub and while he was beaten up it was clearly told to him by his attackers that they now know what he and Director Lincoln are busy with ... It is very clear that certain elements in the SAPS are becoming scared of the results of our investigation and that they are now trying to go all out to shut down this unit.'[32]

But if Lincoln had been looking for support from Fivaz at that point, he was out of luck. The police commissioner wrote back saying that he felt Lincoln's letter indicated 'a total lack of respect' and contained false accusations. 'The style of the letter is furthermore arrogant, and I intend to direct that Departmental steps be taken against [Lincoln],' Fivaz noted.[33]

Lincoln nevertheless pushed ahead with his investigations, uncovering, for example, a police officer attached to the commercial crimes unit who was allegedly involved in counterfeiting and fraud; and, in a probe in conjunction with the American Secret Service, a racket in which counterfeit US dollars, matric certificates and university degrees were being printed in the police head office in Pretoria.[34]

Much more shockingly, however, Lincoln said that his unit took over an investigation, which had previously been put on ice and which he believed had been covered up, into a brazen assassination plot of which Nelson Mandela was the target. The killing was meant to have been carried out at Mandela's inauguration as South Africa's first democratically elected president in 1994. Lincoln said the investigation into this was reopened against fierce resistance, and even though a handcrafted rifle suspected to have been the intended murder weapon was found under a policeman's desk in Pretoria, the probe later again hit a dead end and amounted to nothing.[35] If this is true, Nelson Mandela's potential murderers have never been brought to account.

By 1998, as a result of the Lincoln investigations, and allegations that Cyril Beeka had tried to get Lincoln to see that a case against Palazzolo was dropped, there were warrants of arrest out for Beeka and Palazzolo. This put a strange spy-versus-spy spin on the situation: Lincoln, at that point an undercover state official in terms of nightclub-underworld investigations, was probing, among others, Beeka, a suspected intelligence operative.

Beeka, and whoever was backing him, had the upper hand, however, staying a step ahead of the reach of the law and never being convicted of the crimes of which he was accused in relation to club-security matters.

Lincoln, on the other hand, got entangled in legal troubles. His worries about sabotage relating to the probes he was conducting appeared not to be unfounded – his investigations collapsed because he was suspected of being corrupt and working with the very person he was meant to be investigating, Palazzolo, and this meant that fellow police officers investigated Lincoln and pushed for criminal charges to be instituted against him.

Lincoln believed that a former senior policeman, Leonard Knipe, who at the time was tasked with probing Mandela's investigative unit and who said he had no personal agenda against Lincoln, was among the cops used to tarnish his (Lincoln's) image because he was investigating high-ranking police officers.[36] In effect, if Lincoln is to be believed, he was one of the first-ever victims of state capture in democratic South Africa.

In July 2002 Lincoln's colleague Jeremy Vearey, who by this stage also felt sidelined within the police for reasons of his own, weighed in on what was happening. He told veteran Cape Town journalist Tony Weaver that he believed that apartheid-era police officers had a 'gut hatred' towards himself and three other ex-managers of the ANC's Western Cape Department of Intelligence and Security, including Andre Lincoln, and were sabotaging their investigations. These investigations included in-depth and clandestine probes into underworld figures including Vito Palazzolo, as well as others who had 'worked as apartheid sanction busters, helping procure guns and oil'.[37]

Vearey had said that around sixty of the ANC's Department of Intelligence and Security operatives in the Western Cape had been absorbed into police and intelligence units after apartheid. He cautioned that some individuals couldn't be allowed to push ahead with old agendas in a new environment. 'We didn't want this fight, but they have continually attacked us through a series of actions designed to destroy our integrity as professionals, and to render our actions and persons suspect. ... The police force has to be cleaned up,' he said.[38]

Lincoln had also said that cops from the country's former regime were targeting him and Vearey because of their political backgrounds: 'This is about who we are, it is about the antagonistic history between former ANC operatives and former apartheid-era police.'[39]

Vearey further alleged that hatred for former ANC intelligence operatives stemmed from various police branches, but mostly from members of the former Security Branch's covert unit. These members, Vearey said, were based in the offices of provincial and national police commissioners, and had also been absorbed into crime intelligence and the detective services. If this were true, it would mean that the democratic police service was liberally peppered with apartheid-era moles who still shared the previous government's mindset and objectives.

Andre Lincoln was criminally charged, and in November 2002 he was convicted of 17 of 47 charges.[40] A year later he was unceremoniously discharged from the police.

Lincoln was certainly not defeated, however, and he fought fiercely for his honour, flat-out denying that he'd worked with Palazzolo and launching legal processes to prove what he insisted was his innocence. In 2009 he was acquitted on all charges in the High Court, and the next year he was reinstated into the police.[41] This meant that the ousted officer was back in a working environment with some colleagues who were suspicious about his past, given the claims levelled against him and which had seen him forced from the police in the first place.

Eight years later, the fallout of the Lincoln saga was still playing out – in 2017, in a civil matter in the Western Cape High Court, Lincoln claimed R15 million in damages from the Police Minister for what he termed a 'malicious prosecution'.[42] Lincoln's testimony throughout this civil case is what lifted the lid on details of decades-old investigations, claims of corrupt activities carried out by apartheid-era cops, and twisted political plots and ploys within South Africa's police. He claimed, for instance, that the then head of the National Intelligence Service in Cape Town, Arthur Fraser, had asked him (Lincoln) not to contest a cabinet minister's testimony in a 1998 legal tussle, and also to plead guilty to some of the lesser charges he was facing, in exchange for a guarantee that he wouldn't spend more than a week behind bars.[43]

Lincoln's civil claim was dismissed in September 2017, on the grounds that he'd failed to prove that he'd been framed by his colleagues, but he pushed on and appealed this.

In April 2018 Fraser, then head of the country's State Security

Agency, was transferred to the Department of Correctional Services following a formal complaint by the Democratic Alliance (DA) that he had run a parallel intelligence network about seven years earlier. (Fraser countered that the investigation into himself was a political conspiracy to tarnish his reputation and that of the ANC.)[44] And in October 2018 Major General Andre Lincoln succeeded in the majority of his appeal, and the cop mandated by Mandela was effectively vindicated. This was massive because, following more than two decades of grating up against his police bosses in legal skirmishes, Lincoln's victory added a hefty dose of integrity to the many claims he'd made, starting with the one that his colleagues had framed him.

That same month, Lincoln was appointed to head up a newly created anti-gang unit, which was backed by President Cyril Ramaphosa, in the Western Cape. For the second time in his career he had the overt backing of the president of the country. This promotion meant that for Lincoln the wheel of fortune had certainly turned.

The anti-gang unit faced problems, nonetheless, with the South African Police Union initially claiming that it was operating illegally. This prompted the ANC in the Western Cape to accuse the union of colluding with the opposition party, the DA, to destabilise the unit.[45]

Another possible problem that again seemed to involve internal cop squabbles also arose, with questions swirling about as to whether another Western Cape policing unit, the Major Offences Reaction Team, was actually working against the anti-gang one. The Major Offences Reaction Team, an 'integrated provincial intervention comprising specialised provincial units ... targeting specific identified station precincts' was intended 'to ensure swift response to serious offences' reported in thirteen Cape Town police stations, including Bishop Lavis, Mitchells Plain and Cape Town central. The aim, according to Western Cape provincial head of communication, marketing and liaison, Brigadier Novela Potelwa, was 'to complement existing policing initiatives thereby reducing serious and violent crimes plaguing certain parts of the Western Cape'.[46]

And Lincoln's elevation within the Western Cape police also caused dormant friction to stir once again involving those who vehemently believed he was involved in underhanded dealings. In November 2018 the police ministry approached the Supreme Court of Appeal for special leave to appeal to try and overturn Lincoln's High Court victory of the month before, and so the two-decades-old battle dragged on.

Around the same time, some sources linked to the club-security industry grumblingly told the author that they still believed that Lincoln had covered up dirty dealings, including working for the state and then switching over to working for Palazzolo, as well as paying a woman with state money for activities totally unrelated to his work. And, indeed, in Lincoln's successful 2009 appeal case, the woman in question – an 'agent' referred to as 'PI8' – testified that she'd 'had an affair with [Lincoln] and spent most nights with him in the hotel and that that was the reason for her being with [him] – it was not because she was working for the unit'.[47]

The woman's testimony, although found to be false, seemed to tally with the claims that surfaced late in 2018, of Lincoln having been in a relationship with a sex worker and paying for her living expenses with state money. And this in turn is similar to what Ferdi Barnard had testified to at the Truth and Reconciliation Commission, about he and military intelligence having used sex workers to target members of umKhonto weSizwe. The 2018 claims made against Lincoln therefore had a whiff of apartheid-style military-intelligence operations about them.

Over the years, some of the same figures have repeatedly cropped up in underworld ructions. This applies equally to police officers and investigators, in that some of the same cops have been probing the same phenomena and some of the same individuals for years, with history often repeating itself.

Underworld happenings and clampdowns in Cape Town have become like a pebble tossed into murky water, unleashing a ripple effect involving police investigators and suspects, and while these ripples of activity are intense at first, they eventually weaken into smooth-surfaced murkiness again, with all those involved settling back down into the muddy depths.

As more figures enter the shadowy waters of organised crime, rivals become more wary and new allegiances are formed, and this in turn means various types of organised crime are brought together and start interweaving to create intricate overlapping criminal circles – perlemoen (abalone) poaching and the trade in crystal methamphetamine (locally known as tik), for example; or the illicit tobacco and steroid trades. In these symbiotic and burgeoning relationships, one crime feeds off the other and various crimes become intertwined, so if a perlemoen-poaching kingpin is murdered, say, retaliation may not necessarily target a rival perlemoen poacher or an obviously related grouping, but may be aimed at a figure who's an associate of the kingpin but involved in another illicit trade. This is how a cycle of violence is sparked, and how one murder creates a ripple effect of attacks and counterattacks that may appear unrelated at first glance, but which are all intertwined.

Unravelling these knots of crimes is a problem for the police, especially since some of the criminal activity may actually be facilitated by their own colleagues: when one cop tugs at a thread trying to loosen up information, a corrupt cop may be pulling at the same thread on the opposite end, preventing this.

In September 2017, for example, then Police Minister Fikile Mbalula warned the country's Crime Intelligence unit that he was going after 'rogue elements' within it, and the following year national police commissioner Khehla Sitole told Parliament that the country's Crime Intelligence had been 'infiltrated'.[48]

Police were therefore going after their own and, more specifically, were targeting operatives meant to be gathering intelligence to be used to fight crime, but who were instead possibly using secret information to further crimes; and who may additionally have been planting fabricated details in the public domain to taint some state figures and detract from what their puppetmasters were up to.

The country's intelligence structures were exposed as severely compromised to the point that an extreme overhaul of the state intelligence arena was on the cards, partly because of suspected unshakeable political factionalism within it.[49] Thus, at a critical

Nafiz Modack during an interview with the author at the Cubana bar and restaurant in Green Point, on 21 September 2017. Picture: Caryn Dolley, News24

time on a clock of crime, South Africa's crime-intelligence arena was deeply tainted, with suspicions of turncoats operating within it, compromising any decent work being done by clean operatives.

This highlighted the deep mistrust within the state's crime-fighting bodies and presented itself as another breeding ground for underworld operations, because this is where underworld activities settle, sprout and thrive: in the ruts and ditches of wariness and bickering between policing units and individual officers, proxies and intelligence agents.

The combination of underworld figures, and crooked cops and their clean counterparts, had played out in the late 1990s in Cape Town, when Vito Palazzolo and Cyril Beeka were under investigation, and it played out again two decades later, when Nafiz Modack became prominent on the nightclub-security scene in 2017 and 2018. 'Cyril Beeka, at the time, did exactly what Nafiz Modack is doing now,' is how one cop described the parallels.[50]

Modack and Beeka were, in fact, friends, and in the years running up to Beeka's 2011 assassination, the two were said to have become closer, with some sources suggesting Beeka had become Modack's mentor. Photographs of Modack at Beeka's gravesite on the anniversaries of Beeka's murder have surfaced, suggesting he pays tribute to the underworld kingpin annually on that day.

Modack, like Beeka, was also widely rumoured to be an intelligence agent. 'It appears from detailed billing and phone conversations that Nafiz Modack has contact with various high-ranking police officers, in excess of ten. It's unknown if Modack is a registered informant. Informants usually have one handler,'[51] is how Hawks Lieutenant Colonel Peter Janse Viljoen put it. Speaking to the author, however, Modack denied being an agent.[52]

What is undeniable is that Modack, like Beeka, has links to high-ranking state officials, including police officers. In May 2017 the author discreetly photographed Nafiz Modack in the upmarket

One&Only hotel near the V&A Waterfront in Cape Town, with Northern Cape police commissioner Risimati Shivuri. Later in 2017 another photograph surfaced, this time of Modack with Prince Mokotedi, the controversial head of the Hawks in Gauteng, apparently taken in a restaurant in the N1 City Mall in Cape Town in July of that year. (The Hawks was the name given to the Directorate for Priority Crime Investigation, established in 2008 as an independent directorate within the SAPS.) And in 2017 yet another photograph was leaked, of Nafiz Modack and former president Jacob Zuma's son Duduzane sitting together in the One&Only hotel – Modack had told the author that he'd looked after Duduzane whenever Duduzane was in Cape Town.[53]

But it was Modack's ties to police officers that piqued the interest of some cops. Information suggests, said Lieutenant Colonel Janse Viljoen, that 'there is a possible corrupt relationship between Modack and some of these high-ranking police officers and that he plays a role with them to further his criminal activities. He plays them off against each other.'[54]

Modack countered, 'The state has made much of the fact that I am well connected with senior policemen whom they suggest are corrupt. I deny this allegation ... Because of the regard in which I am held by most of my community, I often receive information which can be used by the police. I have always been available to members of the police force.'[55]

And so the decades-long cycle of claims and counter-claims about an underworld embedded with cops whirred on.

CHAPTER 2

Cyril Beeka's rise to bouncer-racket domination

In the late 1980s and early 1990s, revellers in Cape Town's CBD were mainly white (given South Africa's political climate at the time and the lingering grip of apartheid), and while there were plenty of pumping pubs and clubs catering to a vast clientele, there were also a few standout upmarket establishments, all situated within an approximately two-block radius in the heart of the city. These lured in moneyed partygoers who arrived in fancy cars with the heady anticipation of a good time. Convertibles and Harley-Davidson motorcycles crowded the parking places at these venues; 'It was a carnival vibe with music and all lit up,' recalled one reveller.[1]

Perhaps not surprisingly, robbers and gangsters targeted clubgoers in the Cape Town city centre. After all, they presented soft targets – they carried cash and their guard was often down because they were there to enjoy themselves, not to watch their backs. So the doors to nightclubs such as Hemingways, the Magnet, the Piano Room, Rita's and Comic Strip were guarded by groups of muscle-bound men – the nascent nightclub-security industry. It was on this business that a group headed by Cyril Beeka set its sights.

There are so many tales about Beeka that it's difficult to separate fact from fiction, the man from the myth. Aggravating this is that there were (and are) those who loved him, and spoke about him with affection and pride; and those who didn't, and had only disdain for him.

One source notes that Beeka went into nightclub security only to get a foot in the door of the drug trade, working on the orders of the then boss of the Americans gang Neville Heroldt, better known as Jackie Lonte,[2] who in turn was believed to have been working for members of the apartheid police's CCB.

But others vehemently dismiss this version of how Beeka came to be a dominant force in private security, insisting he was against drugs. If Beeka had links to any gang, some say it was the Americans' rivals, the Hard Livings, which was then under the leadership of Rashied Staggie. Making nice with this gang meant that Beeka wouldn't have had to worry about Hard Livings gangsters (who operated in the city centre, carrying out mostly petty crimes) dominating town or coming up against him.

Born in Wynberg in Cape Town in 1961, Cyril William Paul Beeka was one of six brothers and two sisters. 'He had a very strict and God-fearing upbringing,' according to a source close to him.[3]

At some point the family moved to Faure, an area between Stellenbosch and Strand, where their father was said by the source to have worked at a correctional facility for boys. Their mother worked in administration at the University of the Western Cape. The family later moved to Kuils River.

Beeka became a top martial artist, earning his Springbok colours and a reputation as a physical powerhouse. 'Nobody argued with him for too long,' the same source said.[4]

Under apartheid, Beeka was reportedly linked to military intelligence, and later moved into other intelligence structures involving figures linked to South Africa's new ruling political party, the ANC. The tale goes that on the command of Jacob Zuma, Beeka had, in the late 1980s, helped to ensure the safe passage to Zambia of Dirk Coetzee, a commander of a covert police unit under apartheid, after he'd admitted to the existence of the unit – actually a hit squad based at Vlakplaas, a farm outside of Pretoria. Coetzee said 'dirty tricks' emanating from this unit 'involved stealing cars, murdering people, harassing people, anything but legal police work or as indicated in the directive'.[5]

In the early 1990s, Beeka started a small city-centre outfit known as Pro Security, created, according to police officer Jeremy Vearey, as a front for the apartheid Security Branch.[6] Beeka initially had no office, working instead out of his bakkie and a little Portuguese-owned shop in Cape Town's city centre, situated on the corner of Bree and Riebeek streets, which sold snacks including pies and chips, where he kept a book in which he recorded logistical matters – Beeka would often pop in to this shop and grab a samoosa to nibble on while he jotted down something.

One of Beeka's close friends had a Rhodesian ridgeback which the friend started bringing into the Cape Town city centre at night to help Beeka patrol the doors of certain clubs. Beeka and this friend were remembered by a source as sharp dressers – they both wore waistcoats specially made for them from buffalo hide.[7]

Beeka soon had five men working with him; and at some point, two more dogs, a boxer named Satchmo and a rottweiler named Michka, and then yet more dogs and dog-handlers, were added to the team. 'The quickest way to get rid of a skollie is to set a dog after them – not to bite, but to chase and scare them.'[8] Clubland legend has it that Satchmo and Michka wore specially made green-and-yellow jackets.

As more high-end clubs opened, drawing in celebrities, politicians and high-profile foreign patrons (some of whom went on to pop up on police radar), Beeka's client base grew steadily. And while Beeka's bouncers pitched in to maintain peace when scuffles broke out between booze-addled partygoers, some police officers and other sources have a very different and more extreme view of Beeka's reign – that he ran an extortion racket, forcing establishment owners to use his services or he would send men, including a group of martial-arts experts originally from Morocco, to trash their venues. Andre Lincoln, then a director in the police service, was among those of the view that Beeka and those working for him were deeply entrenched in organised crime.

In a 1997 letter from Lincoln, who at that stage was investigating Beeka and other suspected underworld figures, addressed to (among others) the deputy president, Thabo Mbeki, Lincoln referred to Beeka's company, Pro Security, 'which consists of South Africans and Moroccans [sic] security guards who patrol the city centre's club lands. Beeka, together with his staff at Pro Security, fulfil the role of soldiers for the criminal organisation, Cosa Nostra'.[9]

One former club owner from Cape Town recalled how, some time in the mid-1990s, he was paid a visit by two or three Moroccan men linked to Beeka who, once seated in his establishment, which was full of patrons, casually told him they could offer him prime security services at a specific fee. 'If you said no, they would later send in people to pickpocket patrons, harass them and trash the place, and that's how they got you to use them.'[10]

Beeka apparently expanded his business, moving from club security to rich businesspeople whom he similarly forced to pay him 'security fees'.[11] In 1998 he formalised his security-focused business and took on partners such as Yuri 'the Russian' Ulianitski and Jacques Cronje. (Rumour had it that he also employed Dirk Coetzee and Coetzee's son at some point.)

Cronje, tall and broad shouldered, is a key player who has recently resurfaced on Cape Town's private-security scene. He has a very long track record in the security industry, counting among his many clients the children of former Human Settlements Minister Tokyo Sexwale.[12]

Cronje has firsthand experience of how South Africa's bouncer industry started shaping up in Cape Town in the 1990s. He'd got involved in nightclub security while he was a Permanent Force member – a physical training instructor – of the South African Navy, he said, working part time as a bouncer at various clubs around Cape Town.

Cronje met Beeka around 1997 and the two formed an alliance. 'He [Beeka] approached me and said he would like us to start a security company together ... where we can provide bouncers or doormen at certain venues,' Cronje explained. 'I took the decision [at] that time to basically take the opportunity to go into the corporate world and leave the navy, seeing that maybe I could make some extra money.'[13]

That's when Beeka and Cronje established Wide Props, trading as Pro Access, as a close corporation.[14] In March 1998 they registered the company with the Security Officers Board, which later became the Private Security Industry Regulatory Authority – a wise move, as in later years the non-registration with the private security regulator of the company Specialised Protection Services (SPS), as well as the registration of bouncers, presented itself as a massive problem.

Cronje became Pro Access's security salesman, going around to clubs 'selling the concept of we are going to provide them with a security service and that our company is above board [sic]'. He said that because, at the time, people were unhappy about the clubbing environment 'and they wanted us to clean up certain clubs and restaurants', Pro Access was generally well received.[15]

But then things started changing. In June 1998, as gang wars

Veteran bouncer Jacques Cronje, his wrists cuffed, waits for police officers to lead him away following his arrest for alleged extortion in Cape Town on 15 December 2017. Picture: Caryn Dolley, News24

raged across Cape Town, a police armoury in Faure, situated between the winelands town of Stellenbosch and the seaside town of Strand, was broken into and a mass of weapons – including 32 rifles, 12 shotguns, 49 grenades and several rounds of ammunition – was stolen.

Rashied Staggie was among those arrested for this high-level burglary.[16] An integral character on the Western Cape's gang landscape, Staggie's name has popped up repeatedly in terms of nightclub security, although he has never been convicted for such matters. One of his co-accused alleged that they had planned to use the weapons on members of the controversial organisation People Against Gangsterism and Drugs (Pagad) who were constantly attacking them[17] – Rashied's twin brother Rashaad was infamously set alight and murdered during an anti-gang and -drug march in the

Rashied Staggie (left) with one of his 'guards' a week after the slaying of his twin brother by armed vigilantes. Picture: Adil Bradlow/PictureNET Africa

suburb of Salt River in 1996. Four men linked to Pagad, including its chief coordinator, Abdus Salaam Ebrahim, were arrested for the murder, but were later acquitted.[18]

Pagad has a rich and highly controversial history rooted in the Western Cape. Formed in 1995,[19] it had a predominantly Muslim membership, and while it didn't start out with criminal intent, it became known for extreme acts of vigilantism aimed at drug dealers and gang bosses.

A 2001 report on Pagad for the Centre for the Study of Violence and Reconciliation said that the group's development couldn't be viewed as a master plan being carried out by a group of Islamic radicals, but rather as a culmination of several issues. It said the state viewed Pagad initially as an anti-crime movement, but later as an illegitimate violent vigilante organisation, until, in 1998, it was labelled an 'urban terror group'. 'In line with these altered perceptions, the state's response to Pagad has changed from constructive engagement with it to demonisation and repression.'[20]

There have been constant rumours over the years that national intelligence agents were involved in the grouping.

On 25 August 1998 a popular venue at the landmark V&A Waterfront, Planet Hollywood, was bombed. Two people were killed and about two dozen injured in the explosion.[21] And on 1 January 1999, a pipe bomb exploded in a car park at the Waterfront, the second in what became over a dozen bombs to go off around Cape Town in the ensuing twenty months.[22]

In 2000 in the Cape Town Magistrate's Court, Pagad's Abdus Salaam Ebrahim claimed that Cyril Beeka and Dirk Coetzee were behind one of the two Waterfront bombings. He said that a lawyer representing Pagad had been told by a prosecutor that information at their disposal revealed that Beeka and Coetzee were responsible for a bomb at the Waterfront because they wanted to control security in the area.[23] Ebrahim's allegations don't seem to have been taken seriously, however.

Nonetheless, Beeka's name was around this time increasingly linked to serious allegations of crime. In May 1999 Beeka, together with Germany national Olaf Reucker, and Robert McBride,[24] who at that stage was an official in the Department of Foreign Affairs, were charged in connection with the assault of an escort, Jennifer Morreira, in Cape Town. The Director of Public Prosecutions in the Western Cape ultimately decided not to proceed with the matter,[25] but three months later, Beeka again found himself in hot water with authorities, and this time the allegations were even more serious.

Cronje described what happened as an 'unfortunate incident' at the Saigon Bar, one of the clubs serviced by Pro Access. Beeka, Cronje and another man, one Hamid Zouity, had been walking in the Cape Town city bowl following a meeting, when, as Cronje told it, 'we saw a commotion down the road in Loop Street at one of our clubs. The bouncer was in trouble. We went to the venue to go help the bouncer. A lot of Chinese men, sailor men was around him. [sic] We had to go into the mob.'[26]

According to Cronje, he, Beeka and Zouity managed to get the bouncer away from the mob and the fight ended.

But a few days later a 23-year-old sailor, Hong Laing Wu, who'd been involved in the brawl, died of head injuries.[27] Cronje said members of the Scorpions, then an elite crime-fighting unit in South Africa, investigated the incident, and this culminated in Beeka, who had initially fled the scene, and others – Cronje, Zouity, Patrick Plum, Muktar Fall and Ruben Myburg – being arrested.[28]

It was during the subsequent court proceedings that a curtain was pulled back to reveal hundreds of suspected crimes hinting at widespread brutality and violence, and it became clear just how overwhelming and dominating Beeka's security operations had allegedly become. According to a news report at the time, police investigators alleged Beeka's company would 'send in a gang of Moroccans to cause havoc in a new club, then offer the services of its bouncers to sort out the problem. Dogs and baseball bats were used in the attacks at clubs.'[29] These acts of violence were 'linked to illicit dealing, and/or possession of drugs, illegal firearms, theft, extortion, and acts aimed at influencing state officials'.[30]

More than 400 crimes, including 262 assaults and 10 attempted murders, had been reported to police in Cape Town over three years, but these cases had all been closed because the complainants feared what would happen to them if they pursued the incidents.[31]

All charges relating to the death of the sailor were eventually withdrawn, but by then Beeka had resigned from Pro Access and started working for RAM Couriers, a South African courier company, overseeing national security operations.

'Although resigning from [Pro Access] … he was still directly involved with the company, just more in a quiet way,' Cronje said.[32]

Over the ensuing years nightclub security stabilised somewhat, but the underworld was continuously beset by violence and one by one individuals in this broad arena started being targeted and killed off.

In an early case, the victim suffered a unique fate. In September 2005 the death in Johannesburg of mining magnate Brett Kebble, who was linked to former national police commissioner Jackie Selebi in a dodgy relationship involving money in exchange for certain favours from the then-top cop, shook up the shadowy circles in which he moved.[33]

The Kebble saga had all the makings of Hollywood blockbuster – good guys, bad guys, a shootout and a startling plot twist. It emerged that Kebble had apparently orchestrated his own killing in an 'assisted suicide'; and the trigger men, boxer Mikey Schultz, and bouncers Faizel 'Kappie' Smith and Nigel McGurk, were granted indemnity from prosecution in exchange for testifying for the state.[34] Controversial convicted drug dealer Glen Agliotti was granted a discharge in the case.[35]

And back in Cape Town, a reverberating murder was carried out on 21 May 2007 – Yuri 'the Russian' Ulianitski was assassinated, and his 4-year-old daughter Yulia was also killed in the attack. His wife Irina survived several gunshot wounds.

Ulianitski and a close friend, Igor Russol (sometimes referred to as 'the other Russian'), had a shared history of how they got involved in the Mother City's nightlife – a path that led to 'the Russian's' murder.

Russol and Ulianitski had a titanium-strong bond – their mothers had been friends before they were born, both in 1972. They'd lived next-door to each other in Odessa, Ukraine, played together as children and were in the same grade at school. Their paths forked only when Russol joined the army at the age of 18, while Ulianitski joined a sports university in Russia where he excelled in sambo, a form of Russian martial arts.[36]

Ulianitski's father, an engineer, travelled to South Africa in the late 1980s and started working in Cape Town. Ulianitski followed his father about eighteen months later. In Cape Town, the young Russian took up kickboxing, and it was through this that he met Houssain Taleb, better known as Houssain Moroccan, as well as Beeka.[37]

Taleb, slightly built but powerfully compact, arrived in South Africa in 1994 as a martial-arts fighter and started training local boxers.[38] By 1996 he was involved in the security industry, where he remained for more than two decades; in the late 1990s he did a stint with Beeka and Cronje's Pro Access.[39] Taleb had a conviction for discharging a firearm in a municipal area stemming from a fight between several individuals that unfolded in the Cape Town suburb of Claremont in 1999.[40]

Ulianitski's connections with Houssain Moroccan and Beeka resulted in his foray into bouncer operations in Cape Town. Recalling how Beeka and Ulianitski had once operated, a source said, 'Ja, they'd walk around with long coats and long guns.'[41] Ulianitski also had business dealings with Mark Lifman.

Many years after Ulianitski, Russol followed his path and immigrated to South Africa, where he dabbled in (among other things) the 'gentlemen's club' industry in Cape Town. He too got involved with nightclub-security figures, including Lifman, and his name repeatedly surfaced as tensions in the industry flared and dissipated.[42]

In the same year that Yuri 'the Russian' was killed, 2007, Beeka's shadowy connections to government became more obvious when he accompanied Moe Shaik, a seemingly close ally of Jacob Zuma's who went on to head South Africa's Secret Service, to the ANC's national conference in Polokwane. Beeka was reportedly there as security.[43]

Years later, a Hawks investigator was questioned in court about why Beeka had at times been in the company of Moe Shaik. The investigator said there were rumours that Beeka was working for national intelligence but that the National Intelligence Agency had denied this.[44] These rumours added weight to an unofficial theory that Beeka worked for a parallel intelligence structure with ties to top politicians.

It was also apparently around this time, in 2007, that Beeka was introduced to a man whose name slowly but surely became synonymous with intelligence-driven plots: George 'The Butcher' Darmanović. The two met in Johannesburg and hit it off.[45] Several sources pointed to Darmanović as having been involved in a parallel, or rogue, intelligence structure too. Rumour had it that he was nicknamed 'The Butcher' because his father, who was said to have acted as a bodyguard to Serbia's king at one stage, had decades before run a butchery in Johannesburg where Darmanović was also taught how to cut meat. The nickname became even more significant because of firearm licences and firearms Darmanović later procured.

Darmanović had apparently got involved with South Africa's Security Branch before democracy but at that stage was dabbling in drug use; these habits of his had to be addressed before he could be deployed in earnest as an intelligence operative.

After apartheid, Darmanović, who at some point worked as an intelligence agent on a contract basis for the state, worked closely with various people in the South African government, and while some said he had the best interests of the country at heart, they also said he had a dark side.[46]

Meanwhile, Pro Access under the leadership of Jacques Cronje continued expanding operations, and by 2010 was rendering services to about eighty clubs and restaurants around Cape Town.[47] Cronje, who had by then developed a significant drug habit,[48] met

Czech national Radovan Krejčíř: a prison cell couldn't confine his reputation nor could it silence him. Picture: Thys Dullaart 06/07/2007 © *The Times*

with Beeka at the restaurant Mariner's Wharf in Hout Bay, where they discussed his drug problem. Beeka organised for a personal trainer to help him get his health back on track.

Cronje badly wanted to get out of the nightclub-security industry, but Beeka persuaded him otherwise. 'We had another follow-up meeting where I basically said to him I want to not be a part of the underworld or nightclub industry,' Cronje related years later. 'I want[ed] him to buy me out. He said "no… I want to keep you. I need you for the face for the business." Then I stayed on.'[49]

In mid-2010 another murder rocked underworld circles – in May the 'king of sleaze', Emmanuel 'Lolly' Jackson, the colourful owner of the Teazers chain of strip clubs,[50] was assassinated in Johannesburg.

Cyprian national George Louca was arrested for the killing and extradited from Cyprus four years later to stand trial. He claimed it had been Czech national and prolific criminal Radovan Krejčíř who'd pulled the trigger on Jackson; and he put Cyril Beeka at the scene. Louca also fingered Major General Joey Mabasa, a Gauteng Crime Intelligence boss who was later investigated for his links to Krejčíř and parted ways with the police.[51] The month after making these claims, in May 2015, Louca died of lung cancer while still in custody.

In South Africa in recent years, a few names from other countries have cropped up as powerful kingpins of organised crime, but none more so than that of Radovan Krejčíř, who has managed to dig his fingers deeply into several criminal situations and act as a powerful puppetmaster of some influential police officers.

Having operated mainly in Johannesburg, he's given the city the reputation of being South Africa's most notorious underworld hub. But Krejčíř is also closely connected to several figures in Cape Town, and his name is therefore a toxic glue firmly connecting underworld activities in these two major urban centres.

Born in what was then Czechoslovakia (today's Czech Republic) in 1968, Krejčíř was a flamboyant man with a weakness for beautiful women, but his first love is, reportedly, money. 'Radovan Krejčíř comes from money… Nothing gets in the way if he wants to make money,' is how one source put it.[52]

Krejčíř faced multiple legal battles and criminal charges in his home country, where he'd been convicted of fraud and blackmail. While in custody there in 2005 he managed to escape and eventually, after much country-hopping, he arrived in South Africa in April 2007.

Arrested at OR Tambo International Airport in Johannesburg and detained for extradition to the Czech Republic, where he was wanted for conspiracy to commit murder and fraud, his life over

Mark Lifman (right) chats to his attorney William Booth as he leaves the Bellville Magistrate's Court on 9 February 2018 following his arrest for allegedly pointing a firearm. He subsequently took legal action against police for the arrest, which Booth claimed was unlawful. Picture: Caryn Dolley, News24 the next decade was the stuff of a Hollywood movie plot. He was released from custody then hauled back to prison, was allegedly tied to several murders, was the target of an assassination attempt, was associated with some of South Africa's most prominent underworld figures as well as top police officers, rang up more criminal convictions, including kidnapping and attempted murder, and was allegedly involved in a few plots to escape prison.[53]

On New Year's Eve in 2010 Cyril Beeka and Jacques Cronje were together once again, and Beeka told Cronje that Krejčíř, as well as Mark Lifman, Andre Naude, and the two Booysen brothers, Jerome and Colin, were planning to amalgamate all nightclub-security companies to form one massive security body. 'He also said to me [that] he wasn't too happy with the closeness of Colin [Booysen] and Mark and Radovan, that he was going to have a meeting with Jerome Booysen regarding this,' Cronje said.[54]

By that stage, Beeka had managed to stay clear of courtroom dramas and legal wrangles for several years, but he hadn't shaken the image of underworld figure in the police's mind – the cops' organised crime unit in Gauteng was investigating him for murder, drug trafficking and illegal diamonds.

Although Cronje and Beeka kept in touch by phone following the New Year's Eve they spent together, they never saw each other again.

On Monday 21 March 2011, Dobrosav Gavric, a convicted Serbian hitman going by the alias Sasa Kovacevic, drove Cyril Beeka to a restaurant in Green Point, Cape Town. Leaving the Audi they'd been using in the restaurant parking lot,[55] the pair left in a BMW X5 and drove to Jerome Booysen's home in Belhar. Booysen, who had previously worked for the city council, was supposedly going to advise Gavric on renovating a venue in Parow and getting municipal approval to run it as a sports betting shop and a pawn shop.[56]

After their meeting with Booysen, Gavric and Beeka drove away. When Gavric stopped the vehicle at a red traffic light, two people on a motorbike pulled up next to the car and fired seventeen bullets into it. Beeka was struck in the chest, arms and head, and died on the scene; Gavric was wounded but nonetheless apparently tried to chase the motorbike.[57] He lost control of the BMW and crashed it.

Jerome 'Donkie' Booysen – the only person ever to be publicly named as a suspect in Beeka's murder (according to a Hawks investigator there was evidence and statements to back this up,[58] yet nothing came of this) – was the first person to arrive at the scene of the crash.

On the day of the murder, Nafiz Modack received a message on his cellphone that read 'You next'.[59] A few people close to Beeka apparently also received similar messages.

Beeka's funeral, held in the Cape Town suburb of Ottery the month following his assassination, was a grand affair and drew a vast and motley array of people who wanted to pay their last respects – this included umKhonto weSizwe veterans, Jerome Booysen, former Springbok rugby players James Dalton and Percy Montgomery, and members of the Hells Angels biking group.[60] UmKhonto weSizwe veterans draped the ANC flag over Beeka's coffin.[61]

Given all the stories and anecdotes that built Beeka up into a near-mythical figure, it's easy to overlook the fact that he wasn't just an underworld kingpin, but also a father, husband and friend – a person with a multifaceted and private life. His gravestone bears the epitaph: 'How little we knew that morning the sorrow the day would bring. Gone the face we loved so dear, silent the voice we loved to hear, beautiful memories left behind as solace for our grief.'

Those first four words – 'how little we knew' – encapsulate Beeka's broader public legacy, and some of the unanswered questions that still linger about his role in the underworld, and the previous and current governments.

It later emerged that on the weekend prior to Beeka's assassination, Radovan Krejčíř had allegedly flown three Serbian assassins to South Africa to carry out hits – and that at the top of the list of names of targets was that of Cyril Beeka.[62]

The bad blood between the two men apparently had its roots some time in 2010, when Krejčíř had opened a gold pawn shop, MoneyPoint, in Claremont in Cape Town. 'It had vaults. It was more secure than a bank,' one source said.[63]

The plan was that it would end up being part of a chain of such stores, and that Beeka and a third man, known as Sailor, would be co-managers. But business hadn't gone too well, and the third man had complained that rent and salaries weren't being paid. Eventually Beeka and the third man simply took over the store and renamed it The Gold Father, cutting out Krejčíř. This, sources claim, irked Krejčíř.

Then, around November 2010, Beeka was at a party with, among others, Krejčíř and Modack. Some flexing of testosterone culminated in Krejčíř hitting Modack and Beeka jumping in to calm the situation. Several of those present urged Krejčíř to make peace with Modack. He then apparently walked up to Modack, his hand extended as if in appeasement, before suddenly punching Modack in the face.[64] A brawl ensued, with Beeka splitting Krejčíř's lip.

On the evening of 31 December 2010, so the story goes, Krejčíř was meant to meet Beeka for supper at a restaurant in Green Point, but didn't pitch up; and Krejčíř was also a no-show for a subsequent meeting in Green Point.

At that stage, sources say, Beeka heard there was a hit out on him, with a bounty as high as R5 million rumoured. 'There was money on his head,' the source confirmed.[65] Beeka organised firearms for those around him.

There have been several theories mooted around why Beeka was assassinated, including that he had to be eliminated so that nightclub-security companies could be amalgamated without him standing in

49

the way, and that he was about to spill the beans about strip-franchise owner Lolly Jackson's May 2010 murder in Johannesburg.

One of Krejčíř's former right-hand men and a fellow Czech, Milosh Potiska, later said that he believed Krejčíř had suggested to Mark Lifman that he have Beeka taken out 'to open Cape Town up for Krejčíř and Lifman to control all the night clubs and drugs in Cape Town'. Lifman denied any involvement in Beeka's murder.[66]

Meanwhile, Krejčíř's own take on his dealings with Beeka was befitting of him in that it was as sensational as any of the other rumours and allegations in criminal matters that surrounded him. He claimed that in 2010 Beeka introduced him to the then-president's son Duduzane Zuma, who promised to help him (Krejčíř) obtain asylum papers from the Department of Home Affairs, which would shield him from the actions of politicians in his home country who had it in for him. In return for this help, Krejčíř alleged he was asked to pay Duduzane R5 million, of which he had handed over more than half.[67]

Krejčíř claimed that his relationship with Duduzane had suffered a blow following Beeka's murder, which he said members of the controversial Gupta family had accused him of orchestrating.

After the shooting a small bag of cocaine (just less than ten grams) was found in the car, and it was for this, and fraud relating to concealing his true identity, that the survivor of the Beeka hit, Dobrosav Gavric, was arrested and detained.[68]

Gavric was wanted in Serbia, where he faced a 35-year jail sentence for playing a role in murdering that country's most feared warlord, Zeljko Raznatovic (aka Arkan), as well as killing two of his bodyguards, in January 2000. A pale man with brown hair, meek and reserved, and walking with a pronounced limp, Gavric looked like anything but the idea of a link between two massive underworld killings on two different continents.

Gavric's version of how he came to be linked to the Arkan murder goes along the lines of his having gone to meet friends, including one Milan Djuricic, at the Belgrade Intercontinental Hotel to celebrate the new millennium. While waiting, Gavric had spotted Arkan in the lobby, a large space with several restaurants and bars, but had only realised that there was a killing in progress when he heard gunshots, which spurred him to try and leave the lobby to get to safety.

In court papers forming part of an attempt by Gavric to get refugee status it was noted, '[Gavric] remembered rolling and ducking down to his right side and wanted to reach the exit which was nearby. He immediately got up and started running towards it. As he was running towards the door, he was hit in the back by a stray bullet. The bullet pierced his spine causing serious injury.'[69] Gavric had no clue who'd shot him and caused the wound that resulted in his walking with a limp.

Djuricic spotted the wounded Gavric and, with other friends, got him into his car and rushed him to hospital where Gavric, losing blood and in shock, lost consciousness. Gavric, in a sense, therefore owed Djuricic his life.

The men were both convicted of Arkan's assassination, but Gavric, pointed to as the trigger-puller, steadfastly denied the killing, and claimed he hadn't received a fair trial, noting, 'Until today there are different various reports about Arkan's killing. Marko Milošević, the son of Yugoslavia's president at the time, Slobodan Milošević, was said to have had a harsh quarrel with Arkan over control of oil-smuggling rackets.'[70] Arkan, Gavric said, was also behind an ethnic cleansing campaign against Bosnian Muslims: 'Some 1 400 Bosnian Moslems were killed in various ways starting on 6 April 1992 with the arrival of Arkan's army and other paramilitary groups.'[71]

As a young man in the late 1990s, Gavric had attended a training camp of the Serbian Secret Service in Serbia. 'Arkan and members of his Volunteer Guard visited the camp frequently to receive instructions from government superiors and obtaining ammunition [sic]... I had firsthand experience of this,' he said.[72]

Gavric went on to work for the Serbian special forces. In the meantime, Arkan shed his warlord cloak and, while still viewed as an underworld figure, reinvented himself. 'He was a very powerful and feared man as he amassed a large personal fortune in the war. He owned a number of businesses, football clubs, he started a political party and he married a popular Serbian singer ...' Gavric said.[73]

He claimed that Arkan had criminal connections and that his January 2000 murder could have been a result of a gang or turf fight.

Gavric – much like some local underworld suspects who've alleged police are orchestrating cases against them – believed that evidence had been manufactured to ensure that he was convicted and jailed in Serbia,[74] and said that this was the reason he'd fled the country in 2006. 'The reason for my escape was due to the fact that I genuinely feared for my life; I knew that if I was sent to jail I would be murdered,' he said. 'I simply could not envisage a situation where I would be killed before I had time with my daughter. I regard myself as a committed father and play an active role in the lives of my children, whom I love dearly; I do not want to be separated from them.'[75]

Using a Bosnian passport in the name Sasa Kovacevic, Gavric fled to Ecuador, where he stayed for about a year.

'The reason why I opted to come to South Africa [in 2008] was because I heard that it was a stable country with new opportunities. I wanted to build a new life and raise my children in a solid society. I thought me and my family would be safe,' he said.[76]

Still using his alias, Gavric got into business importing and exporting, and later in secondhand goods. And he met Cyril Beeka. 'We became friends and when Cyril [who was then based in Gauteng] visited Cape Town we would usually go out together. I was really fond of Cyril and enjoyed his company. I regarded Cyril as a friend,' he said. He also mentioned that he'd heard that Beeka was 'connected to the police and if ever there was a threat to me, my family would be warned'.[77]

Gavric denied categorically that he was involved in the contract murder. 'I maintain I had nothing to do with the death of Cyril Beeka. I was seriously injured during the incident and was shot in the right arm and in the chest.'[78]

After the murder he was faced with 'very hard choices'. 'I had attempted to keep a very low profile in South Africa and to ensure that the followers of Arkan [did] not trace me to where I was staying. I knew that I had come in to South Africa under another name. I also knew that the local authorities did not know who I was but I suspected that the Crime Intelligence had a fair idea as to who I was.'[79]

Gavric, who's in a high-security prison in South Africa, claimed that he hadn't fled the country following Beeka's murder, despite the risk of his true identity being discovered, because 'out of respect for Cyril Beeka, [I] felt that I owed it to him and his family to in fact tell the authorities exactly what I saw, as I am clearly a material witness in this murder case. I want the perpetrators who killed Cyril Beeka and shot at me to be caught.'[80]

CHAPTER 3

Enter by blood, exit by death

Johannesburg may bear the unofficial stamp of 'underworld capital of South Africa', but Cape Town has an extra, very potent ingredient that in itself is deadly, and which brings with it myriad unique problems that roil through the province. This ingredient curdles the Western Cape's idyllic visual veneer – waves caressing a pristine coastline and mountains rising majestically to create its iconic landscape – to expose a province that's a formidable dot on the local organised-crime map and which bolsters its position on the global map.

This ingredient is gangsterism.

Gangs fight to control criminal syndicates that include drug dealing, human trafficking, illicit cigarette channels, prostitution, and the security and entertainment industries. Embroiled in corruption, the gang hierarchy starts with street-level thugs and climbs to the second-highest tier, who operate interprovincially and work to expand their businesses, including club security rooted in

Gauteng, and hitmen being hired out from the Western Cape.

The top tier of gangsters are involved in transnational crimes and syndicates – 'specific activities that are the most pertinent threat to [the] national security of the country', according to a senior police officer.[1]

In the Western Cape, underworld tentacles form invisible turf lines that slash through suburbs, demarcating which gangs and groupings may operate where. Stepping over an invisible gangster-etched line can quickly end in murder.

Back in November 2001, the province's gangsterism issue was discussed in Parliament in a joint Safety and Security Portfolio meeting, and a simple truth was faced head-on: there was no quick fix for the problem, and blame for it couldn't be apportioned to one entity or person. It was acknowledged that gangsterism was so entrenched in society – with at least 150 gangs with 120 000 members operating in the Western Cape at that point – that there was no end in sight. Increased policing wouldn't help; 'the social culture of South Africa had to change to eradicate crime'.[2]

Fast-forward sixteen years and the situation hadn't changed much, if at all. In mid-2017 a police presentation in Parliament identified three provinces in the country as having to grapple with structured gang groupings – the Western Cape, the Eastern Cape and KwaZulu-Natal. The Western Cape stood out by far, however, with 73 gangs in the province (a more streamlined count compared to years earlier, with gangs having become more formalised, and with factions of gangs grouped together instead of counted individually), compared to fifteen in the Eastern Cape and six in KwaZulu-Natal.[3]

Gangsterism in the Western Cape is deeply linked to policing and not just in the obvious cop-versus-gangster way. Former apartheid-era hitman Abram 'Slang' van Zyl confirmed, for example, that in the late 1980s a fellow CCB operative had asked him 'to gather information relating to radical people in the Western Cape'.[4] Van Zyl had then involved Edward 'Peaches' Gordon, a member of the Dixie Boys gang, in a murder plot to try and assassinate anti-apartheid activist Dullah Omar.[5] Gordon and two associates were provided with a Russian-made Makarov pistol for the job, 'so that it could then not lead to police or army activities, so that it could lead away from the state in other words'.[6]

Gordon was murdered in Athlone in 1991, weeks after giving evidence to a commission set up to probe apartheid death-squad allegations. Isgak Hardien, also a member of the Dixie Boys, said in 2000 that Americans gang boss Jackie Lonte, who was widely believed to have worked for the CCB, offered him 'R20 000 and a Grenada [sic]' to have Gordon killed,[7] although he later said this was a lie. Gordon's mother believed gangsters acting on the orders of members of the CCB had had her son murdered.[8]

Lonte himself was murdered outside his Athlone home in November 1998; a source said the weapons found at the scene were from either the police or the army, and further suspicions were that members of Pagad had had a hand in the killing.[9]

Gangsterism in the Western Cape is, like policing, also intrinsically linked to politics. This had its genesis in the 1950 Group Areas Act, which laid down legal provisions on the specific areas where different population groups could own property, reside and work. This meant forced removals of 'non-white' residents from the Cape Town city centre to poorly resourced areas farther afield, and this indirectly facilitated the spread of gangs in the Western Cape, because dispersing and isolating residents, and callously chopping up their familiar social matrix, contributed to the formation of loosely structured groupings which later calcified into gangs.

In the mid-1960s, for instance, District Six, a vibrant and close-knit suburb of mainly coloured people in the inner city, was declared a whites-only area, so thousands of residents were forcibly removed, many of them to Lavender Hill, about twenty kilometres distant. Today this suburb with its serried blocks of dreary flats is often the scene of gang shootings.

Another apartheid-era dumping ground and a gang stronghold is nearby Manenberg, a 3.35 km² suburb[10] in which over 61 000[11] mostly coloured people live. It consists of blocks of dull maisonette flats separated by courtyards across which washing lines zigzag, and cramped houses; graffiti and scrawls abound on peeling walls and grey vibracretes. Two notorious gangs – the Hard Livings and their rivals, the Americans – have been among the groupings that have plagued the suburb for decades, their squabbles and battles igniting shootouts and shaping the environment in which children grow up and with which their parents have to contend.

Manenberg is 'a place where life is treated cheaply, and killings and revenge killings are the order of the day'.[12] The circumstances there are such that some residents 'are under significant temptation and enticement to become involved in gang membership and activity. This comes about not only because of pervasive poverty and unemployment, but also because of the prevailing social norms in the area, which seem to accept gang culture as part of the way of life. This is manifest by the way in which the various gangs that operate in the area have carved out territories within the suburb in which one or other of them holds sway and influence. It is also borne out by the evidence that such is the hold of gang culture in the area that there is little respect for the forces of law and order. The police are openly defied and disregarded on occasion.'[13]

An example of just how deeply saturating and commonplace gangsterism in Cape Town is emerged in 2015, when the municipality conceded it may have inadvertently, via subcontractors, hired gangsters to provide security at construction sites in Manenberg.

Several residents said it was common knowledge that a Hard Livings gang boss ran the company hired by a city subcontractor, and that he'd recruited his gang's members as security guards.[14]

And there's another political wrinkle: while South Africa is led by the ruling party, the ANC, the Western Cape has been governed by the opposition DA since the general election in 2009; and this means that while the DA can blame the ANC for poor policing strategies that form part of national operations, the ANC can point the finger back at the DA for failing to properly govern the province.[15] Political blame games often centre around gang violence, and this political fingerpointing ping-pong has played out in the province for several years.

As the nightclub-security saga has evolved, historic gang turf lines have extended from suburbs chronically plagued by gangsterism, to right into Cape Town's city centre. If you've got the cooperation of a gang, your power base is immediately extended to that gang's turf, and your notoriety, or so-called muscle, is strengthened; plus it means you've neutralised a potential enemy. This is how gang boundaries have been pushed closer and closer to the public-dense business district and very busy nightlife areas, as well as to prominent places of policing and authority.

When Cyril Beeka was at the helm of Cape Town's nightclub security in the late 1990s, the Hard Livings, in turn linked to its former leader Rashied Staggie, was the gang associated with the industry. As the 2017 nightclub-security battle developed in Cape Town, the names of three particular gangs kept cropping up – the Sexy Boys, the 27s and the 28s – a trio of groupings each with a deep and entrenched history that has affected how violence around the city has played out over decades.

By 2018 there were the two clear-cut groupings identified by police and a Hawks investigator[16] as vying for control of nightclub and restaurant security in Cape Town, and each grouping had suspected ties to a gang. The one grouping was allegedly headed by Nafiz Modack and Colin Booysen, among others; the other was allegedly run by Mark Lifman, Andre Naude and Jerome 'Donkie' Booysen.

Bear in mind that, over the years, the Booysen brothers – like Modack, Naude and Lifman – had insisted they were simply businessmen and in no way involved in crime, whether drugs or gangsterism.[17] But a Hawks investigator alleged that Jerome Booysen headed the Sexy Boys gang,[18] and police pointed to his brother Colin, a convicted murderer,[19] as also being heavily involved in gangsterism.

The 28s are massive and multi-layered, operating within prisons and on the streets. A crushingly powerful gang, with several factions and offshoots, it's structured similarly to a political party, in that it has a leadership, members and cliques that control specific areas, or turf.[20] Members are identified by tattoos and hand signals.

The state believes 28s gangsters are embroiled in a noxious cocktail of underworld crimes including murder, assault, the intimidation of witnesses, drug trafficking and the possession of unlicensed firearms and ammunition.

A faction of the 28s is the Mobsters, a lesser known but equally ruthless organised group of hitmen who carry out killings and are contracted by others to perpetrate murders. A witness alleged that the Mobsters leadership was connected to detectives who either helped members who were arrested to get released on bail, or tried to ensure that the cases against them were withdrawn.[21]

Members are said to have worked for George 'Geweld' Thomas, once the most notorious 28s street-faction gang kingpin in Cape Town. In September 2012, while Thomas was in the dock along with seventeen other men in the biggest gang trial in South Africa to that point, the then-44-year-old had no bank accounts and no driving licence, and had been in jail for about twenty years, nearly half his life.[22]

Thomas was responsible for a reign of terror mainly in Bishop Lavis between 2006 and 2008; a slideshow encapsulated the sheer horror he and his henchmen had unleashed on the suburb, with many illustrations of murdered men, some with gunshots to the head and blood seeping across the concrete they'd died on, others with their heads awkwardly tilted back in vehicle seats after being assassinated, one crumpled up with a small bicycle he'd been riding, and another (murdered to guarantee his silence about other crimes) splayed out on long, dry grass. The slideshow said the gang operated only after dark and that its primary purpose was to get into and remain in power, and to be seen as exceptionally notorious.[23]

Over just three years at least twelve people linked to the massive trial, six of them state witnesses, were murdered.[24] Bodyguards were assigned to those involved in the trial, including the prosecutor.

In 2015 Thomas was sentenced to seven life terms for an array of crimes, including ordering hits from behind bars.

By 2019 the name most publicly linked to the 28s in Cape Town was Ralph Stanfield, the nephew of late drug lord Colin Stanfield. Colin, who had been under intense investigation for suspected involvement in a high-level mandrax-smuggling syndicate with international offshoots, was jailed in 2002 for tax evasion. He was released from custody as he was terminally ill and died of lung cancer in 2004.

A speaker at Colin's funeral in 2004 expressed a complex conundrum more broadly experienced in Cape Town – he noted that Colin was regarded by the residents of Valhalla Park, where he'd lived, as a saviour of sorts because he made time to listen to their problems and provided some of those who needed it with food. 'Those who vilified him, including the intelligence services and police, stand here ashamed,' the speaker said.[25]

Ralph Stanfield, far from appearing to be a dominant leader of the 28s gang, portrayed himself as a man focused on business and family. Stanfield has homes in the upmarket Cape Town suburb of Newlands as well as in the generally impoverished area of Mitchells Plain, where he grew up, raised by a single mother.

'She earned a small income and with very limited resources available to her ensured that I was able to attend school, complete Grade 12 and enrol at university. ... [I]t turned out that there was not sufficient money for me to continue my studies ... so I entered the business world as an entrepreneur,' he said. He became a property developer and owned a service station from which he ran several feeding schemes for the poor of the area, and also supported a local high school. One of his 'principal goals' was to see that his children received a good education.[26]

In April 2017 photographs emerged of Ralph Stanfield handing out money from a wad of cash to residents in Beacon Valley in an apparent gesture of goodwill to try and improve their Easter period.[27] These actions echoed what his uncle Colin Stanfield was remembered for, and it appeared Ralph was keeping his uncle's legacy alive.

The notorious Sexy Boys gang has never been on the same page as the 28s – friction between the two gangs dates back decades, and several shootings over the years appear to have been sparked by this ongoing strife. Sexy Boys strongholds are mainly in the northern suburbs of Cape Town, some twenty kilometres from the city centre, and include the areas of Bellville South and Belhar.

There were three active gangs in the Belhar area in the 1990s – the Sexy Boys, the Dixie Boys and the Back Street Kids. According to Hennie Erasmus, a Western Cape High Court judge at the time, 'The gangsterism in Belhar is characterised by battles which

Suspected 28s gang boss Ralph Stanfield (front left pallbearer) at the funeral of murdered advocate Pete Mihalik on 10 November 2018. Picture: Caryn Dolley

sometimes take on the form of a guerrilla war, with the Sexy Boys on the one side and the Dixie Boys and the Back Street Kids on the other side... The community was completely conditioned to the shooting in their environment.'[28]

This multiple-gang scenario gets complicated because the Sexy Boys had ties to the 26s gang, while the Dixie Boys and Back Street Kids had ties to the 28s gang.[29] On top of this, the 28s, the Dixie Boys and the Back Street Kids formed part of an overall gang organisation, or cartel, known as The Firm, headed by Colin Stanfield, and this meant The Firm posed a powerful grouping of which the Sexy Boys were not a part.

In the late 1990s there were attempts to make peace between various gangs operating in the broader Cape Town area. The grouping driving this was called Core, short for Community Outreach. It was led by gangsters-turned-pastors Albern Martins and Ivan Waldeck. Individuals with strong followings took part in this process: Colin Stanfield; Ernie 'Lastig' Solomon,[30] who was once the leader of the 28s gang; Rashied Staggie; and brothers Jerome and Michael Booysen.

But Michael felt that Core later became a smokescreen for crime (a policeman agreed with this view),[31] with members allegedly going after protection money from taxi and shebeen operators, who in some cases had to fork over R200 000, and more than R2 million was collected. According to Michael, this protection money was earmarked for bringing drugs into South Africa from India.[32] This tied into what Colin Stanfield was under investigation for – allegedly distributing mandrax, some sourced from India, around Cape Town.

Later Core's leadership, according to Michael Booysen, made a decision to take on Pagad, the grouping focused on disrupting gangsters and trying to quash drug dealing. Targets were identified and weapons handed out to be used on those identified.

Michael Booysen didn't want to go ahead with this, so the Booysen brothers withdrew from Core, and this apparently angered The Firm, which included a large grouping of 28s gangsters, members of which were said to have then launched a full-scale war on the Booysens. In the ensuing violence Llewellyn Booysen, another Booysen brother also known as Percy, was shot dead, in an attack of which Michael was apparently the target.

Some years later, in December 2011, Ernie Solomon once again apparently tried to smooth over gang clashes and was involved in mediation talks between rival gangsters in hot spots including Lavender Hill.[33] The attempts at making lasting peace between rival gangs did not work.

After Core collapsed, Albern Martins, apparently a friend of the Booysen family,[34] tried forging ahead with Core II to broker peace in Belhar, but that wasn't successful either.

A decade later, by July 2012, Core II was long forgotten and in its place was Western Cape Community Outreach, or Wecco, based in Bellville South. Wecco's work involved continuing efforts to broker peace between gangs, and attempts to reintegrate former gangsters into everyday life by providing them with, among other things, social skills and basic professional tools. Rashied Staggie worked at Wecco in 2013 after being released from custody on day parole, and in 2014 he gave a lecture to ex-gangsters at the Wecco building in which he emphasised that crime does not pay.

Nonetheless, Albern Martins, who had been a founder of the original Core and was now part of Wecco, was apparently deeply involved in alleged criminal activity; certainly, strange rumours surrounded him.[35]

The author visited Wecco's centre in Bellville South in May 2013 to see how the organisation was operating. There, 36-year-old ex-gangster Brian Alexander of Belhar admitted to having been a 28s member and said he had murdered three people in 1996 and then a few years later had stabbed someone to death. (He didn't say if he'd been prosecuted for these crimes.) Alexander threw light on the South African prison system which, far from being a rehabilitative environment, was 'a birthplace for the worst'; it was where, he said, he'd been transformed into a hardened, tough-minded criminal who felt no remorse.[36]

Of trying to leave a life of gangsterism, Alexander had a prophetic view, part of which, as nightclub-security, gang and policing

Jerome 'Donkie' Booysen in a room in his home at the end of May 2018. Picture: Caryn Dolley, News24

ructions developed, repeatedly proved true: 'You enter by blood and you exit by death.'[37]

The Sexy Boys gang has somehow over the years become synonymous with nightclub security in Cape Town, although recently tensions within the Sexy Boys have apparently split the gang into several factions.

Jerome 'Donkie' Booysen was in 2012 named in court as a leader of the Sexy Boys and, even though nothing came of this and he was not arrested, his name in the ensuing years remained publicly associated with the grouping. He's tried to shake this off.

Jerome Booysen is a father and grandfather. A former rugby player and ardent fan of the game, he's the president of the local Belhar rugby club that was started by his father in 1983. He was a building inspector with the Cape Town municipality for more than twenty years. Although he has owned legally registered nightclubs,[38]

Colin Booysen outside the Cape Town Magistrate's Court after being released on bail on 28 February 2018. Picture: Caryn Dolley, News24

since 2001 he's been involved in the property industry, buying properties through sales of execution, and then selling or renting these. Nonetheless, his home in Cape Town's northern suburbs is fronted by bulletproof glass, and he has a long history of brushes with the law. While acknowledging that in the past he was 'no angel', he's recently said that he's now a businessman and simply wants to be a good father to his children. 'Gangsterism is not the way to go,' he's said.[39]

Jerome's brother Colin Booysen left school in Standard 9. 'I could not complete my schooling career due to financial constraints and therefore had to seek work in order to support my family,' he explained.[40]

Although described by one cop as 'just a gangster' ('He opens his mouth and people are scared'),[41] Colin has a hand in the highly competitive – and sometimes lethal – taxi industry, as the owner of four taxis with five operating permits servicing both local and long-distance routes.

Colin, who lives in a comfortable home in upmarket Loevenstein in Bellville, has a history of run-ins with the law. In 1992 he was sentenced to eighteen years in jail for the murder of a policeman; he was released on parole in 2005. He's since been arrested for fraud and assault, but both cases were withdrawn.[42] Towards the end of 2018 he again faced a murder charge.

Although in the past there seems to have been a 'code' among gang members and underworld operatives, similar to the Mafia 'omerta', which demanded no snitching to police or other authorities, this seems to have weakened over the years, with poor choices of allegiances and personal greed eroding loyalty. This has made the already-tense gang situation in the Western Cape even more volatile.

For instance, a rift apparently developed between Colin and Jerome Booysen some time in 2016. Jerome and an associate of his, Kishor Naidoo, at some point allegedly swindled Colin out of money in a drug transaction.[43] (The Hawks later pointed to Naidoo, informally known as Kamaal, as a funder for the grouping of men they linked to Mark Lifman.) In May 2016 a tyre shop of Kamaal's in the Cape Town suburb of Observatory was set alight.[44] While neither Colin nor his brother was arrested or charged for this, rumours suggest that the incident may have somehow played a role in creating the rift between him and Jerome. Further rumours were that when the distance widened between Colin and Jerome in 2017, Colin branched off and aligned himself to nightclub-security disruptor Nafiz Modack.

This manoeuvre is what apparently caused fractures within the Sexy Boys – if gangland folklore is to be believed, several members of the gang backed Colin Booysen, leaving Jerome Booysen and the

Sexy Boys who stayed with him to pair up with the 27s gang. This, according to the unverified tale, is how the two nightclub-security factions came to be aligned to two different gangs.

The third Booysen brother, Michael, like Jerome, denies being a gang leader and insists he's a legitimate businessman. He's serving a life sentence for killing Jason Idas in 1999 in Sexy Boys stronghold Belhar.[45] Major General Jeremy Vearey, who has serious clout in parole matters, is one of those ensuring Michael doesn't go free.[46]

Aside from being viewed as a thorn in the side of Michael Booysen – and therefore by some as a thorn in the side of the Sexy Boys – Vearey has also been credited for being among the cops who played a role in having had Rashied Staggie and Colin Stanfield locked up,[47] thereby significantly denting the Hard Livings and the 28s gangs, respectively. More recently Vearey has been involved in investigations into Ralph Stanfield.

CHAPTER 4
Where the dog lies buried

Jeremy Alan Vearey is one of the cops in the Western Cape who has weathered mounds of claims of his having dodgy relationships with equally dodgy figures. At the same time he's widely known as the province's leading gangbuster, and, with a rich history in policing, he's no stranger to controversy: he's made enemies of several suspected gangsters and politicians, is known for being outspoken, and over the years has vigorously rubbed several of his colleagues and bosses up the wrong way.

Countless claims against him have surfaced, including that he received money from an alleged gang boss, protected another and worked with yet another, and that he was involved in the murder of an attorney. He's never been criminally charged for any of these claims.

Given all the allegations levelled against him and the sensitive investigations he's conducted, he's recently taken to moving around with bodyguards.

Major General Jeremy Vearey outside the Cape Town Magistrate's Court in December 2018. Picture: Caryn Dolley, News24

An avid storyteller whose pinprick eyes dart back and forth when he reminisces, as if keeping imaginary track of the people he's describing, Vearey began his career in a classroom. He got a secondary teacher's diploma in 1984, and that year also became a member of the ANC (which was banned at that stage) and was involved in umKhonto weSizwe.

Vearey first worked at a school in Elsies River in 1985, then, in 1987, at a school in Mitchells Plain, both suburbs among Cape Town's historic gang hotspots.[1] But that year, 1987, he was arrested for his involvement in umKhonto weSizwe. Convicted of terrorism, he was imprisoned on Robben Island from December 1988 to April 1990.

Following the February 1990 unbanning of political parties in South Africa and the subsequent release of political prisoners, 'The euphoria that everybody experienced ... was not a reality for us... to me. A lot of us thought, Now the boers will, the enemy will, really target us, and comrades were eliminated,' Vearey recalled. 'A lot of the guys I shared these cells with – off [the top of] my head I can think of about five – were killed. We're talking within two months after their release.' Vearey cites this as the reason he decided to 'go back into the organisation': 'don't have a gap in between, go back to the intelligence environment of the ANC, continue in the war'.[2]

On his release from prison, therefore, Vearey went to Zimbabwe, Canada and the UK for further intelligence training. On his return to South Africa, he was deployed by the ANC's Department of Intelligence and Security, involved in the covert collection of information involving politics, crime intelligence and counterintelligence. Appointed regional manager of the VIP protection section of the Department of Intelligence and Security in the Western Cape, he planned and managed operations to protect senior ANC leaders when they were in the province and was among those ensuring the safety of Nelson Mandela.

By the late 1990s Vearey was part of police senior management and the provincial commander of intelligence coordination. Between 2000 and 2002 he headed up a Western Cape gang-investigation unit ominously, or appropriately, named Slasher. Vearey managed about thirty investigators responsible for dealing with 4 600 murders and attempted murders linked to gang activities (the case dockets were from the years 1984 to 2000).[3] This is when gangsters started feeling the heat, and also when Vearey started getting under the skin of certain colleagues.

While at the helm of Slasher, Vearey claimed to have uncovered gross police corruption, which included members of a former gangbusting unit lying and making misrepresentations, 'losing' exhibits and evidence, neglecting to send forensic and ballistic evidence away for analysis for up to two years and more, or closing dockets without reason, as well as the falsification of charges against some officers.[4]

'I know the dockets reveal widespread corruption and gross negligence in the investigation of gang-related crimes of murder and attempted murder, because I conducted the initial investigation leading to the creation of the Slasher team and have overseen its work,' he said. 'This evidence may well be the only proof available to show the nature and extent of corruption and gross negligence in relation to gang-related crimes in the Western Cape.'[5]

In May 2002, in what was said to be a temporary move, Vearey was ordered to drop his Slasher duties and instead carry on with other cop duties in the evaluation-services component.[6] He refused to budge,[7] however, because he believed this order equated to strangling the investigations the unit was busy with, and would result in the corruption allegations against some cops being promptly and conveniently swept aside.

Two months later Vearey publicly aired his belief that apartheid-era police officers were intentionally scuppering critical cop investigations, and he vowed that he and his allies would defend the ANC's previous intelligence structures. 'If it involves exposing the [Security Branch] informers within the liberation movement, we will do so ... If it means exposing covert operations of the former statutory agencies for which they did not apply for amnesty, we will do so,' he said, adding that he had access to 'documents that were not shredded in time'. 'This is a cold war from an intelligence perspective, and right now we are wasting our time fighting ridiculous battles when we should be fighting organised crime.'[8]

Just weeks later Vearey was suspended without pay. It was reported that he faced disciplinary action,[9] and that the police's counterintelligence unit was probing both Vearey and Major General Andre Lincoln (whom Vearey had appointed to represent him in disciplinary action stemming from the Slasher saga) for being a possible threat to national security, related to the apparently unshredded documents that could expose covert apartheid schemes.

Many years later, Vearey explained that around 1992 Nelson Mandela had appointed the Motsuenyane Commission, which was apparently set up to look into human-rights violations by ANC personnel of people captured in Angola, and that this had sparked fears among Security Branch cops of a possible 'Nuremberg' situation about to unfold – 'Nuremberg' referring to war-crimes trials held in Germany in 1945 and 1946 against former Nazi leaders. In preparation for this 'ANC Nuremberg', Security Branch members had been ordered by their superiors to detail exactly what they'd got up to in the past, which would have included highly sensitive details such as who their informants, some probably within the ANC, were.

'All that information was put on stiffy disks,' Vearey said. 'An informer handed me the disks. What was on the disks is the issue… It included handler reports of all sources they, military intelligence, handled. We didn't publicise it. We used it. We said, "You'd better choose a side. We know this and this. You're afraid of Nuremberg, change sides before it's too late."'[10]

If Vearey was telling the truth, it meant that certain Western Cape members of the ANC's intelligence structures, just before the start of a democratic South Africa, would soon be absorbed into the amalgamated democratic police service with a wealth of incriminating information against their future colleagues.

Vearey said that many Security Branch police officers had hastily decided to become informants and that, as a result, 'we know things from the past. They know people like us have old access and sources. We don't need intelligence sources now. We know where the dog lies buried.'[11]

In Andre Lincoln's civil-court matter in 2017, he, independently of Vearey, had said that five Security Branch members were among his informants who had divulged details about an array of individuals.[12] It appeared that the Security Branch in the Western Cape had indeed been successfully infiltrated by ANC intelligence-operatives-turned-cops.

Vearey said that at some point (he didn't say when) the crucial stiffy disks with sensational and incriminating details about apartheid secrets were handed over to the National Intelligence Agency, now known as the State Security Agency. Vearey, and his colleagues who'd perused what was on those disks, have the information filed in memory.

Others in exceptionally powerful positions may have had, or still have, access to this information.

In August 2002 Vearey approached the Labour Court to try and have his temporary transfer from Slasher declared unlawful, on the grounds that its aim was 'to remove him from his post as commander of the Slasher team and to terminate or minimise the work of the team'. He wasn't prepared 'to accede to unlawful instructions aimed at ensuring that the work of the Slasher Team would cease', he told the court.[13]

Vearey said that he wanted a commission of inquiry set up to probe the corruption he claimed to have uncovered, and the then-Community Safety Minister in the Western Cape, Leonard Ramatlakane, asked for the names of seventeen high-ranking police officials allegedly involved in the corruption.[14] But Vearey didn't supply this information because he believed it would end up being delivered to those involved in the corruption. His Labour Court application was dismissed with costs.

In January 2003 Vearey was found guilty of insubordination following an internal disciplinary hearing and he was warned that he would immediately be fired if found guilty of a similar offence within twelve months.[15]

The matter then went dormant, and Vearey went on to fill

various positions within the police and was stationed in various areas, most of them gang hotspots around Cape Town.

Fourteen years after Jeremy Vearey's effective transfer from Slasher, history repeated itself.

Cape Town police officer Lutfie Eksteen was a valuable member of the Western Cape cops' anti-gang strategy known as Operation Combat.[16] On the evening of 13 October 2014, some men arrived at the house Eksteen shared with his mother and brother in Manenberg. They opened fire.

Eksteen wasn't home at the time, but his brother and mother were, and they were both shot; his 71-year-old mother was killed. It's believed that Eksteen's family was targeted because of the work he was doing in trying to quell gang violence.[17] Eksteen's brother, critically wounded, may have been mistaken for him.

But this sorry tale has an even more sobering twist – a firearm seized by police during another incident in another gang hotspot, Bishop Lavis, widely viewed as 28s gang turf, was believed to have been used in Mrs Eksteen's murder – and it was suspected this firearm was one of more than a thousand smuggled from within the police to gangsters.[18]

The previous year, 2013, police officers investigating crimes unfolding across the Cape Flats – suburbs a substantial distance from Cape Town's city centre to which 'non-white' residents were forcibly removed under apartheid – had begun to suspect that certain firearms that were meant to be with police so that they could be destroyed, were instead being circulated illegally in the Western Cape.

A presentation by police experts showed that several firearms circulating among Western Cape gangs showed 'identical ballistic signatures'; each firearm had been altered, with the identification number filed off, but – chillingly – each had been altered in exactly the same manner, one 'peculiar to armourers and ballistic experts in the police'. 'Because of the sheer number of firearms in circulation we eventually concluded that the mass of firearms in gang possession had to have come out of the SAPS system,' Major General Jeremy Vearey said. 'They came fully loaded ... and had been adapted to be untraceable.'[19]

This is how South Africa's biggest-ever gun-smuggling investigation, codenamed Project Impi, was born, in December 2013, headed by the police's Vearey and Lieutenant General Peter Jacobs.

Peter Jacobs, like Vearey, is from the Western Cape and comes across as unassuming while paying acute attention to what's happening around him – seeing beyond the obvious is what he's been trained to do. A member of umKhonto weSizwe in the 1980s, he was arrested, like Vearey, in 1987. Hauled off to Culemborg, the police's anti-terrorist unit base in Cape Town, he was tortured through the use of near-suffocation and electric shocks.[20] Following a lengthy trial in the Western Cape High Court, Jacobs was convicted of terrorism and sentenced to time behind bars on Robben Island.

Released in April 1991, Jacobs joined a non-governmental organisation involved in developing community education in the Western and Southern Cape. Four years later, when umKhonto weSizwe members were absorbed into the SAPS, Jacobs became a major within the police. This was during the period that Lincoln said was marred by deep mistrust among cops – and this tension seemed to be lingering two years later, in 1997, when Jacobs said apartheid-era 'structures' were seemingly still in place and presenting 'a serious danger to the present state'.[21]

Jacobs continued climbing the ranks, and in January 2014 he was named the Western Cape's head of Crime Intelligence, an appointment that coincided with the early stages of Project Impi created the month before.

By 2015, Project Impi was leading police investigators back to within their own ranks, and what had started out as a provincial probe in Cape Town began expanding into a national one with international offshoots. In that year, Vearey, also heading up the provincial police's operation focused on clamping down on gangsterism, said that some apartheid-era police officers, wanting to destabilise certain areas in Cape Town when the apartheid regime switched over to democracy, were suspected of having helped gang bosses fraudulently obtain firearm licences so that they could get guns to disrupt these locations. 'The practice of corruption through the supplying of firearms predates our democracy,' he said. 'We have to interrogate the integrity of every firearm licence obtained by gang leaders right back into the 1980s.'[22]

Firearms meant to be in the custody of the state had for years ended up in the wrong hands, fuelling an array of crimes and arming the very people the police were meant to be clamping down on. Criminals viewed police not as state officials maintaining law and order, but as easy sources of firearms, and this guns-to-gangs issue impacted with severe negativity on the fundamental right to safety of residents in the Western Cape.

A June 2016 police ballistics audit revealed that smuggled guns meant to have been destroyed by police had been used in various gang hotspots across the Western Cape between 2010 and 2016. 'They had been used in 1 666 murders, 1 403 attempted murders and 315 other crimes. Victim analysis revealed that a disturbingly high number of murder and attempted murder victims ranged from the ages of 18 to infants. The list of children shot with Project Impi firearms consists of 261 child victims,' Vearey noted.[23] Most of the shootings happened in Cape Town suburbs that were synonymous with gang violence, such as Bishop Lavis, Belhar, Elsies River and Manenberg.

What had also become obvious was the potential for civil liability on the part of the SAPS. They'd been in possession of thousands of firearms that they were supposed to destroy; instead, the weapons had been released to gangs who'd used them in murders. Vearey said, 'The SAPS has an obligation to solve these crimes and prevent more crimes involving use of these firearms. However, [the] SAPS is now compromised. It has a duty to link the stolen firearms ballistically to murders committed with them. Should [the] SAPS carry out this duty it will prove its own civil liability to inhabitants of South Africa who are killed or injured by these firearms.'[24]

The guns-to-gangs scandal lifted the lid on extreme fragmentation within the police – divisions that may have cost countless residents their lives. The saga, if those who investigated it are to be believed, is an absolute and undeniable threat to national security and a shameful case of state-facilitated killing.

On 13 June 2016, Peter Jacobs was moved from the post of the Western Cape's Crime Intelligence head to that of the Wynberg cluster commander, while Jeremy Vearey was transferred from his position of acting deputy provincial commissioner of crime detection in the province to the head of the Cape Town cluster of police stations, a role he'd previously filled. Major General Mzwandile Tiyo replaced Jacobs and Major General Patrick Mbotho replaced Vearey.

For Vearey, being summarily removed from Project Impi was strikingly reminiscent of his fate in the 2002 Operation Slasher saga, during which he claimed to have uncovered rampant police corruption. Vearey was moved from that task team, and it remained unclear what had happened to the approximately 1 500 case dockets that he would have used to prove corruption and gross negligence within the police.[25]

Following his 2016 transfer, Vearey, this time along with Jacobs and the Police and Prisons Civil Rights Union, took on national and provincial police management, as well as the successors to their own positions, in the Cape Town Labour Court, demanding that their transfers be effectively reversed. And it was through affidavits deposed for this case that, in 2017, extraordinary and unprecedented details of Project Impi and the intense internal police skirmishes came out.

Firearms in the police's possession in the Western Cape destined for destruction were being destroyed within the province, but firearms destined for destruction in other provinces were channelled to Pretoria for this purpose, so Vearey and Jacobs began to investigate police officers in Pretoria responsible for destroying firearms.

Ex-police colonel Christiaan Lodewyk Prinsloo became a focus, and businessman Irshaad 'Hunter' Laher, a reservist at the De Deur police station, an area south of Johannesburg and where Prinsloo had been stationed (and who later based himself in Cape Town), was identified as his alleged middleman.[26] A dedicated firearm shooter, Laher belonged to the SA Hunters Association, as well as a shooting club in the Cape Town suburb of Kenwyn.[27]

Prinsloo was arrested in January 2015. He confessed to selling at least 2 000 firearms meant to be destroyed by police, allegedly to Laher and Alan Raves, a Vereeniging firearms collector. Raves was also a registered and licensed firearms dealer, and had been a heritage inspector with the South African Heritage Resource Agency in 2012, which meant he'd had access to firearms with potential heritage value.

In June 2016, a week after Vearey and Jacobs had been yanked from their positions and therefore from Project Impi, Chris Prinsloo was sentenced to an effective eighteen years in jail after accepting a plea deal with the state.[28] If Prinsloo were ever charged with the murders of those killed with Project Impi firearms, he would become South Africa's most prolific mass murderer without himself ever having pulled a trigger.

The state's indictment of Raves and Laher,[29] who were arrested in August 2015 and June 2016, respectively, as part of the Project Impi clampdown, noted that unlicensed firearms, those that were voluntarily surrendered, homemade firearms and those with unknown owners, were taken to the confiscated-firearms storeroom in Silverton, Gauteng, where they were kept under lock and key. They were then sent for ballistics testing, after which each firearm was allocated a specific number for the destruction process. However, Prinsloo and another former police colonel, identified in court papers only as Naidoo, both of whom had been responsible for the destruction of firearms forfeited to the police, had opened an unauthorised firearms store in Germiston.

It was the state's case that Laher, together with others both known and unknown to authorities, had operated together as a group of criminals. 'The state alleges that the core function of the criminal enterprise was to steal firearms and ammunition destined for destruction for themselves and also provide the firearms and ammunition to criminals including Alan Robert Raves for his own benefit and Laher who supplied firearms and ammunition to members of gangs on the Cape Flats that displayed a continued and considerable demand for illicitly obtained firearms and ammunition to further gang wars in the Western Cape from 2006 onwards.'[30] In a later court document, however, the state said that 'there is no direct evidence that [Laher] sold or supplied the firearms personally to members of street gangs.'[31]

During a July 2016 appearance in the Bellville Magistrate's Court, Laher and Raves seemed rattled when protesters, including members of Pagad, gathered there. Abdus Salaam Ebrahim, the coordinator of this grouping, confronted Laher, shouting, 'How many children

Where the dog lies buried

Alleged firearms smuggler Irshaad Laher conceals his face as he leaves the Western Cape High Court on 22 September 2017. Picture: Caryn Dolley, News24

have died because of him?'[32] Police officers had to step in and Laher had to leave the court via a back exit for his own safety.

(By April 2019 the case against Laher and Raves was slowly unfolding in the Western Cape High Court. The trial was expected to be massive and lengthy, with more than 3 000 dockets forming part of it. Raves had wanted to have his case separated from Laher's because he felt he was simply being dragged along in that matter, which barely overlapped with the charges he faced. The author understood that both Laher and Raves were set to argue that they had not been involved in channelling firearms to gangsters.)

On 7 November 2016, attorney Noorudien Hassan, who had been among a team of lawyers representing Irshaad Laher in the Project Impi case, was shot dead in his car outside his home in the suburb of

Lansdowne in Cape Town. The bullets ended an illustrious career in law, which had involved representing several alleged gang members, including Jerome Booysen and Ralph Stanfield, as well as others linked to nightclub security. No one was arrested for the shooting.

Hassan's close associate, advocate Pete Mihalik, who was also on the defence team in the guns-to-gangs case, at the time noted, 'We [are] entering a very dangerous period but it won't stop us defending the right to have a fair trial.'[33]

Noorudien Hassan once told the author that he was not a 'gangster lawyer'. Nevertheless, Pagad national coordinator Haroon Orrie was of the opinion that Hassan had been part of a problem. He said, 'We're not claiming responsibility; however, we are saying our full support is behind those responsible. His death is long overdue.'[34]

Startling claims started surfacing following Hassan's killing, including that the lawyer had inappropriately accessed (via a Crime Intelligence officer) an investigation diary and documents in the case involving Laher. This paperwork contained the details of an informant linked to Project Impi – details that would likely have sent shockwaves through gang circles and sown seeds of mistrust and suspicion among members of the Hard Livings.

The state accused the defence team in the Laher case of having got hold of the documents without its consent,[35] which the defence team, including Mihalik, disputed.[36] In fact, when cops, on behalf of the state, later delivered another set of the documents to the defence team, the team refused to receive the paperwork, fearing they would again be accused of having inappropriately accessed it.

Perhaps the truth about the initial batch of documents was a combination of the state and the defence's stance: that certain cops had formally delivered the documents to the defence, but, that this, unbeknown to the defence, had happened against the state's will. This tallied with the rumours that a Crime Intelligence officer was involved in getting the documents to Noorudien Hassan.

Where the dog lies buried

In May 2017 Jeremy Vearey added to the claims swirling around Hassan's murder – he said that he was aware that a Crime Intelligence officer had visited Hassan about concocted claims to be made against him (Vearey). 'We are aware of what they are up to,' he said. 'There is definitely something everybody is hiding. We are coming after them systematically.'[37]

And he made another startling claim, that some police and Crime Intelligence officers were conspiring with gangsters and politicians to try and snuff out investigations he was busy with. 'This is a various convergence of various people. This is the politics of organised crime,' he said.[38]

In 2018 Nafiz Modack made shocking claims that Vearey was a 27s gang member working with a leader of that gang, known as Red, and that Vearey had played a role in Hassan's murder.[39] Modack claimed that Hassan had introduced Vearey to Red because the two had issues to iron out – serious issues, because it was claimed that Red had wanted Vearey murdered. The two had apparently smoothed over their problems, but some gangsters had found out about the meeting and were unhappy because they felt Red having Vearey's backing meant the gang boss was becoming too powerful.

Vearey, according to Modack's claims, had had Hassan murdered to prevent the lawyer ever confirming that he'd facilitated the introduction of the top cop and the gang boss, which, if Vearey's superiors found out about it, would have resulted in Vearey being fired.[40]

These claims didn't amount to much and Vearey wasn't charged for Hassan's killing.

With the identification of the Gauteng arm of the gun-smuggling racket involving Chris Prinsloo and his alleged associates, the

Western Cape investigation morphed from a provincial one focused mainly on certain cops and gangsters, into a critical national investigation. Then-national police commissioner Riah Phiyega was briefed on it, and those running it were instructed that it should continue.

Vearey identified other illicit firearms networks. 'One network funnelled firearms through Laher to gangs in the Western Cape; the other distributed illicit heritage and military weapons. Our investigation identified role players involved in cross-border trafficking of military armaments,' he claimed. 'The investigation … also demonstrated that firearms were possibly being stockpiled for crimes against the state by right wing groups.'[41]

When Vearey and Jacobs were suddenly transferred, there was allegedly no handing over or any process to bridge the gap between the outgoing team and the one taking over the Project Impi investigation. 'The whole operation [was] simply … allowed to grind to a halt. The team has been reduced from twelve to four. The inhabitants of the Republic of South Africa have therefore been exposed to violent crime and dereliction of SAPS duty to prevent, combat and investigate such crime, and to protect and secure the inhabitants,' Vearey said.[42]

But it wasn't just Vearey and Jacobs who were frustrated by the ever-tightening path along which Project Impi seemed to be stumbling. The Director of Public Prosecutions in the Western Cape expressed concern in a two-page letter to provincial police commissioner Khombinkosi Jula in August 2016. The letter stated that Lieutenant Colonel Clive Ontong, a key police officer who was investigating the illegal firearms channels, had revealed that within three days he would no longer be the lead investigator, or even part of, Project Impi. Ontong's removal from the project could, the letter pointed out, prove detrimental because as the lead investigator under Vearey's command, he had conducted all searches, secured evidence and followed up all leads, as well as identified, located and interviewed several witnesses, including expert witnesses.[43]

It said developments had seen Project Impi's focus increase. Aspects that still needed investigation included tracing outstanding firearms that had been sold to gangsters on the streets. Witnesses had also identified loopholes in firearms legislation making it easy to smuggle guns out of South Africa.

'Further investigation is therefore required into the import and export of firearms by individuals and/or arms dealers for illicit means and the possible violation of South Africa's arms embargoes and international protocols of which South Africa is a signatory,' the letter said.[44]

Ontong was in September 2016 still trying to push ahead with Project Impi work despite the apparent resistance it was up against: he applied to go to Gauteng for purposes of the investigation – to have a witness placed in protection. However, a police colonel from the provincial finance office told him that 'Project Impi was not renewed and he would not make funds available'.[45]

It was clear that Project Impi was of national, and even international, importance, but that it was not getting the support needed for it to continue and expand.

Jacobs said that his transfer, and that of Vearey, had interrupted their investigation at a critical time and that the investigation team was then reduced, meaning that, far from increasing resources to boost Project Impi, police powers had done the exact opposite.[46]

Having been advised that Project Impi's investigations would end with the Prinsloo case, Jacobs pointed out that about 1 200 firearms Prinsloo had supplied were not at that stage accounted for, and that their job was therefore not yet over. 'Part of our investigation was to trace and recover the firearms, identify the people using them and to bring them to justice,' he said.[47]

And he emphasised that there was a foul symbiotic link between cops and gangsters, naming alleged 28s gang boss Ralph Stanfield. 'Our investigation has revealed that police officials, of whom three have been arrested at this stage, have colluded with gang leaders to facilitate the provision of firearm licences to gangs illegally and fraudulently,' he said.[48]

Back in 2014 Ralph Stanfield had become the focus of a splinter investigation stemming from Project Impi. In June that year Stanfield, his partner at the time who later became his wife, Nicole,[49] and his sister Francisca were arrested for allegedly getting hold of firearms using gun licences that were fraudulently created. That same month three police officers who were based at the Central Firearms Registry in Pretoria – the head office where cops deal with gun-licence issues – were taken into custody[50] and added as accuseds in the Stanfield case.

While still facing these charges Stanfield become the focus of further cop action – but this time he pointed a finger back at them, insisting that police infighting had turned him into a target. (A common claim by those in the underworld targeted by police is that they've been picked on because they've somehow become caught up in fights between cops or individuals in other state agencies.)

On 25 March 2016 – Good Friday – police officers arrived at Stanfield's mother's home in Mitchells Plain, 'armed to the teeth with firearms, bulletproof jackets and a whole arsenal of weapons'. 'They broke open the gates, handcuffed my mother, got her to speak to me [presumably on the phone], took photographs of her, mocked her openly in front of my sister... who is a special needs child, assaulted her, pulled her around and then threw her into a van,' Stanfield later claimed.[51] It isn't clear how he was aware of the details of this event as he wasn't present, but he was presumably filled in afterwards by those who were.

Against the advice of his legal representatives, Stanfield then went to his mother's home. 'I was met by several massive police officers who merely grabbed me, assaulted me, threw me into a van and drove me to Mitchells Plain police station,' he said. He alleged that there had been no warrant for his arrest, nor for his mother's, and described the police's actions as 'apartheid-style militia conduct'.[52]

Stanfield said that a cop, whom he knew as Detective Titus, was present and told him 'in no uncertain terms' that he could not 'rely on General Veary's [sic] protection anymore and that he [Titus] will come for me. He threatened me, intimidated me and then left with various other police officers.' Detective Titus was known to him, Stanfield claimed, 'because several years ago he made the vexatious allegations that I was being protected by General Veary [sic]. He testified this in court in a matter where I was not an accused.'[53]

Ralph Stanfield said he had no relationship with Vearey, and that he understood that after Detective Titus had made these 'spurious' claims relating to him and Vearey, the detective was demoted.

'It is also apparent that I am caught in the middle [of] a dispute between General Veary [sic] and General Goss who seem to be vying for certain positions in the police and who have huge animosity between one another. I am not going to be a "whipping boy" for either of them. The allegation against me is nothing more than a ruse. I have been set up by design,' Stanfield insisted.[54]

The General Goss Stanfield referred to was Gregory Goss, previously a major general in the police. In August 2014 Goss was appointed to head the Mitchells Plain cluster of police stations, a role Vearey had filled from March 2010 to the same month in 2014 that Goss was appointed to the position. Goss and Vearey reportedly didn't see eye to eye.

Goss's son, Greg Goss Junior, was shot dead in gang-related violence in July 2014 in Elsies River, with a firearm later believed to have been used in fifteen different murders and possibly obtained by gunmen via cops as it was identified in Project Impi investigations.[55]

Two suspects were arrested but later acquitted.

Goss said that he was disappointed in the poor quality of his colleagues' work and that he believed the 28s gang had been behind his son's murder.[56] He lodged a formal complaint, and four police officers were subsequently investigated and two state witnesses charged with perjury.[57]

In October 2016, four months after Jeremy Vearey and Peter Jacobs were suddenly shifted away from Project Impi, the state provisionally withdrew the firearms-licence charges against Ralph Stanfield and his co-accused.

According to Jacobs and Vearey, politics is what crushed Project Impi; and there were rumours in cop circles that the investigation was doomed because certain officers had been expressly tasked with ensuring it ended because of the high-level individuals who would've been identified as suspects had it continued. Jacobs said he and Vearey had been incorrectly perceived as siding with then national police commissioner Riah Phiyega, and as such, had been incorrectly viewed as 'Phiyega's people',[58] and that during December 2015, in the run-up to their transfers, there was a purge of those perceived to have been in her camp.

Phiyega, by that point, was facing serious allegations and was the centre of another ugly controversy dogging the police – in October 2015 she was suspended for her role in the Marikana massacre in which 34 miners were killed during a strike at a mine in Rustenburg in the North West province.

And there was another facet to the politics of the situation, this one revolving around outspoken former member of Parliament Vytjie Mentor. Vearey had been responsible for ensuring the recording of a contentious statement by Mentor to the SAPS in May 2016, while he was in the position of acting deputy provincial commissioner of detective services. Although Mentor had requested that he, Vearey, take down her statement, it had been routinely recorded by police officers under his command.

Mentor's allegations of corruption in the statement pointed directly at the highest government official in South Africa: '... The Gupta family, the son of the President [Duduzane Zuma] and some ministers ... as well as the President to a certain extent: All have a corrupt relationship that gives unfair advantage to the Gupta family and their associates at the expense of the state using state resources and agencies all the way for their own benefit.'[59]

The national police commissioner's office directed Mentor's statement to the head of the Hawks, Berning Ntlemeza; and it was also leaked to *City Press*. The subsequent 'political storm ... related to vexing political issues of state capture', plus the fact that Mentor revealed that Vearey had arranged for the recording of her statement, 'fuelled an ulterior motive which led to my transfer, contrary to the interests of the SAPS, the public interest, and the prevention of criminal gang activity in the Western Cape,' Vearey noted.[60] In seen as siding with Mentor, Vearey may have been viewed by some as taking a stance against Jacob Zuma, given the contents of Mentor's statement.

And yet more bad blood was exposed – this time between Peter Jacobs and the successor to his position as Crime Intelligence head in the Western Cape, Mzwandile Tiyo.[61] Jacobs said that he'd received information that Tiyo didn't have a matric, and nor did he 'meet the requirements of the clearance applied for' in order to qualify for the job.[62] When the author asked the SAPS in August 2017 about Tiyo's qualifications, however, they responded that documents in their possession showed that Tiyo had obtained a matric certificate in 1993 and his security clearance in 2016, and they were therefore satisfied that he met the requirements for the role he filled.[63]

It's understood that Tiyo, who had previously felt 'ridiculed' and 'humiliated' by Jacobs,[64] lodged internal complaints against

Jacobs, but was later asked to instead settle the disputes through a reconciliation process.[65]

Police management fought Peter Jacobs and Jeremy Vearey in their attempts to be reinstated to the posts from which they had been removed. Lieutenant General Bonang Christina Mgwenya, the police's deputy national commissioner of human resources management, painted the duo as egotistical. She found what Vearey and Jacobs had outlined in their affidavits to be 'extravagant, unfounded and displaying a concerning lack of insight and humility' – 'they display a lack of due modesty and inappropriately and unfairly overtook [sic] the important roles played by others', she said.[66]

Mgwenya insisted that the police had no political perceptions when it came to the duo and that this hadn't influenced their placements – the police bosses viewed the Vearey and Jacobs redeployments not as transfers or demotions, but rather as part of organisational structuring.

Bosses including Western Cape police head Khombinkosi Jula and acting national police commissioner Khomotso Phahlane[67] found it 'little short of ludicrous'[68] that Vearey and Jacobs believed that it was impossible for police to tackle the gang problem in the Western Cape unless they were deployed back to their original positions. While conceding that Vearey and Jacobs had played a massive role in Prinsloo's arrest, Mgwenya went so far as to imply that Jula felt that Jacobs had not been meeting the expectations of his job. Jula had, she said, 'expressed dissatisfaction' with the level of intelligence with which Jacobs was providing him.[69]

Nonetheless, on 3 August 2017, the Cape Town Labour Court ruled that the transfers of Jeremy Vearey and Peter Jacobs be set aside.

The duo said the court ruling was particularly poignant because the Labour Court was situated opposite a building that had once housed the apartheid's security police and it was where many years earlier they had been harshly interrogated. In both instances – in the Labour Court and with the security police – they had been up against cops, first under apartheid and then during democracy.

After the Labour Court ruling, the author requested documents stemming from the case, which had been handed up in court thereby becoming public documents. Over the next two days the author wrote several articles, based on these court papers, which were rich in previously unpublished details about Project Impi, and which went up on the News24 website.

On the afternoon of 4 August the author received an SMS that read, 'Ms Doley! That. same. guns. that. the. cops. sold. is. going. to. be. used. on. your. head. at. work. or. your. house. or. your. mom. house and. your. Dog.' The author was provided with private security officers and lodged a criminal case with police.

Major General Jeremy Vearey (left) and Lieutenant General Peter Jacobs near the Cape Town Labour Court in August 2017 after hearing they had been successful in having their transfers within the police service set aside. Picture: Caryn Dolley, News24

During the first few months of 2018 Vearey and Jacobs were still in limbo following their Labour Court victory, their reinstatements not yet having been effected.

Around this time, the political landscape changed drastically – on 14 February 2018, Jacob Zuma stepped down as president, making way for Cyril Ramaphosa to become South Africa's head of state. Twelve days later, Ramaphosa reshuffled his cabinet, and among the key changes was that outspoken Minister of Police Fikile Mbalula ceded his position to the equally flamboyant Bheki Cele. The change brought about a shift in power in the police, inevitably shaking up connections between crooks and corrupt cops.

Shortly after this there were still attempts from within the police to try and take down, or to pin crimes on, Vearey and Jacobs. On 14 March a criminal case was opened against Jacobs and Vearey by a fellow police officer and, according to sources, it related to allegations that Jacobs had destroyed documents from Goodwood prison.[70] However, the complaint wasn't taken seriously and the Western Cape's head of correctional services was even quoted calling it 'fake news', considering that the information had emanated from the Western Cape's Crime Intelligence.[71] No arrests were made and the case was closed.

Six days after this, on 29 March 2018, freshly appointed Police Minister Bheki Cele announced that Peter Jacobs had been promoted to become the new head of the country's Crime Intelligence unit.[72] And a couple of weeks after that, on 12 April 2018, it was announced that Jeremy Vearey would fill the role of deputy provincial head of crime detection.

Jacobs's promotion to a national post and Vearey's redeployment to the position he'd fought for meant that the fortunes of others who had stood in their way had taken a massive knock, and that implicating information the duo had gathered as part of Project Impi could again see the light of day.

Jacobs, however, faced an immense task, as he'd taken over a Crime Intelligence unit infested with rogue elements and which had become porous with both information and misinformation.

In April 2018, while the country was still getting its head around the shift from the Zuma to the Ramaphosa administration, and just weeks after Vearey was transferred back to head up the Western Cape's detective services and Jacobs was promoted to national Crime Intelligence head, it emerged that not only had the firearms-licence charges against Ralph Stanfield and his co-accused been reinstated but the case had grown much bigger, with more charges and more suspects – a further seventeen of Stanfield's associates, including relatives, had been added to the charge sheet.

The renewed charge sheet said Stanfield and his co-accused were suspected of either being 28s gangsters or being associated with the gang's operations; that the three (now former) police officers who had been based at the Central Firearms Registry in Pretoria had in 2014 allegedly been involved in 'facilitating the destroying and/or disappearance of all documentation relating to the competency and all firearm applications that was received at the Central Firearms Registry office' by Stanfield and his co-accused (it was not specified if the officers had resigned or had been fired since last facing charges); and that Stanfield and his wife had had several firearms and rounds of ammunition illegally in their possession.[73]

The same month that the reinstatement of the Stanfield firearms charges became known, the Western Cape's problem of cops allegedly facilitating the issuing of firearms licences to those who didn't qualify for these surfaced afresh – two police officers based at the Lentegeur police station in Mitchells Plain were arrested on allegations that they'd accepted a bribe to declare someone fit to own a firearm.[74]

Early in 2019 it emerged that those that Jeremy Vearey and Peter Jacobs had legally taken on following their 2016 'redeployments' had once again entered the fray – they planned to appeal the ruling that had ordered that the transfers of the two men be set aside.

But in late February this was withdrawn[75] so the airing of further dirty cop laundry in this saga was avoided.

CHAPTER 5
Strength in numbers: amalgamation

In December 2010 Cyril Beeka had told Jacques Cronje that word on the street was that Cape Town nightclub-security companies were planning to amalgamate to form one large security body. And, indeed, mere weeks after Beeka's March 2011 murder, well-oiled wheels were in motion to have the security company he'd created, Pro Access, merge with Professional Protection Services to become part of one nightclub-security grouping.

Professional Protection Services had been in operation since 1993; from 2003 it was run by Andre Naude.[1] Naude's version of events was that a few days after Beeka was killed, Jacques Cronje contacted him about merging the two companies.[2]

Cronje's story was, however, markedly different: '[A]bout two weeks after the [Beeka] funeral I was approached by Andre [Naude and] Mark [Lifman], to have a meeting regarding the security, the bouncing industry.'[3]

Andre Naude, a tall man with muscular upper arms, and a

self-described 'family guy', had been in the bouncer business since the early 1990s, and had a history of personal protection, including having worked for some international celebrities.

Mark Roy Lifman, meanwhile, was referred to by close associates as an astute businessman who'd climbed the money-making ladder rung by rung, from owning some taxis and a pie shop at Cape Town's central train station to becoming a major property mogul. He'd also dabbled in the fashion industry.

Lifman has consistently denied being involved in crime; nonetheless, his name consistently comes up in discussions about underworld dealings, and legal action has repeatedly been instituted against him. In 2001 the Jockey Club of South Africa[4] banned him for life from any role in horseracing over claims involving two incidents in which jockeys were intimidated.[5] And in 2005 he was charged with indecently assaulting seven boys, plus the attempted murder of a man who had allegedly procured the boys; he was acquitted in 2009 due to 'contradictory and poor evidence' and when a state witness suddenly recanted.[6]

A few weeks after first being approached by Lifman and Naude in early 2011, according to Cronje, Lifman, Colin Booysen and Leon 'Lyons' Davids from the Sexy Boys met at Cronje's office; and there was a follow-up meeting at Lifman's Sea Point offices at which Lyons was also present.[7] (Lyons's presence at these meetings was apparently no coincidence: there were whispers that the high-ranking Sexy Boys gang member had pulled the trigger on Cyril Beeka.)

There was another meeting between Cronje, Lifman and Naude in April 2011, and Cronje reported feeling positive about the amalgamation. 'I was keen to do it at that stage. I found it ... sounded like a good idea. They came across very honest that time.'[8]

The new company, Specialised Protection Services (SPS), was registered on 13 April 2011 involving, among others, Naude,

Lifman, Jerome Booysen, Colin Booysen and one Richard van Zyl. A group of Moroccan men under Houssain Taleb, the martial-arts expert and kickboxing champion known as Houssain Moroccan ('he knows how to enforce maximum force ... he's actually a weapon by himself')[9] was included as part of the amalgamation.[10]

The stories about the Moroccan bouncers gave the impression that they acted together like a tornado – swiftly, viciously and leaving a trail of destruction. But Taleb insisted that the seven Moroccan bouncers working in the city centre were not a 'mafia' but rather a brotherhood who had each other's backs. The aim, he said, was make the city centre a safe place for those who wanted to enjoy what it had to offer. 'One message I want to send to any drug dealer, gangster or pickpocket is that you're not welcome here. I'll be here all the time. I'm not scared. I'll take a bullet if I have to.'[11]

It was agreed that club and restaurant owners would be told that the security services being rendered to them would remain in place and that basically only the name of the security company providing the services would change. Although its first contract was signed on 23 June 2011,[12] SPS was officially launched several months later, on 1 November 2011.[13] Its logo, of a lion's face flanked by wings, gave off an air of power and dominance.

A few months after the meetings with Lifman and the others about merging Cape Town's security companies, Jacques Cronje was becoming increasingly uneasy about the amalgamation, and later his attitude towards it changed completely. 'I didn't feel too comfortable with signing over my contracts to SPS but I also felt threatened, that's why I did it ... because the Sexy Boys are a well-known gangster group in Cape Town. When I then decided that I basically didn't want to go ahead with the signing of the contracts, it was too late.'[14]

Towards the end of 2011 Cronje had found himself unable to attend another meeting with the heads of the amalgamated security grouping and claimed that when he phoned Colin Booysen to tell him, Booysen had sworn at him, trying to force him to get to the meeting. Bad blood therefore developed between the two.

Cronje claimed that at a later meeting about the signing of SPS contracts and between management of several security companies, held at the Ritz Hotel in Sea Point around November 2011, Colin Booysen had approached him with two men from the Sexy Boys who 'had long knives in their jackets'. Cronje further claimed that he and Colin Booysen started swearing and shouting but the situation eventually cooled down.[15]

Cronje's contracts were handed over to SPS, and he insisted that around February 2012 he was unfairly forced out of the company. 'It took me ten years to ... build that and they took it in nine months

Andre Naude, backed by private security officers, waits for his friend Mark Lifman outside the Bellville Magistrate's Court in February 2018. Picture: Caryn Dolley, News24

from me,' he lamented. 'It was really hard at the time, it was hard work getting these contracts and by losing it in nine months, to look at it, it gets a bit emotional, I must tell you that. ... I have put a lot of passion into this ... and to lose it in nine months is quite hard – heart sore, heart broke, to know that how people can get away with it and do it with a smile. [sic]'[16]

However, later in court an alternative version emerged of what had happened: Mark Lifman had been unhappy with Cronje's conduct as he was apparently once again using cocaine and was accused of misappropriating company funds.[17] Cronje denied this.[18]

'We try our best to curb drugs in clubs... We're not part of any underworld gangs. We run a clean operation.'[19]

This is how Andre Naude described SPS in an interview in 2012. He said that the company employed about 350 doormen, trained in karate and jiu-jitsu, in 146 clubs.

Expectations of SPS employees, according to the company's eight-page code of conduct, included 'a positive public image, instilling public confidence, integrity, a culture of honesty, loyalty' and 'maintaining credibility'. Members of the company were expected to be 'polite, helpful and non-aggressive', and conduct themselves lawfully; they were not to 'assault, threaten, victimise or intimidate persons at the venue', and were not to use excessive force while performing their duties.[20] Smiling genuinely and using words instead of fists was strongly encouraged.

Despite all this attention to detail, the following month – February 2012, just three months after its official launch – SPS was shut down. Because the company had not been registered with the Private Security Industry Regulatory Authority, it was deemed illegal. Arrests followed, with several bouncers, including Houssain Taleb, being taken into custody on charges including working for a security company not registered with the relevant authority.

Mark Lifman and Andre Naude were also arrested and faced a

whopping 313 charges relating to running the company without the necessary registration.

While Lifman and Naude turned their attention to the legal wrangle that would last more than three years, their associate Richard van Zyl didn't let the grass grow under his feet, registering a new security company called Lifestyle Entertainment Security Services[21] just two months after the arrest of his erstwhile partners.

Lifman, it emerged much later, had also had contingency plans in place, and had approached one Alwyn Landman, whom he'd first noticed as a doorman-cum-car guard at the Atlantic seaboard seafront establishment the Grand Africa Café and Beach, and to whom he'd offered a job at another seafront venue, Shimmy Beach Club, which opened in December 2011. Lifman had been involved in the conception and opening of Shimmy Beach Club, although he later cut ties with the establishment.

After the SPS debacle in 2012, Lifman had asked if Landman would like to be the name associated with a new security company.[22] 'He [Landman] was very excited and began the process of becoming compliant with grading and registration. For about six months he kept me in the loop with the progress and we had many discussions and meetings. Then all of a sudden he went quiet on me and would just say things were moving along slowly,' Lifman said.[23] He added that Landman had gone on to create PPA Security, in which he (Lifman) had not been involved.[24]

For his part, Alwyn Landman denied ever having been involved with Mark Lifman.[25]

In March 2013, gangster-turned-pastor Albern Martins, who had been instrumental in running Core and other subsequent initiatives to apparently try and quell gangsterism, was gunned down outside the Blue Downs Magistrate's Court in Cape Town, where he was expected to appear as a suspect in a perlemoen-smuggling case involving racketeering, drug dealing and fraud.[26]

A few weeks after this murder, on 28 March 2013, the Glenhaven home of Jerome Booysen (who, together with his brother Michael, had withdrawn from Core several years earlier) was targeted when a petrol bomb was thrown at the garage door and shots fired at the house.[27] Then, on 9 May, another Booysen brother was targeted – Colin was wounded in the arm and leg in a shooting outside his home in Belhar.

And just three days later Martins's sidekick Ivan Waldeck, who had also been involved in Core and other apparent plans to snuff out gangsterism, was shot several times and his wife wounded in a targeted gun attack.[28]

Sources believed the shootings that had targeted Martins, the Booysen brothers and Waldeck were linked, and suspected the triggermen were carrying out orders for someone.

In March 2016 Ruben Adams, the gunman convicted of pulling the trigger on Martins, said that in return for protection for his family from the 26s (which is affiliated with the Sexy Boys), The Firm (which includes 28s members) had demanded that he carry out a murder.[29] 'One day they came to fetch me at home and took me to Blue Downs Court and said I would get what I need if I killed someone for them,' he explained. He eventually admitted that 'they' were 'Lastig's people',[30] presumably referring to former 28s gang boss Ernie 'Lastig' Solomon, who had been a member of Core in the 1990s. (Solomon was never officially linked to the Martins killing.) Adams's words implied that the historic fighting between the Sexy Boys and the 28s was ongoing.

After the first bout of attacks in Cape Town in 2013, violence snaked over to Johannesburg where it erupted spectacularly – on

24 July a remote-controlled device was used in a failed apparent attempt to assassinate Radovan Krejčíř outside his Bedfordview business premises.

The attack was reported to be linked to the Cape Town movie industry, but it was also reported that a source said that the bizarre shooting may have related to Krejčíř's dealings with Cape Town gangsters over territory – a meeting the previous week between Krejčíř and 'one of Cape Town's most notorious members of the underworld' in an attempt to iron out their differences 'didn't go well'.[31]

Back in Cape Town, on 30 July, it was reported that a 30-year-old woman and her boyfriend had been shot in Hard Livings and Americans gang stronghold Manenberg. The boyfriend had been killed outright; the woman had been taken to hospital with a bullet in her neck. The woman, a police informant, was the survivor in a rape and kidnapping case for which Rashied Staggie had been convicted and sentenced in 2003 to fifteen years in jail.[32] At the time of the rape the woman was 19 years old and had a 3-year-old daughter.[33]

After the shooting, the woman's mother said that the woman had been in witness protection but had missed her family and eventually left the protective service, returning to Manenberg, where her family had constantly feared for her safety. A week after the shooting, the mother said, she'd switched off her daughter's life-support machines.[34]

Jeremy Vearey, in his capacity as a police officer, told reporters that the woman had died. But it later emerged that this was all an elaborate ruse. 'I exploited the fact that the Hard Livings thought they had gotten rid of her,' Vearey said in September 2013. 'I know there were gang members scouring the hospital wards looking for her as well as going to her family's houses. We needed to protect her. I am responsible for the life of a person, [and] I will do whatever is necessary to ensure their safety.'[35]

Cape Town's city centre became the next scene of the 2013 violence, and this time it unfolded daringly close to a court of law. Suspected 28s gangster Saliem John, Ralph Stanfield's cousin, was shot on the steps of the Western Cape High Court on 9 October. John, who was based in Valhalla Park and was on trial for several crimes,[36] survived the shooting.[37]

This attack was particularly brazen, given that there was a CCTV camera located near the entrance to the building; in addition, the court is located on a fussy little street nearly always clogged with cars, providing no clean getaway route.

The attempted hit on John was viewed as an attack on the 28s, so it was no surprise when an apparent retaliatory attack on the Sexy Boys then unfolded. Leon 'Lyons' Davids, the man suspected of having pulled the trigger on Cyril Beeka and therefore a critical witness to the assassination, was killed hours later on the same day John was wounded, 9 October, in a hit while at a braai in Sexy Boys-stronghold Belhar.

Following Beeka's assassination, Davids had gone into witness protection – there were strong rumours suggesting that Davids had started talking to cops and Hawks investigators about Beeka's murder (including who was with him when he'd pulled the trigger) and that these officers had convinced Davids to accept state protection given the extremely sensitive information he had about this high-profile Western Cape killing. But, the story goes, Davids had been lured out into the open by the promise of being able to run an upmarket club in Loop Street in the Cape Town city centre.[38]

Further and wilder rumours went along the lines of a senior police officer having sold affidavits relating to Beeka's murder to underworld figures who then, seeing in the documents what Davids had initially told cops, had had him eliminated.

Just three days after Davids was murdered, a killing again rocked

Johannesburg – this time Sam Issa was the victim. A Lebanese drug dealer and once an associate of Krejčíř, Issa was fatally shot in Bedforview.[39]

And the following month, on 12 November 2013, in the same Joburg suburb, at the business linked to Krejčíř and where the 007-style assassination attempt had been carried out barely three months earlier, a bomb detonated, leaving two people dead. Krejčíř wasn't there at the time.[40]

There was a long lull following these extreme bouts of violence, during which the focus shifted back to Mark Lifman. This time, however, the issues weren't directly linked to nightclub security. In May 2014 Lifman found himself under intense scrutiny by the South African Revenue Service (SARS), which launched an enquiry covering the tax affairs of Lifman himself 'and 35 other entities'.[41]

Others being looked into, with the authorisation of Ivan Pillay, then acting SARS commissioner, included Andre Naude and Jerome Booysen.[42]

Lifman conceded that some problems had indeed been picked up during the inquiry, in that some of the entities in which he had an interest weren't compliant with SARS tax laws. He said he'd instructed his accountant to remedy the identified problems, and in September 2014 appointed a company to assist the accountant. However, 'the amounts of outstanding tax due to SARS pursuant to the compliance backlog were much larger in scope that any of us had initially fathomed, if the assessments proposed to be raised by SARS was [sic] correct'[43] and towards the end of 2014 Lifman signed an agreement with SARS, undertaking not to dispose of certain assets, including all vehicles registered in his name and five of his watches, while the inquiry was underway.

While Lifman had the criminal charges relating to running SPS and

Strength in numbers: amalgamation

the SARS investigation to worry about, Andre Naude had his own set of problems. On 4 October 2014 Naude and his friend, martial-arts fighter Jan 'The Giant' Nortje, were shot in a parking area in front of Eastwoods Entertainment Lounge in Bellville in Cape Town's northern suburbs. Eastwoods was one of the businesses that had been paying SPS for its services.[44] Naude, who was shot in the lower legs, claimed the incident stemmed from an argument relating to a woman.

Turkish national Bora Unuvar, who was also wounded in the incident, said that he and a friend had gone to Eastwoods that evening, and after a verbal tiff over a woman, had been 'helped' out of the establishment by some bouncers. As they were leaving, he said, he'd turned back towards the venue and seen what appeared to be a security guard pulling out a firearm, so he pulled out his own and shot into the air as a warning. A BMW full of bouncers, who were not security providers at Eastwoods, had reportedly been parked outside the establishment and had started shooting at Unuvar. Police reported that in total about fifty shots were fired during the skirmish.[45]

'I never fired my gun at living entity in my life. I do not have any criminal record in my life too [sic],' Unavar insisted.[46]

After roughly eight months of public-domain calm, nightclub security in the heart of the city became a major focal point again, dragging names including those of Mark Lifman, Andre Naude and their associates back into the news and into muttered conversations about the underworld.

In early June 2015 a group of men – including Houssain Taleb, who at that stage still appeared to move with figures linked to SPS – had spent a little time at the Beerhouse, a popular establishment on Long Street. On exiting, there was an altercation with the doorman, Joe Louis Kazadi Kanyona.

105

In a second incident, on the evening of 20 June, Kanyona, the father of a four-month-old girl at the time, was fatally stabbed in an attack that was shrouded in mystery because the attacker somehow managed to evade being captured on CCTV. It was suspected that Kanyona had been killed because those running the Beerhouse had refused to pay protection money.

The targeted killing, late on a Saturday night when clubs in Long Street were pumping and the area was busy with pedestrians swarming on pavements and cars and taxis clogging the street, was particularly bold, yet it would have needed to have been meticulously planned, or guided by powerful figures, for Kanyona's killer to somehow slip through the fingers of police, which is what happened.

After the stabbing, three suspects were initially arrested for conspiracy to commit murder, but Kanyona's actual killer was not taken into custody. At the time of these initial arrests, police claimed in court that at least one of three suspects was a member of the Young Gifted Sexy Bastards, a gang with ties to the Hard Livings and with a stronghold in Woodstock, a suburb just outside the Cape Town city centre.

In August 2015, in a court case relating to the three arrests, a statement by one suspect noted that a man named Ashley was to stab a bouncer and that others would form a wall around the bouncer as this happened. This Ashley was not arrested at the time.[47]

Following Kanyona's killing, there was an outcry about safety in Long Street and establishments in the Cape Town city centre, but not much detail about what had led up to the murder emerged at that stage; there were rumours it was linked to the underworld, but these weren't officially substantiated. More than two years later, though, an official police theory went along the lines of the Crime Intelligence unit having ascertained that Ashley Fields, alleged to be 'a well-known and respected gangster in Salt River and Woodstock', had been involved in the killing; and that Colin Booysen had allegedly recruited Fields to be part of 'the muscle'.[48]

It was never made clear if Ashley Fields was the same Ashley referred to years earlier in the 2015 court case. Neither Ashley Fields nor Colin Booysen was charged for the killing and, as such, their involvement remained tales from the lips of cops.

———

Mark Lifman got a major reprieve in October 2015 when he and Andre Naude were cleared of all 313 charges relating to their running SPS without being registered with the necessary authority. They'd successfully applied for a discharge, on the grounds that they believed the state had targeted them for 'ulterior reasons', which they never elaborated on. Lifman felt the state (and the Hawks in particular) had 'manipulated evidence' and driven a 'malicious prosecution' against them.[49]

But just because Lifman was off the hook in the criminal case didn't mean he was off the hook with SARS, and he was hit with a staggering tax bill. 'The total amount of tax estimated to be claimed by SARS, cumulatively, exceeded R388m, which is in my estimation at least six times the value of the net worth of all the assets of the affected entities and my personal assets together,' he said. 'The figures were unrealistic and grossly unfair.'[50]

On 25 May 2016, six years to the day after an auction during which assets belonging to Lifman and Yuri 'The Russian' Ulianitski had gone under the hammer, Lifman's possessions were the focus of yet another auction, this second one linked to the taxman saga.

Other than both being public sales, however, the two couldn't have been more different. At the 2010 auction, in Cape Town's swish Belmond Mount Nelson Hotel, things seemed to be going well for Lifman. His assets up for sale included a 'gentleman's club' in the city centre named The Embassy, four other properties, and a 1971 Rolls Royce. The proceeds were to be split, in accordance with a March 2010 court order, between Lifman and Ulianitski's widow Irina.[51]

At the 2016 auction it was two Porsche Cayennes and two Lexus vehicles of Lifman's that went under the hammer, and this time around it was for the benefit of SARS. Held in considerably less swanky surrounds – at the Sheriff for Cape Town's warehouse in the industrial area of Montague Gardens – the auction was attended by about thirty people, including Jerome 'Donkie' Booysen, who bid successfully on a Porsche and a Lexus.[52] Colin Booysen was also at the auction, nursing a swollen hand; he said he was recovering from a shooting.[53]

Over the next few months it emerged that there were deep divisions within the revenue service about the review of Lifman's tax matter. Lifman himself said he believed that 'there were various irregularities relating to the decision to launch the initial tax inquiry and the manner in which it was thereafter conducted'. He claimed that information had surfaced that showed the enquiry may have been 'based on untested covert intelligence procured by what is now known as the "SARS rogue unit"'.[54]

Lifman was referring to allegations surrounding an apparently illegally constituted unit within SARS, the very existence of which eventually came into question: it became clear that claims of a rogue intelligence unit had been created and used as a tool against figures including former SARS commissioner Pravin Gordhan, to protect Jacob Zuma and those close to him (among others).[55]

'Since the start of the inquiry, I got the feeling that the SARS team prosecuting the inquiry had an ulterior motive over and above simply prosecuting an inquiry into my tax affairs, but that their intention was to ruin myself and the affected entities that belong to me,' Lifman continued. 'I have formed the apprehension that I was perhaps the target of illegal spying by government functionaries, especially after realising that a known spy had arranged to meet with me in November 2013.'[56]

The 'spy' in question was attorney Belinda Walter, who Lifman believed had, acting on the instruction of her handlers, secretly recorded their meeting in order 'to infiltrate' him.[57]

A panel of inquiry, separate from the Lifman SARS saga, was launched into allegations targeting SARS officials and this resulted in the controversial Sikhakhane Report,[58] which many felt had excluded critical information and overlooked legislation, and was yet another product of state capture. In this report, Walter was acknowledged to be a covert agent, while Lifman was named in the so-called Operation Honey Badger, specifically aimed at clamping down on the illicit tobacco industry. Lifman had, according to a newspaper report, met businessman Adriano Mazzotti, a director of local cigarette manufacturing company Carnilinx, and Jerome Booysen, with a view to doing business.[59]

The tax probe into Lifman was still hobbling along in court in 2019. His name seemed inextricably linked to illicit-tobacco shenanigans, as well as upsets within the nightclub-security arena – two notoriously shadowy industries.

Towards the end of 2016 there were murmurings in underworld circles about a businessman from Pakistan by way of the United Kingdom, the man known as Choudhry,[60] who was shaking things up, making inroads and disturbing the peace in bouncer operations in Cape Town and Johannesburg, but there was no outright and continuous violence. Yet.

In November this changed drastically, when attorney Noorudien Hassan was murdered (a hit in which, Nafiz Modack would later claim, Major General Jeremy Vearey had played a role); and just a day later, Craig Mathieson, the night manager of Hotel 303, an establishment belonging to Mark Lifman, was shot dead. Hotel 303 is located on Sea Point's busy Main Road, despite which the two gunmen carried out the brazen hit in a remarkably casual and unhurried fashion.[61]

It later emerged that the murder of Mathieson had allegedly been ordered by Colin Booysen and that it followed an altercation between Booysen and Lifman. Ashley Fields (the same man who, along with Colin Booysen, had been identified by police as allegedly having been involved in the murder of bouncer Joe Kanyona in June 2015) was allegedly tasked to 'take care of the night manager' at Hotel 303. Fields then supposedly recruited members of 'The Gifteds' – the Young Gifted Sexy Bastards – to carry out the murder.[62]

Colin Booysen denied any involvement in the Mathieson killing. 'There is no evidence linking me to the murder and I will go so far as to say that if there were any evidence the state would have charged me accordingly,' he said.[63] And, indeed, neither Booysen nor Fields was charged for the Mathieson murder.[64]

By December 2016 the ominous murmurings in Cape Town about Choudhry, whom one source described as a terrorist, had put underworld operatives on edge, although it wasn't yet clear exactly what they were nervous about.

Then, twenty days into 2017, Russel Jacobs, a suspected perlemoen-poaching kingpin based in Cape Town who was allegedly a member of an offshoot of the 28s prison gang's top tier of leaders,[65] was shot in the stomach and back in the Cape Town suburb of Blue Downs. He died in hospital the next day.

Jacobs, described by one source as a 'most intelligent psychopath',[66] was allegedly the mastermind of an operation that involved the illegal acquiring, processing and distribution of perlemoen in the Western Cape. Perlemoen is a sought-after black-market commodity and is so coveted that both legal and illegal consignments are targeted while in transit, necessitating security to protect it. Illustrating how much clout Jacobs seemed to have in gang circles, there were suspicions that 28s gangsters under the command of George 'Geweld' Thomas had years earlier been tasked with protecting Jacobs's perlemoen consignments.[67]

Jacobs, who some sources suspected was a police informant, had apparently travelled to China shortly before he was killed and had planned to start his own perlemoen-smuggling channel. It was thought that a rival faction within the 28s, with a fierce and unrelenting grip on illicit perlemoen routes, may have ordered the pulling of the trigger on Jacobs.

At the time of his killing, Jacobs was facing charges relating to the illegal perlemoen industry in a case involving about a dozen other accused, and had been the focus of a police operation named Project Ogies. Between July and November 2008, as part of the operation, a police agent had infiltrated Jacobs's alleged organisation. Surveillance cameras had also been used in the agent's home, as well as on a farm in Riviersonderend, a village about 140 kilometres outside of Cape Town where the perlemoen was processed. Jacobs was a step ahead of the authorities, however, because he'd discovered and destroyed the cameras.[68]

'It is anticipated the accused may dispute that abalone was transported and possessed. It is also anticipated that the usual attacks will be made on the credibility and reliability of the agent,' the prosecuting authority noted, insinuating that the smearing of police investigators' characters was so commonplace that it was expected.[69]

After Jacobs was murdered, some sources claimed that he had been paid R500 000 by Jeremy Vearey and fellow senior police officer Peter Jacobs, who had wanted Jacobs to gather information for them.[70] However, others dismissed this, saying the allegations formed part of a larger smear campaign to tarnish the images of certain police investigators.

CHAPTER 6

Money, murder, plots and politics

As the recharged nightclub-security takeover was developing in Cape Town in late 2011 and early 2012, Daniel 'Dan' Plato, at the time the Western Cape's Minister of Community Safety, heavily involved himself in trying to crack down on underworld activities in the city centre.

Plato had been a fulltime politician since 1996, operating as a ward councillor for areas including Belhar, a suburb that happened to be a stronghold of the Sexy Boys gang. In 2009 he was elected mayor of Cape Town in place of Helen Zille, a title he relinquished two years later to Patricia de Lille – from whom he took over again in November 2018.

Around early 2012 Plato was deeply involved in trying to unravel club-security and related crimes. He met with Mark Lifman and Jerome Booysen as part of his attempted crackdown, made several public statements – including that underworld businessmen operating in Cape Town were behind the channelling of drugs around the Cape Flats – and conducted several interviews with other figures who claimed to have knowledge of what was transpiring in the underworld arena.[1]

Plato is a member of the opposition DA, which runs the Western Cape province and the city of Cape Town, while senior career policeman Jeremy Vearey has a long and loyal history with the ANC, so tensions that emerged between the duo were inevitably, if not intentionally, steeped in politics. The roots of these tensions, which were planted around 2011, indirectly involved none other than the then-president of the country, Jacob Zuma.

In May 2011 Cape Town's underworld suddenly garnered national attention when Zuma reportedly held a meeting with several known gangsters at his official residence in Cape Town, supposedly as part of a plot to have the ANC take over control of the DA-led Western Cape.[2] Zuma's son Duduzane had, it was reported, met the delegation at the gates of the presidential estate and ensured that security guards didn't record the identities of any of the visitors.

While the ANC labelled as baseless the allegations about the gangster meeting, two independent sources confirmed[3] a media report that Zuma had met with alleged crime bosses Quinton 'Mr Big' Marinus, suspected Americans gang leader Igshaan Davids, and Durban businessman and 'alleged gangland enforcer'[4] Lloyd Hill.[5] A source high up in government and with ties to policing claimed that Hill[6] – who had spent about two decades in prison for crime and was released roughly the same time as the ANC was unbanned – was invaluable to Zuma in that he was highly connected in circles in which the South African president was not – with those on the ground and with a vast array 'ordinary' individuals, not in the upper echelons of political office.[7]

Another source, with decades of experience in policing, insisted that under the presidencies of Nelson Mandela (1994-1999) and Thabo Mbeki (1999-2008), while police corruption involving the

Dan Plato, who's been in politics since 1996, and in 2019 was mayor of Cape Town. Picture: Esa Alexander © *The Times*

underworld existed, it was neither particularly deep nor wide. It was only under the watch of Jacob Zuma that the problem became amplified and the corruption flowed in, saturating the police. As this source put it, 'The corruption goes right to the top.'[8]

There are many claims of dubious links between the former president and questionable characters. For example, a startling photograph, dated to some time in 2012, shows Zuma with state-security operative and known double agent George Darmanović, and Frans Richards, who'd previously worked in intelligence circles, in Zuma's offices in Pretoria.[9] And in April 2014 a photograph of Mark Lifman at Zuma's birthday rally in Athlone, Cape Town appeared in the *Sunday Times*.[10]

Meanwhile, controversial Cape businessman Jeffrey Franciscus – who was apparently one of those who knew about the May

Money, murder, plots and politics

2011 meeting Zuma allegedly had with the gang bosses – claimed that Zuma had flown Lloyd Hill from Durban to Cape Town for the meeting.[11] This indirectly became part of the foundation on which claims of a smear campaign against Vearey settled because Franciscus also apparently made a startling range of allegations involving politicians and the policeman.

In a letter apparently written and signed by Franciscus, dated 26 October 2011, Franciscus claimed he had recorded conversations between people in business and politicians, including those from the ANC, that would prove that they (those recorded) had planned to commit fraud. The letter said that Franciscus intended to approach police about the matter because he'd started receiving threats, including from members of the 28s prison gang, who had told him that if he disclosed details to the cops, he would be killed.

Eighteen days later, in November 2011, Franciscus died in a car crash on the N1 near Kuils River in Cape Town as he was returning from a meeting that had reportedly included Lloyd Hill.[12] He apparently lost control of his vehicle. The police said no foul play was suspected,[13] although some sources remained sceptical about what had caused the crash.

After Franciscus's death, Dan Plato compiled a dossier of conversations and communications that he said he'd had with Franciscus before the latter's death. The dossier made sensational claims against top politicians and police officers. Jeremy Vearey was named in it as working with certain suspected top gang bosses.[14]

But Franciscus's character came into question: it emerged that in 2011 he'd spent nine months in Cape Town's notorious Pollsmoor Prison relating to a fraud matter, and several sources labelled him a liar. Marius Fransman, then heading the ANC in the Western Cape, claimed Franciscus was mentally ill.[15] Franciscus's claims were therefore widely dismissed as delusional ramblings, or part of a smear campaign. (Five years later, in April 2016, following more claims made against Vearey, the Western Cape ANC claimed that 'Franciscus was not party to any allegations against the ANC but had, instead, refused to implicate General Vearey in exchange for a tender from the DA administration'.[16])

In February 2012 the author accompanied Plato to interview a man who said that a particular city-centre venue, which he claimed was a brothel, was a front for drug-dealing operations that involved rich foreign clients and included steroids being illegally imported from China. 'You pay your R70 and go into a room. You tell the girl you want cocaine and she goes to the security guys from the Congo. They'll make a call and the cocaine will arrive ... There are cameras in each room and the footage is used to bribe policemen who get caught on tape in the act,' he said.[17]

About whistleblowing, he noted, 'It's dangerous. They wouldn't think twice about popping someone off. But how do we prove it? They'll wipe me out. They'll follow your car and then get you.'

In any case, the informant said, he didn't want to go to the police, as he believed police officers were working very closely with underworld figures. 'The cops are connected in this, with the result that when there's a raid, they get tipped off so when the police get there, everything is hunky-dory.'[18]

In his community safety budget speech in the Western Cape legislature at the end of March 2012, Dan Plato said, 'The ANC is not looking to stop the violence and bloodshed, and they do not care about the safety of the people. What they do care about is power. The violence we currently experience in the Western Cape is nothing other than politically motivated. People attending these meetings [at which gangsters were allegedly present] reported that one of the topics discussed is how to make the Western Cape ungovernable with the assistance of the gangsters.'[19]

Other informants linked to Dan Plato also made shocking claims against Jeremy Vearey, all effectively alleging that Vearey was deeply involved in organised crime.[20]

An affidavit made by self-styled informant Pierre Mark Anthony Wyngaardt, which was apparently provided to Plato in September 2012, implicated senior ANC members and high-ranking police officers in a shocking swathe of crimes, including ATM bombings, drug trafficking, money laundering and corruption.[21] It contained claims that Vearey was working with, among others, relatives of dead 28s gang boss Colin Stanfield.[22] Early the following year a possibly incriminating voice recording surfaced in which Plato and Wyngaardt apparently discuss Vearey's alleged links with gangsters.[23] But Wyngaardt turned out to be not the most watertight of sources: he later claimed to be a prophet who was 'guided by angels' and described himself as having had a colourful past as a top spy who worked for the National Party then the ANC.[24]

When Jeremy Vearey accused Dan Plato of running a smear campaign to tarnish his name, Plato denied trying to discredit Vearey.[25]

Then, early the following year, 2013, one Pierre Theron, an information peddler who also goes by the name Jason, claimed in an affidavit that he'd met Dan Plato in June 2012 at a restaurant in Stellenbosch, where he'd told him (Plato) that he (Theron) wanted to expose members of a syndicate that included 'Creicer' (Krejčíř) because they owed him R749 000 and wouldn't pay it. The syndicate, said Theron, was involved in deep-underground crimes, including assassinations, gold dealings, ammunition and human trafficking, and the members had an array of state officials on their side, including police officers and those in the judicial system.[26]

Theron claimed Plato asked him to gather information on top police officers and politicians, and that for this Plato had paid him nine sums between July 2012 and January 2013.[27] To back up these claims, bank statements stamped by a branch of a well-known bank were leaked to the author. Plato later denied paying Theron for information, saying that he'd provided money for Theron's medical expenses.[28]

The author met Theron in Plato's offices in the Cape Town city centre in 2012. A tall, frail-looking man, who limped and sometimes made use of a walking stick, he made a range of startling and fascinating claims, including that he'd been present when National Party politician Robert Smit and his wife Jean-Cora were murdered in their Springs home in Gauteng in 1977 – high-profile political killings that were never solved.[29]

In 2013 the Western Cape Director of Public Prosecutions, Rodney de Kock, said that the Hawks had forwarded an enquiry to his office relating to allegations the Public Protector had received via Plato 'that a senior politician and an SAPS officer have involved themselves in various alleged criminal activities. The source of the allegations is a witness who lacks credibility and whose version is unable to be corroborated in any respect'.[30]

With that, the claims against Vearey fizzled into nothing.

But information peddler Pierre Theron suddenly resurfaced in October 2015, and with him the smear-campaign-claims saga. This time, Theron deposed a detail-dense affidavit saying, among other things, that Radovan Krejčíř had paid several prominent figures substantial amounts of money. The affidavit – which was leaked to the media – named a few top police officers, including Jeremy Vearey, as being recipients of the money. Vearey, according to the claims, received R6 million; the reason for this alleged payment wasn't provided.

Theron, who said he'd met Krejčíř in 2007 through Cyril Beeka, also stated that in early 2013 he'd transported R700 000 from Johannesburg to Port Elizabeth which was to go to the state team prosecuting Nelson Pablo Yester Garrido, an ex-Cuban intelligence officer who was facing drug-smuggling charges relating to a stash of cocaine discovered in 2010.³¹ Theron's reason for supplying the information was that ill health had prompted him to 'become part of the solution to the crime problem' of which he had been part for some time.³²

Theron turned state witness against Krejčíř in the murder trial of drug dealer Sam Issa, but Krejčíř's lawyers said that information had been received that Theron had been paid to make the affidavit.³³ In the event, Theron wasn't called as a witness in the case, which by March 2019 was still limping along in a Joburg court.

Confidential and/or manufactured data is a rich underworld currency that increases in value as political happenings, as well as criminal investigations, develop. False claims presented as fact or leaked information, or a combination of both, can prove as dangerous as a weapon, ruining lives or putting them at risk. It's in this opaque realm that the aptly named 'grabber' fits.

Properly called an international mobile subscriber identity (IMSI) catcher, it's an extremely expensive kind of 'fake' mobile tower, a telephone-eavesdropping device used for intercepting cellphone traffic and tracking the location of cellphone users. In South Africa, a grabber is 'listed equipment', meaning that a certificate is needed from a relevant government minister to obtain one.

Double agent George 'The Butcher' Darmanović had, in 2015, allegedly illegally imported a grabber from Libya, in conjunction with (among others) an ex-South African National Defence Force lieutenant who was, like Darmanović, apparently a member of one of former president Zuma's parallel intelligence structures.³⁴

A grabber was also linked to the May 2015 arrest of Crime Intelligence officer Paul Scheepers, following a raid at his office at the police's provincial Crime Intelligence headquarters in Bishop

Lavis – a Cape Town suburb widely known as 28s gang turf – as well as at the offices of his private-investigations company Eagle Eye Solutions Technology in Southfield.

In 2010, the year after the DA had taken over the running of the Western Cape province from the ANC, Eagle Eye Solutions Technology had been awarded a tender to sweep the Western Cape government offices for bugs. Years later, in 2015, the ANC in the province voiced its belief that Scheepers had actually been a spy – illegally monitoring members of the ANC – for the premier of the Western Cape, who at that stage was Helen Zille and who vehemently denied this.

In any event, Scheepers – an unassuming man who by all accounts was exceptionally skilled at discreetly acquiring information of all kinds – was arrested in May 2015 and faced charges including allegedly violating the Electronic Communications Act by being in possession of a grabber. The device, as alleged in the charge sheet, was delivered to Scheepers in Cape Town and installed in a Toyota Fortuner, a fleet vehicle for a Johannesburg-based company providing cash-in-transit security services.

Scheepers unsuccessfully tried to get a court to order that items seized from him during the raid at his private office be returned, stating that he believed the search warrant had been obtained for 'ulterior purposes'.[35] He explained that he'd been a unit commander in the Western Cape's Crime Intelligence division, and that his duties had included gathering information on alleged crimes and working with informers and sources relating to drug-trafficking syndicates. Most of his work was done covertly because he worked with undercover informants and agents, he said.

'During early 2015 three of my informers reported to me on various occasions that a high-ranking officer in the SAPS regularly attends meetings with very well-known drug lords and criminal gang bosses ... in the Western Cape. During such meetings discussions took place about undermining rival gangs and the way of ensuring distribution of drugs in the Western Cape,' Scheepers claimed. 'The senior officer, on several occasions, received huge amounts of money for the exchange and delivery of drugs.'[36]

This echoed similar claims made by informants who'd approached Dan Plato and who added to the growing mountain of claims being made against Jeremy Vearey.

A warrant officer attached to the Western Cape's Crime Intelligence unit, who'd been present when Scheepers was arrested, said the removal of items by police from the office was irregular. He also gave Scheepers a glowing character reference, calling him a brave and highly experienced officer who operated 'with honesty and integrity'.[37]

In October 2015 Helen Zille, in her capacity as Western Cape premier, wrote about the saga, saying that Scheepers[38] had alleged that items had been unlawfully seized from his private office 'after three of his informers had provided him with sensational information asserting the involvement of high-ranking police officers in corruption, and of links between the drug trade, gangs, and politics in the Western Cape'. 'Could it be that there is a deliberate political strategy, involving high ranking police officers and politicians, to ensure that gangs, drugs and crime continue to destabilise the Western Cape?' she asked.[39]

In November 2015, while the Scheepers matter was still being picked apart by politicians, Zille turned the tables on those in the ANC claiming Scheepers was acting as a spy for her, saying it was in fact her phone that had been bugged, and that she'd been tipped off to this by a police officer. 'The ANC should be in the dock, answering very serious allegations about intercepting people's calls, and of collusion with police and ganglords, to influence the 2016 election in this province,' she said.[40]

Zille's words about cops, politicians and gang bosses conspiring to influence an election were along the same lines as the claims made by the late Jeffrey Franciscus in his 'Plato dossier'; and informant Pierre Mark Wyngaardt had also touched on the subject.

And then there was the other theory: that intelligence operatives with longstanding apartheid-rooted grudges could have created the idea that figures within the ANC were working with gangsters; and these operatives may have used proxies to feed this narrative to those who most craved it, the politically opposing DA.

The start of 2016 in Cape Town was marked by another major gangland killing. Nathaniel Moses, the head of the Mobsters, a brutal faction of the 28s known for carrying out hits, was murdered in January – he was shot repeatedly in the head outside a car-rental dealership in the Strand main road.[41]

Moses had an intense history with the Mobsters. In 2010, after the gang's leader, McNolan Koordom, was killed in Bishop Lavis (nobody was convicted of the murder),[42] it was decided that Moses was the man for the job of leading the Mobsters.

The Mobsters were involved in drug dealing and illicit firearms, and under Moses's command, turf from which to sell drugs was to be used strictly by the 28s; if rival gang members tried to stand in their way, they were to be eliminated. The Mobsters' turf included parts of Belhar, Macassar, Kuils River and Blue Downs. Drugs were to be sourced from Russel Jacobs, the suspected perlemoen poacher who was later murdered (in 2017).[43]

Moses decreed that the vehicles used by the Mobsters were to look similar to vehicles used by police, and that these were to be hired from a particular contact who had access to stolen cars which were to be burned after use. 'The group also hijacked vehicles from tourists and foreigners. These vehicles were also burned after use.'[44]

Six years later, however – in the weeks leading up to his murder – Moses was showing a more humane side. Said to have started attending church and going for guitar lessons, he may have been trying to distance himself from the Mobsters. In fact, he apparently suspected that he was the target of a pending hit as he'd received death threats, some said because he was 'getting soft' and displaying behaviour unbecoming of a ganglord.[45] It seems likely that Moses was murdered by a rival within his own gang.[46]

Mention of Nathaniel Moses's murder cropped up in a surprising quarter – the smear-campaign-claims saga involving Jeremy Vearey and Dan Plato.

In April 2016, yet another a startling affidavit emerged, again naming Vearey, this one by self-proclaimed whistleblower Sylvano Hendricks, a transgender woman going by the name Queeny Madikizela-Malema, with alleged links to the 26s and 28s gangs.

Queeny's affidavit, under the spelling 'Queenie' and with a note beneath her signature stating 'real name known to author', contained several striking claims, including that she was 'well acquainted' with 'the various "hits" on persons that was carried out and the names of senior police officers, correctional services and the navy [sic]'. Moses's killing, for instance, had been 'planned to perfection right down to the very last detail and would most likely end up being an unsolved murder'.[47]

Queeny claimed that she'd made a detailed statement to three police officers stationed in Cape Town under Vearey's command, but that she didn't trust police officials because she knew there were officers stationed around the Western Cape who were on the payroll of an alleged gang boss, and that Vearey had, in one instance, been advised by this gang boss to apply to be the Western Cape's police commissioner.

There were, however, several problems with Queeny's affidavit. One of the stamps, which read 'Department of Community

Safety Western Cape' (Plato's remit), turned out to have been discontinued.[48]

And while the provincial police ombudsman's office said that Plato had asked a staffer there to help Queeny draft a statement, the advocate from the police ombudsman's office who'd signed off on the affidavit was formerly a policeman who'd admitted to cooking crime statistics, and had been expressly prohibited 'from associating the [affidavit] with the office of the WC police ombudsman'.[49] Queeny herself wasn't an altogether reliable deponent,[50] with a history of whistleblowing subsequently found to be baseless[51] dating back some thirteen years, including a 2005 bomb scare made to the Public Protector at the time and a 2016 warning to Public Protector Thuli Madonsela that she was the target of an alleged hit.[52]

And so Jeremy Vearey once again accused Dan Plato of driving a smear campaign against him to tarnish his image, an accusation that Plato once again denied.

Finally, at the end of April 2016, the ANC in the Western Cape decided to retaliate. 'Not only has Plato violated the rights of General Vearey by spewing forth vague and embarrassing untruths about him in public, but he has also violated the confidentiality of those who use him to peddle their agenda's, [sic] no matter how untrue they may be. The danger is that Plato sets himself up, by his own misfortune, for citizens to mistrust him in future for fear of their identity being revealed to suit the DA's own narrow-minded political agenda,' the party's statement read. 'Dan Plato has become a master of engineering perception around something that has not been tested and, in this way, he maliciously pre-empts the investigative due process that is meant to operate in a normal democratic dispensation.'[53]

In May 2016, members of the ANC in the Western Cape lodged criminal complaints of perjury, conspiracy to commit perjury, defamation and defeating the ends of justice against Plato – all related to the 2012 affidavit made by Pierre Wyngaardt in which Wyngaardt had claimed that senior ANC members and top police officials were involved in an array of crimes including corruption and drug trafficking.

A press statement by the Western Cape ANC on the lodging of the criminal complaints alleged that Plato had got hold of this affidavit in September 2012, but that instead of taking it to the police or the police watchdog, the Independent Police Investigative Directorate (Ipid), for the allegations to be officially probed and tested, he'd gone to the media. 'Plato determined that he would leak the information to embarrass the ANC prior to the national elections in 2014 and now again prior to local elections in 2016,' the statement read. 'The ANC is proud of its MK cadres who faithfully serve the nation in all spheres of government and in particular in the Police Service in the Western Cape.' The press release also expressed the concern of the ANC 'that so called Police Ombudsman' [sic] 'allowed his office to be used by a rogue official to peddle false information against the ANC and General Jeremy Vearey'.[54]

Plato wasn't at all perturbed by this and welcomed the ANC's act of lodging criminal complaints, saying that allegations and affidavits handed to him would be thoroughly investigated and the truth chiselled out. 'My actions in office have always been above board, transparent and in the best interest of the safety of communities in the Western Cape,' he said. 'The ANC's allegations and half-truth concocted conspiracies are a desperate attempt to deflect attention away from how much they feature in the affidavits supplied to my office.'[55]

Dan Plato was the common denominator between the apparent informants – Pierre Wyngaardt, Pierre Theron and 'Queeny' – who'd made claims against Jeremy Vearey. Vearey used this factor in the Labour Court matter relating to his 2016 transfer, in which he'd been shifted from Project Impi, arguing that it had been one of the reasons he'd been effectively demoted. 'The publication of their false allegations were facilitated by the Office of the MEC [Plato] without any processes being used to test the truth of the allegations. It appeared to me that the MEC's office was conducting intelligence operations in which informants were being paid from public funds for information they gathered and provided,' Vearey said. He viewed the 'false statements as having been made by persons linked to gangs' as a way to discredit him.[56]

Fresh claims about the Nathaniel Moses murder resurfaced the following year, 2017, suggesting that Vearey had worked with an alleged gang boss to have Moses killed,[57] something that Vearey said was 'another attempt by certain senior officers within the SA Police Service, in collusion with a 28s gangster', to discredit him.[58]

CHAPTER 7

Modack makes his move

In South Africa the thriving private security industry is much bigger than the police service and its sheer size makes it difficult to monitor. But this is what the Private Security Industry Regulatory Authority (PSIRA) is meant to be for – regulating individuals not necessarily mandated by the state to maintain law and order.

Private security providers need to be registered with PSIRA in order to operate legally (this was where SPS fell foul of the law). In mid-2017 about 495 000 employed private security officers in 27 000 companies were registered with PSIRA – more than double the nearly 195 000 police officers in South Africa.[1] Despite this, in 2018 PSIRA had only sixty inspectors. It emerged during a PSIRA presentation to Parliament that '[t]he ratio [of inspectors] to individual security guards [is] 1:6 800' which was 'unacceptable in terms of monitoring'; the ideal would have been more along the lines of an 'inspector to security business ratio of 1:120'.[2]

Not surprisingly, then, as the nightclub-security takeover

developed in Cape Town in 2017, several sources noted that starting a private security business was a convenient way to access firearms for nefarious means under a legitimate guise. A gang boss could task those without a criminal record to submit the paperwork to PSIRA in order to register a security company, and once this was taken care of, the boss's proxy could apply for firearms licences, motivating that these would be used in carrying out official services for the company. In fact, by early 2018 PSIRA as much as admitted that there appeared to be abuse of firearms in terms of private security because there was a lack of control of these.[3] The authorities were, however, doing what they could: seven PSIRA and Hawks operations had been carried out over ten months in relation to club security in the city, and compliance inspections were continuing.[4]

But this didn't mean PSIRA had the upper hand – it became apparent that the layer of protection between members of the public and private security was stretched and fraying, and at some points had in fact snapped, thus leaving holes for criminality to slink through.

'The people out there are too afraid to lay complaints against these people [those involved in nightclub security]. They fear for their lives,' police investigator Edward Edwardes insisted, saying that even PSIRA inspectors were worried about being killed when they had to take on certain security companies.[5]

On 15 February 2017 Raymond 'Razor' Barras, who had links to Brett Kebble, was shot dead in Johannesburg, outside his home in the suburb of Kensington. Barras, who was in the car-restoration business, had previously been in business with Faizel 'Kappie' Smith, one of those involved in Kebble's 2005 assisted suicide.[6]

Sources in underworld circles several months later claimed that soured business relations had led to the murder, and one source believed that the firearm used in it was later to have been planted in a property linked to Nafiz Modack, or someone aligned to him, so as to trip up Modack's operations.[7]

But it was an auction that turned out to be the powder keg that reignited the nightclub-security power battle in Cape Town. On 29 March 2017 a property belonging to Nafiz Modack in the suburb of Richwood went under the hammer as part of a sequestration, and Mark Lifman was the highest bidder. Both Lifman and Modack were present. Shortly afterwards, on that same day, a second property belonging to Modack, in the nearby suburb of Parow, was auctioned, and Lifman and Modack were also both there. This was where the violence erupted, and there are three main versions as to how this event unfolded.

The first version, an eyewitness account, was that while the auction was in progress, a van with a registration plate including the letters VIP pulled up and several men got out and stationed themselves across the road. Three or four more minibus taxis then arrived, disgorging men, whom the witness identified (without saying whether by recognition or by their clothing) as security guards linked to a controversial private security company, The Security Group (TSG).[8] These apparent guards then allegedly ambushed Lifman (who, according to this version, did not bid on this second property) and those with him, running amok with knives.

It later emerged that police were of the view that Modack was directly involved in TSG, which Modack denied, conceding only that he sometimes subcontracted security guards to the company for specific events and at a fee.[9] The company's website (which was taken down some time in mid 2018) boasted that 'TSG maintains a strong association with ex-military personnel and employ [sic] many former SADF and SAP officers so that our clients can benefit from the very best in a trained, experienced and motivated security presence. We also actively maintain close networking relationships with the police and intelligence services to further enhance our services to clients.'[10]

As nightclub-security skirmishes unfolded and escalated, police investigators came to view TSG as more of a mob than a formal security outfit. A police officer claimed that 'essentially, if they have control over the door, over the bouncers, they have control over the drugs'. 'Members of TSG would ... approach nightclub owners and restaurants and force them to use their security. If the company doesn't want to use the services of TSG security, there will be individuals sent to the establishment. [sic] Your whole business will be disrupted and in extreme cases ... there will be hits taken out on owners who do not comply with the request of TSG ...' The same officer alleged that Colin Booysen and Nafiz Modack were linked directly to TSG security.[11]

The second version of the pivotal auction is the official one from the Hawks. It goes along the lines of 'the Lifman group' having bought Modack's house in Richwood 'for a very low price by intimidating bidders', and then Lifman arriving at the second auction 'with approximately fifteen bouncers who were also heavily armed to intimidate the other potential bidders. At this auction a fight broke out between the two groups and Modack told Lifman that if he were to take what belonged to him, then he would take what belonged to Lifman.'[12]

The third version is that of Modack, who said he'd pulled up at the second property and seen Lifman there with about fifty other people. 'I walked up sole [sic] alone to stop the auctioneer,'[13] he said, not elaborating on why he'd wanted to interrupt the auction. Modack claimed Lifman then ordered ten men to remove him from the scene and that one of them, a bodyguard, had tried to smack Colin Booysen, but missed. Another man then allegedly pulled a gun on Booysen, and that was the tipping point – a mass brawl erupted that, according to several sources, involved men being stabbed and punched, and firearms being drawn. Realising the escalating fight could end fatally, men started running away and eventually they all dispersed. Some sources claimed that Andre Naude, who had been present, had run so fast that he'd left his flipflops behind in the street.[14]

Modack said, 'I did warn [Lifman and his associates] u wana take wats mine il take wats yours 2nyt an I dun just that, im no gangster im a busineesman and only fear god no one else [sic].'[15]

Nafiz Modack[16] and the men he moved around with were rumoured by some to be violent bullies who believed themselves totally above the law; others believed that Modack was a good person who was simply hellbent on ridding clubs and venues of drugs.

Nafiz Modack (second from left, in checked shirt) outside the Cape Town Magistrate's Court on 13 November 2017. Picture: Caryn Dolley, News24

There were also claims that he was an informant gone rogue and bought information from Crime Intelligence operatives, so was in a powerful position, with sensitive information on several people and situations. And there were stories that Modack had worked with Radovan Krejčíř to help him escape from jail; or that he'd worked against Krejčíř to prevent him from escaping from jail.

Nafiz Modack was born in 1981 and grew up in Bonteheuwel, a Cape Town gang hotspot. As a child he'd dreamed of becoming a doctor. His family ran supermarkets, petrol stations and car showrooms, while Modack referred to himself as a 'security advisor', involved in security companies in both Cape Town and Gauteng, and in debt collection.[17] 'I also provide security for vulnerable persons and/or corporate security and/or corporate events,' he said.[18]

In addition, Modack was involved in the auto industry, earning 'between R80 000 and R100 000 per month' in commission on vehicle sales. A sequestration, which he said happened 'some years ago' (prior to 2017), had left him 'deeply' humiliated, but hopeful of rehabilitation.[19]

Happily married and keen on starting a family, since 2007 he had lived in the suburb of Plattekloof; he shared his comfortable home with his wife, a businesswoman who was a full partner in a successful beauty business with assets worth about R4 million.[20]

Certain aspects of his work, he said, weren't without risks: he claimed he'd received about fifty threats in less than a year. 'We're in the security business. Obviously, my life is in danger, because other people want to be doing what we're doing, taking the clubs,' he said.[21]

Later in the evening of 29 March 2017, hours after the disrupted auction, a group of men allegedly under Modack's command, and including Modack, descended on Mavericks, the popular city-centre

Modack makes his move

strip club situated alongside the Cape Town Central police station, and, according to claims, told security there that they would be working for Modack from that point on.

Several uniformed police officers reacted to what was happening. Some of them lined up against a wall of the building opposite Mavericks, keeping a close eye on Modack and the group of men who were milling around just outside the entrance. The group, which included prominent Cape Town advocate Pete Mihalik, were clustered together, and it was clear that some of them were viewed as potentially dangerous: at one point a man asked people to move away from them as they had a firearm.[22]

The group's presence at Mavericks marked the first incident hinting that a nightclub-security takeover was really and truly taking off. What followed was a shocking surge in shootings, claims of brash extortion, and some police officers having to nimbly juggle tipoffs to try and pre-empt and extinguish violence before it broke out.

The Hawks crime-fighting unit was tasked with investigating the fresh 2017 nightclub-security turf war, and according to Hawks officer Lieutenant Colonel Peter Janse Viljoen, who handled informants, there were two groups involved. Security at several venues in the Cape Town city centre had been handled by 'the Lifman group' which he alleged consisted of Mark Lifman, Andre Naude, Jerome Booysen and Kishor Naidoo, the man better known as Kamaal, who apparently controlled the group's finances. 'This group has been in charge of the club security/bouncer environment for a very long time. They are known to use strong-arm tactics to take control of the bouncer industry by intimidating and threatening club owners with threats of violence and have at times resorted to violence if the owners rejected their services,' Viljoen alleged.[23]

Then, in March 2017, a new grouping came on the scene. This one, 'the Modack group', included Modack, Colin Booysen and Jacques Cronje. (After being ejected from SPS by Lifman in 2012,

Cronje had left Cape Town to go to Durban, where he'd stayed until the nightclub-security turf war started heating up in Cape Town; he'd then returned 'to be the muscle' for Nafiz Modack.)[24] Viljoen said this group hadn't replaced any bouncers with security of their own, but had simply offered bouncers working for the Lifman group more money to work for them instead.[25]

'Both the Modack and Lifman group is [sic] being investigated for serious offences ... Both these groups use intimidation tactics and force to reach their goals.'[26]

Just three days after the skirmish at the auction, the underworld was dealt a violent double whammy. In the early hours of Saturday 1 April 2017, Long Street nightclub venue the Iconic Lounge, which was owned by Mark Lifman, was targeted by those allegedly linked to Nafiz Modack, with patrons and staff being assaulted and R22 000 in cash stolen.[27]

That same day Shamiel Eyssen,[28] an alleged leader of the Fancy Boys gang, was shot dead in Bishop Lavis, apparently because he was owed money in a massive illegal cigarette deal. The illicit tobacco trade was widely said to be a vital connection between an array of crimes ranging from street shootings to white-collar thievery. Eyssen's murder was viewed by several sources as an attack on the so-called Lifman group – because they viewed Lifman, by name if not by official businesses, as being linked to the tobacco trade.

According to several sources, a cigarette delivery vehicle had been hijacked in Woodstock, a stronghold of the Young Gifted Sexy Bastards gang. This delivery van, they claimed, contained a consignment of cigarettes belonging to Eyssen and destined for delivery to one of his associates, a businessman. The businessman, who had thus not received his cigarettes, had not paid Eyssen and had instead fled, leaving Eyssen fuming. Eyssen was therefore killed to eliminate any retaliation plans.[29]

The following day the takeover was allegedly moving ahead at full speed – a seven-vehicle convoy arrived at the Grand Africa Café and Beach, an upmarket seaside establishment in Granger Bay on Cape Town's Atlantic seaboard. Two men emerged from one of the vehicles and they told Radley Dijkers, a brand manager for the venue, that they were taking over security with immediate effect.[30] It was alleged that later that same day a man by the name of Carl Lakay, who was affiliated to Modack, arrived at the Grand Africa Café and confirmed that TSG would be handling the security there.[31]

Grant Veroni, a tall, hulking man with a soft, deep voice, was introduced to the management of the Grand Africa Café as a TSG manager. Identified by cops as Colin Booysen's bodyguard, Veroni was involved hands-on in running TSG. He described himself much as others in underworld circles: as a breadwinner and businessman with no ties whatsoever to gang bosses and suspected criminals. The father of five from Kuils River in Cape Town said that as a director of TSG he earned R10 000-R15 000 a month, depending on how many contracts the company managed to secure, and that his income went towards, among other things, supporting his elderly mother.[32]

Veroni's past seemed to give the lie to this clean image, however, with various brushes with the law through the years: a 1997 conviction (later expunged) for attempted murder, a 2012 charge of assault (later withdrawn), and a 2016 charge of indecent assault (on which he was later acquitted).[33]

The Grand Africa Café's business operations did not change under TSG, apparently, and it was a smooth segue to the new security company, with only invoicing shifting to TSG instead of the previous company in charge of security, Leisure and Lifestyle Security.[34]

A week later the underworld heat was turned up another notch. On the evening of 9 April 2017, a group of security guards and bouncers gathered outside a McDonald's fast-food outlet in the suburb of Sea Point. They were believed to have been preparing to disrupt nightclubs (which cops did not identify by name) in the city centre.

Hawks, Crime Intelligence unit and other officers got wind of this and went to the McDonald's, where they discovered an abandoned vehicle – a black Jeep without registration plates – with the doors left open. On the back seat were two firearms, as well as vehicle registration plates. A cellphone was also found, allegedly belonging to one Matthew Broderick Breet.[35] Breet therefore became a 'person of interest' to the Hawks.[36]

Just hours later, very early on 10 April, at a location on the very opposite side of the Cape Town metropole, in the vicinity of Goodwood, something similar was happening. Police officers got wind that a large group of men, who they suspected had links to the so-called Lifman group, was preparing to attack clubs in Cape Town's city centre where the rival Modack group was providing security. It was very early on a Monday, so the city centre wasn't particularly busy but a potential attack still meant that several innocent people stood in harm's way.

Police officers intercepted the group, which included 63 people allegedly aligned to Cape Town's notorious gangs,[37] at a McDonald's near a mall in Goodwood. Officers questioned members of this group before releasing them. According to several sources, this grouping had been comprised mainly of members of the 27s gang.

Based on the events of the evening of 9 April and early morning of 10 April, it appeared the police had thwarted a pincer-type attack by two groupings that had planned to close in on clubs in the city centre allegedly serviced by Modack's security operations. If police were to be believed, the heart of Cape Town had again become a bull's eye seen through an underworld scope.

But cops weren't able to entirely snuff out these sparks of violence. In the early hours of Monday 17 April 2017, two people without any ties to the underworld were wounded in a shooting in Café Caprice, a popular beach bar and restaurant in the upmarket Atlantic seaboard suburb of Camps Bay. Ironically, one of the wounded men and his friends had gone to Café Caprice because they'd wanted to avoid the city centre, as the security turf war and its risks to revellers had become common knowledge. But it seemed that the tentacles of the turf battles had spread beyond central Cape Town. 'Young people in Cape Town can't go out and enjoy themselves. This indicates the city has a huge problem ... We're paying the price for this,'[38] a relative of one of the wounded men said afterwards.

Nafiz Modack later claimed that he'd been the intended target of the Café Caprice shooting, as he'd planned to have a meeting there that evening, but a Hawks investigator believed the bullets had been intended for Modack's associate, Choudhry, and that figures linked to 'the Lifman group' were behind the attack.[39]

Curiously enough, Grant Veroni had been present at Café Caprice around the time the shootings unfolded and was involved in apprehending three people at the establishment following the incident.[40] It wasn't clear if this was in his capacity as director of TSG and whether the company was officially providing security at Café Caprice, and police didn't regard Veroni's actions as official arrests.[41]

The cops themselves initially took three suspects into custody for the Café Caprice shooting, but the trio was released days later when the case against them was withdrawn, presumably because of a lack of evidence.[42]

Shortly after the Café Caprice shooting, the Hawks took over the investigation into it because it became clear it was linked to the club-security turf war. Veroni and TSG members gave Hawks officers statements about what had transpired,[43] and about five months later several suspects were arrested.

Barely five days after the Café Caprice shooting, very late on the evening of 21 April, several vehicles drew up and parked outside a building just off Riebeek Street in the Cape Town city centre.

Near to the building, which housed a club on its 31st floor – Club 31 – a few men stood still and alert. One, dressed all in black, blended into the shadows; he was carrying what appeared to be a big black shield. Another carried an item shaped like a long firearm.

A few steps away from them was a bigger group of men, standing in a circle. This group uniformly moved into the building, then, moments later, swiftly made their way back out, nimbly getting into waiting vehicles, which were then slowly driven away in a convoy.

The convoy headed to Mavericks, where the outside area appeared as usual, with a person or two loitering there, and several private cars and metered taxis parked nearby. But a few minutes

Police officers make their way from the Cape Town central police station towards strip club Mavericks on the night of 21 April 2017 where they seized firearms from private security guards linked to Nafiz Modack. Picture: Caryn Dolley, News24

later, and almost as one, in an eerie and silent exodus, several of the taxis moved off. [44]

The convoy of vehicles then pulled up and stopped, and several burly men got out, stationing themselves outside the strip club.

A group of police officers who'd been positioned outside the police station moved in on the group, at first walking from the station, then picking up the pace and nearly jogging.

The cops, it later emerged, were led by Captain Althea Jeftha, a short, strong-looking woman with a no-nonsense attitude. Despite her height, Jeftha stands her ground, looking up at those taller than her, never cowering, and her intense gaze never wavering. Once, while searching a car linked to Nafiz Modack outside the Cape Town Magistrate's Court, she walked up to him, pointed at his chest and barked, 'You are not the police, we are the police.'[45] This illustrates how she conducts herself on the job.

The police officers told everyone in the immediate vicinity outside Mavericks to line up against a wall so that they could be searched. It turned out that the men gathered outside the strip joint included Modack and others linked to him. 'Information was received that [the] Modack group were going to attack Mavericks... The Modack group was found at the scene heavily armed,' a Hawks investigator said later.[46] Police seized eight firearms, including three shotguns; the firearms were linked to Eagle VIP Security[47] and some apparently to TSG.[48]

The men were then taken to the Cape Town central police station where their details were checked on a police system that showed they weren't facing any criminal matters. Officers photographed those they'd searched but no one was arrested and no charges were lodged.

Among those present outside Mavericks and later photographed by cops were Jacques Cronje and one Mathys Visser, both providing security to high-profile clients. Visser, a top-heavy, thickset man with a placid expression who's called 'Vissie' by those close to him, was, according to police, Modack's personal bodyguard[49] and represented Eagle VIP Security.

Visser said that Jeftha had explicitly stated that she was acting on Jeremy Vearey's instructions. Jeftha had also, according to Visser, said that the seized firearms would be ballistically tested to see if the guns could be linked to the shooting that had unfolded in Café Caprice in Camps Bay four days earlier.[50]

But Visser took exception to the cops' behaviour. He viewed the police's action as totally uncalled for, complaining, 'I find this plainly irrational, as the media reported that the Camps Bay shooting was perpetrated with a handgun, whereas Captain Jaftha [sic] seized three shotguns during her search.'[51]

Visser further elaborated on the alleged behaviour of the police officers, claiming 'Captain Jaftha [sic] and her SAPS members conducted themselves in the most abhorrent and unprofessional manner. They swore at the individuals they searched, using foul language and heavy-handed tactics that are unbecoming of a public official.'[52]

Visser turned to the Western Cape High Court to demand that the police, including Jeremy Vearey and Western Cape police commissioner Khombinkosi Jula, be ordered to return the seized firearms immediately. The court action became the first of two major legal clashes between underworld suspects and cops over the firearms.

Very early the next morning, Saturday 22 April, during a short period that possibly overlapped with the firearms confiscations outside of Mavericks, information filtered through to authorities about suspected happenings at a city-centre 'gentleman's club' called The Embassy, said to be under the control of the Lifman group. The club, discreetly tucked away in a side street, was one of the properties that had been auctioned off in 2010 when Lifman and Ulianitski's assets had gone under the hammer. Ulianitski's widow, Irina, believed that Lifman's associates had simply bought it back for him, which appears to have been the case.[53]

The Embassy had been closed since November 2016 but a group allegedly planning to attack clubs under Modack's suspected control had gathered there, possibly using it as a sort of operations centre.[54] When police got there, however, no one was found on the premises although there were clues – wet towels, a warm TV[55] – that whoever had been there had just left, although whether as a result of lucky timing or because they'd been tipped off was never established.

There were two sets of intense and increasing rumours about what was unfolding in Cape Town's club-security industry. One was that it was an elaborate high-level intelligence operation involving proxies to conceal and divert from the activities of corrupt cops; the second was the opposite – that it was an intelligence operation to uncover the work of criminals and criminal police officers.

State Security Agency spokesperson Brian Dube effectively poured cold water on both these theories by denying that its agents were involved in influencing nightclub-security industry activities. 'It's a known fact some in this industry have always claimed or alleged that the security services are busy trying to destabilise the industry,'[56] he said.

But several sources steadfastly believed that what was happening was the work of parallel, or rogue, intelligence operatives.

About a week after the firearms confiscations outside Mavericks, a double killing rocked the Mother City and rattled the underworld. On 30 April 2017, alleged 26s gang boss Mayon McKenna and a second man were killed outside McKenna's house in the suburb of Ravensmead. The fatal attack on McKenna followed several attempts on his life dating back many years.[57]

McKenna had reportedly helped provide security to high-profile underworld figures, particularly those involved in the taxi industry who were said to extort money from drivers using certain routes, and he was also allegedly involved in the drug trade.[58]

There was no respite after McKenna's murder and the first few days of May 2017 proved pivotal to underworld happenings. At the beginning of that month, the author received messages from an unfamiliar cellphone number that said Modack was preparing to bring sniffer dogs into the city to boost security operations. These dogs, German shepherds, were said to be trained in sniffing out drugs and explosives and were worth about R20 000 each, but this plan (if it was indeed real and which sounded very similar to the way Cyril Beeka had operated when at the helm of club security) never came to fruition.

Round about the same time, on 3 May, Jeremy Vearey met Nafiz Modack and former State Security Agency official Russel Christopher,[59] who had trained with Vearey in the ANC's intelligence structures prior to 1994.[60] Vearey had, for some or other reason, recorded this meeting.

In the recording, Modack, who referred to Christopher as 'Uncle Russel', had, according to a police investigator who'd listened to the relevant audio clip, said he was dealing with high-ranking police officers, and that if ever there was a problem, he could approach 'Tiyo and Mbotho'.[61]

Modack, if he had indeed used these words, may simply have been name-dropping but it was intriguing that the two surnames he'd apparently mentioned referred to the very same high-ranking police officers who had taken over the positions occupied by Jeremy Vearey and Peter Jacobs before they were suddenly yanked from Project Impi in 2016.

Northern Cape police commissioner Risimati Shivuri (left) and Nafiz Modack in the One&Only hotel in Cape Town on the evening of 4 May 2017. Picture: Caryn Dolley, News24

During the meeting with Vearey and Christopher, Modack also referred to another police general. This general had apparently wanted Modack to obtain statements from police officers about firearms that were seized (presumably from the men who were searched outside of Mavericks), and these officers were supposedly meant to make allegations against Vearey.[62]

On the afternoon of Thursday 4 May 2017 the author received a tipoff that Modack was going to have a meeting with a high-profile figure that evening. The name of this figure wasn't divulged at the time but the author later established it was Northern Cape police commissioner Risimati Shivuri. The venue was the upmarket One&Only hotel near the V&A Waterfront in Cape Town.

Late that evening the author did indeed spot Modack and a second man, who she later realised was Risimati Shivuri, sitting at a table at the hotel, leaning forward, heads bent towards each other, in quiet and intense discussion. They were clearly ill at ease, poised in tense positions.[63]

Hours later, shortly before midnight, a patron and a DJ were wounded in a shooting outside Coco, a popular luxury nightclub in Loop Street in the Cape Town CBD. Sources linked to policing said that the Coco incident appeared to target those aligned to Modack.

The next morning the author received a message from an unidentified source claiming to be communicating on behalf of those linked to Modack, condemning the Coco shooting and saying that the police should have been working with legal and registered private-security providers, instead of against them and targeting them for unknown reasons. The source claimed that months before this shooting, members of the 27s gang had been causing havoc in the city centre, selling drugs to youngsters, and alleged that police were supporting gangsterism. Apparently, the newer grouping muscling in on security and, by implication, linked to Modack, planned to deploy former armed military personnel in plain clothes in central Cape Town and around Camps Bay to catch those who thought they were above the law, as well as their bosses.[64]

Later that day, 5 May 2017, cops investigating underworld happenings were dealt a significant blow when the Western Cape High Court ordered that the firearms confiscated by police officers from TSG and Eagle VIP Security outside Mavericks two weeks earlier had to be returned.

On 8 May 2017 Ravensmead was once again the scene of a shooting, when Deon Williams, better known as Igor (or Iger), who was alleged to be linked to the 26s gang, was gunned down there.

Jerome Booysen was on his way to the Williams's home to offer his condolences when he himself was shot in the neck by an assailant who was unknown to him.[65]

It was clear that Cape Town's club-security operations were slap-bang in the middle of a volatile turf war. While the police didn't publicly say so, their actions soon proved that they were fully aware of the seriousness of, and risks posed by, what was happening on the streets.

There was an unprecedented police crackdown in the heart of Cape Town on the evening of Friday 26 May 2017, when city-centre clubs and restaurants were packed with weekend revellers. Members of the special task force and national intervention unit, two elite policing units tasked with clamping down on especially high-risk situations, descended on the hub and blocked off the area, while a police helicopter hovered above. The operation, signed off by Western Cape police commissioner Khombinkosi Jula, said officers could conduct searches on people, at premises and in vehicles without a warrant 'in order to seize illegal firearms, ammunition and explosives'.[66]

It emerged that a month earlier the Hawks had received alleged information that 'the Modack group is in possession of a M26 hand grenade, which they plan to use against the Lifman group.'[67] It was suspected the grenade was being kept in a club that the Modack group was servicing.

No explosives were found during the intense operation, which police declined to give specific details about, but it gave insight into how seriously cops were viewing the private-security situation. Officers were perhaps also showing that they were the ones in control in the Cape Town city centre, not those allegedly embroiled in underworld activities.

Three days after this flexing of cop muscle, in the very early hours of Monday 29 May, officers again showed their might. Jerome 'Donkie' Booysen's northern-suburbs house in the Glenhaven area was raided, with officers using an armoured police vehicle, a nyala, to ram their way through a garage door to gain access. Policemen in camouflage gear, wearing helmets and carrying torches and automatic rifles, made their way into the home.

Booysen afterwards claimed that police officers had traumatised his daughters and grandchildren by pointing machine guns at them, and that they'd seized R137 000 cash from the property (which they later returned). Booysen said he planned to take civil action against the police because of the raid.[68]

Three weeks later, on 18 June, Jacques Cronje found himself in legal trouble. He was taken into custody for a matter relating to a drug that had given him problems in the past – cocaine. His arrest was for the alleged possession of cocaine worth about R8 000.

Acting on a tipoff about drugs being transported into the city centre, police had stopped and searched the white Nissan bakkie that Cronje was driving that day, in the Cape Town CBD, finding a legal firearm plus a brown envelope containing the cocaine, divided up into twenty packages, apparently ready for sale in clubs.[69]

But it transpired later that Cronje could have been set up by Igor 'the other Russian' Russol, who, it was claimed, had planted the cocaine in the bakkie. 'The whole investigation of this matter is ... highly suspicious,' Cronje's legal counsel Chad Levendal would later state.[70] The case was eventually dropped.

Mark Lifman's name, at this point, wasn't firmly in the centre of underworld ructions, whereas Nafiz Modack's was. But this was to swiftly change.

On 22 June 2017 hard drugs worth hundreds of millions of rands were discovered on a farm in Villiersdorp, a town about eighty kilometres outside of Cape Town. Three sources claimed the farm belonged to Lifman, who vehemently denied this. 'I don't own or rent any farms, so I'm happy to say, that has nothing to do with me,' he said. 'And I've told you before, when it comes to drugs, [it has] nothing to do with me.'[71]

It turned out that Lifman did not, in fact, own the farm, and was not linked to the drug stash. In a Bell Pottinger-style move,[72] claims to the contrary appeared to have been intentionally planted.

Halfway through 2017 yet another double murder rocked the Mother City. On 28 June Marwaan 'Dinky' Desai – who had alleged ties to the 27s – and Shaheem Mohamed were shot dead in a vehicle in Pinelands. This residential area, about eight kilometres from the city centre and home to the mayor of Cape Town at the time, wasn't known for gang violence. Two balaclava-clad gunmen were involved in this double murder and afterwards sped off in a Hyundai. A tracking device was allegedly removed from underneath the victims' car after the shooting.[73]

Claims later emerged that Desai and Colin Booysen had been in a physical fight before the murder, and video footage reportedly existed of Booysen hitting Desai.[74]

With gun violence spiralling further out of control and shootings shaking up several suburbs, at the end of June 2017, Hawks officers approached the firearms, liquor and second-hand goods unit, better known as the Flash unit, and asked that its members help investigate TSG's compliance with the Firearms Control Act, as well as law relating to private security. 'The request, we were advised, came about as a result of the fact the [Hawks] had convened a task team to investigate the incidents of shootings and other violent acts at various nightclubs in Cape Town,' Colonel Jacques van Lill, the Western Cape Flash team's commander, said.[75]

Van Lill was also a coordinator of an investigation conducted by police into contraventions relating to the flouting of regulations by, among others, firearms manufacturers, the suppliers of ammunition and guns, and security service providers. 'The investigation was initiated as a result of the well-publicised and increasing incidents of violent, gun-related criminal activity in the Western Cape,' he said. 'South Africa is plagued by violent crime. Some of the crime committed is well organised, often spontaneous, and always contrary [to] and contemptuous of the values and human rights enshrined in our Constitution. Gun-related violent crime ... poses a serious threat to our democratic order.'[76]

On 4 July 2017, Van Lill and other officers, along with PSIRA members, went to TSG's premises to suss out the situation. There, Grant Veroni produced TSG's PSIRA registration documents, which showed that the company was indeed operating as a service provider registered with the authority. He was also asked to produce a firearms register, showing which firearms had been booked out and returned and when, and an incident register detailing the discharge of firearms, but was allegedly unable to do so.

Van Lill alleged that only 'a purported firearm control register' had been produced, and that it lacked an array of necessary details including the names, identity numbers and PSIRA registration numbers of security officers who'd been issued with firearms. Other inconsistencies, including where firearms were stored when security officers weren't on duty, were also allegedly picked up, and Van Lill said, 'It was clear to me, from the inspection, that (TSG) was not exercising any form of effective control in respect of the issuing and/or returning of firearms to security officers.'[77]

On 11 July a warrant was issued for the seizure of weapons. The next day eight firearms and certain documents were confiscated from TSG. Some of these firearms had apparently been among the guns seized from men, also linked to the company Eagle VIP, outside Mavericks back in April.[78]

TSG hit back and launched an application in the Western Cape High Court to try and force the police to return the seized weapons, but this time around, unlike the successful application launched a few months before by Eagle VIP Security, it wasn't so easy. Van Lill argued that 'the potential safety of any person would be put at risk were the firearms to be returned'.[79]

This argument was shored up by Michael Barkhuizen, a lieutenant colonel with the Hawks who in 2015 had been tasked with investigating alleged fraud being committed by businesses and private gun owners when applying for firearms licences. TSG had been flagged as a company to keep an eye on.[80]

Barkhuizen said that Grant Veroni had, in July 2014, applied to license ten firearms. Part of this application was a motivation relating to TSG, saying that the company offered premium services to, among others, government departments throughout South Africa, multimillionaires who owned companies and, curiously, the South African Police Service.[81]

Included in the application was a list of security guards who were employed by TSG but, according to Barkhuizen, 'Investigation has since proven that the list of security guards – submitted as part of the motivation – was fraudulent. It is suspected that TSG placed an advertisement on the internet offering employment to registered security guards and obtained their CVs in this manner. The particulars of these guards (including their PSIRA registration numbers) were then fraudulently used, in that Veroni falsely alleged they were employees of TSG, whereas they were never employed at TSG.'[82]

The Hawks kept the names of the guards secret for their safety 'given the volatile and sensitive nature of the investigation into the nightclub industry.'[83]

Two days after the raid on TSG's office, police action got uncomfortably close to home for Nafiz Modack. He claimed that 'about 12' officers attached to the police's Operation Combat, an anti-gang strategy in the Western Cape, had burgled his house in Plattekloof.

Modack claimed that on Friday 14 July 2017 officers in police vans from the Brackenfell station had broken into the house, and a 'police rogue unit' had deactivated security cameras so that their faces wouldn't be seen (but in the process had inadvertently activated a silent alarm), then smashed items in the house and stolen an undisclosed amount of money before fleeing.[84] He warned these cops to be careful in case their homes were raided by 'straight cops'.[85]

A Western Cape police spokesperson confirmed that an operation had been carried out at a residence in Plattekloof.

Modack claimed that entries about the police operation had been made by officers at the Parow police station, but that they had scribbled their ranks and names, making this information illegible. Modack further claimed that the police had had no search warrant, didn't know whose house it was that they'd targeted, and had stolen 'high [sic] sensitive classified docs ... out the safe with big names on it re generals and officails [sic]', although Modack didn't say what he was doing in possession of these documents in the first place.[86]

CHAPTER 8
Dodging bullets in the City of Gold

Nafiz Modack didn't limit himself to Cape Town when targeting security operations. He started moving farther afield, setting his sights on another city in South Africa with a glitzy and upmarket nightlife: Johannesburg.

According to cops, in mid-2017 Jacques Cronje visited nightclubs around Johannesburg, trying to get owners or managers to sign contracts for security services, while both Cronje and Modack began recruiting bouncers at various venues to get easy access to these places. If an owner or manager refused their services, Modack and Cronje allegedly threatened them.[1]

In July 2017 the manager of The Grand, a nightclub in the moneyed surburb of Rivonia offering exotic dancers and speciality cuisine, opened a criminal case relating to allegations of death threats, extortion and intimidation. Cronje had allegedly contacted the manager and stated that they wanted to take over security there but was told that security operations were already in place. Modack and

Cronje had then allegedly sent threatening SMSs saying they would burn down the establishment. Modack reportedly called the manager and told him to 'get your fucking boere [police officers] ready with their guns, we are on our way and there is going to be fireworks'.[2]

Cronje had allegedly tried to extort half of the value of the business, which was worth a total of R20 million, by threatening to reveal that the owner, Andrew Phillips, was linked to the May 2010 murder of Lolly Jackson, a titbit of information Cronje was said to have heard from Radovan Krejčíř.[3] Cronje's claims came to nothing.

On 6 July 2017, Ralph Stanfield, who was visiting Johannesburg, was wounded in a drive-by shooting in the suburb of Melrose. He was reportedly wearing a bulletproof vest, which saved his life; and, despite being wounded, he managed to drive himself to a nearby medical facility.[4]

That afternoon rumours flew thick and fast: Stanfield had been killed, they said, and Andre Naude had also been shot. Probably intended to instil fear in those falsely identified as having been targeted or killed, all proved false.

The wounding of Stanfield was widely viewed among police and underworld figures as a pointed attack on the 28s gang, and everyone braced for retaliation. But the anticipated tit-for-tat violence didn't pan out as expected.

In the early hours of Friday 18 August 2017 international steroids smuggler Brian Wainstein was shot dead in his Constantia, Cape Town, home while in bed alongside his girlfriend and child (both of whom were physically unhurt).

Originally from Ireland, Wainstein had a long criminal history that spanned half the globe. In July 2007 he'd been sentenced to an effective four months in jail after pleading guilty in the Dublin Circuit Court to nine charges relating to the possession and sale of banned drugs in a case that stemmed from 2003.[5] In January 2013

Dodging bullets in the City of Gold

he was arrested in Cape Town following an altercation outside his home in the Waterfront area, where he'd based himself at that point, and his identity and legal situation had been revealed – authorities in the USA wanted him extradited because he faced charges there relating to 'the illegal importation and marketing of various drugs, including anabolic steroids'.[6] He was released on bail while the extradition process was underway.

It was claimed that a week before Wainstein was murdered, the men who later become suspects in the case had met in Cape Town to discuss the hit. Then, just hours before, the killers had allegedly scouted out Wainstein's home and, when the coast was clear, one of them had pumped five bullets into the so-called Steroid King. This sensational murder, which led to further outrageous claims and revelations, lifted the lid on a boiling pot of claims that drastically turned up the heat in the underworld kitchen.

Several rumours suggested that while in Cape Town, Wainstein had forged ties with the 28s gang and his killing was therefore viewed as yet another attack on this gang.

Another of the claims was that a firearm stolen during the fateful 29 March auction brawl had later surfaced in the offices of Advocate Pete Mihalik, whose clients included Ralph Stanfield. Mihalik had allegedly told Andre Naude that he would return the firearm to its owner in exchange for R20 000; and Brian Wainstein had apparently paid this.[7] Mihalik had gone to the murder scene after Wainstein was killed but later explained, 'I go to everyone when shot … [I've] never discriminated in my life. My higher power has a purpose for me.'[8]

And Mark Lifman's name came up again. In an audio clip that was recorded either hours before Brian Wainstein was murdered or after the shooting of Ralph Stanfield (depending on who is to be believed),[9] the Irishman can be heard threatening Lifman during a cellphone conversation. It's an understatement to say that Lifman and Wainstein hadn't been friends around the time of the latter's murder, and the recorded conversation, initially between Lifman and a second unidentified man, was ample illustration of the deep distaste the two had for each other.

In the recording the second man tells Lifman via phone that he's on the way to see 'Brian'. However, it turns out this man is actually with Wainstein, who's keeping quiet so that Lifman doesn't know he's present and privy to the conversation.

'You guys were told to be careful of who you got involved with,' Lifman responds. 'I warned you, okay? Remember that... Including that fat fuck that you're going to see now, that piece of peasant shit.'

Wainstein suddenly breaks in, yelling, 'You motherfucking poes. You're a fucking dead bastard. You're a fucking dead bastard, you cunt. I'm going to fuck you up, I'm going to fuck you up, you faggot little cunt. Come, Mark, come, you little shit. Fuck you... I'm here in Cape Town. You're a fucking brave little cunt. You've got fuck-all. If I see you I will destroy you. Do you understand me?'[10]

The state later made clear its stance on Wainstein's murder, and highlighted a growing problem in Cape Town and its surrounds: 'The offence of murder is particularly prevalent in South Africa. However, it is a notorious fact that the number of contract killings has reached alarming proportions in the Western Cape, especially those killings linked to the high prevalence of organised crime and criminal gang related crime in this region... The offence must be seen in the context of the ongoing public and violent executions of organised crime figures and the threat of collateral harm which may be inflicted on the community when attempts are made on the lives of these persons.'[11]

On the evening of Thursday 7 September 2017, two groups of men clashed at the massive and gaudy Emperors Palace Casino near Johannesburg's OR Tambo International airport. Sources claimed that this incident had to do with a debt collection that Modack personally was carrying out. Chairs were apparently overturned and bottles smashed as fistfights broke out.

'Security guards from the establishment then stepped in … but were attacked by the two groups fighting each other. The two groups of men then went outside and apparently drove away.'[12]

Modack's simple take on this skirmish was 'We out numbered [sic] their VIP protection security at [E]mperors.'[13]

Coincidentally, the very next day, in the early hours, Andre Naude's home in Loevenstein, Bellville, was raided. Naude was out of the country at the time but noted[14] that the officers had traumatised his children when they bashed through the front door to effect a search warrant for tik, mandrax and dagga.[15] No drugs were found but several items, including laptops and memory sticks, were seized.

Back in 2013 Project Impi had picked up that firearms that police were meant to have had destroyed were instead being smuggled to gangsters around the Western Cape, and this same problem continued to hound Cape Town as the nightclub-security turf war was in full swing.

At the end of August 2017, a firearms audit and inspection was held at the Mitchells Plain police station's community service centre and it was discovered that fifteen police handguns, loaded pistols containing a total of 225 rounds of ammunition, were missing. Just two days later it was realised that eighteen handguns were missing from a trunk in the Bellville South station's exhibit store. Some sources insisted that among the firearms missing from Bellville South were R5 rifles.[16]

Then-Police Minister Fikile Mbalula said the stolen weapons would probably end up in the hands of gangsters.[17]

On 2 September 2017, crime prevention unit police officers in

Manenberg responded to tipoffs received from residents and found a 9mm pistol with thirteen rounds of ammunition hidden in rubble in the back yard of an empty house; it was discovered that this firearm was one of those stolen from the Mitchells Plain police.

On 13 September, Jerome Booysen was targeted for the second time that year by gunmen. He was shot at by four men in a silver SUV while driving in Bellville South. Six cartridges from a 9mm pistol and an R5 cartridge were found at the scene, and Booysen handed over two 9mm projectiles, as well as an R5 projectile, which he'd apparently found in his vehicle, which had 21 gunshot holes in it.[18] The discovery of the R5 remnants was rattling because it was R5 rifles that sources had claimed had been stolen from the Belville South police station the previous month.

The situation became even more worrisome because about a week later, on 21 September, police officers patrolling in Sexy Boys gang hotspot Belhar responded to a complaint that someone was pointing a firearm; it turned out to be one of those stolen from the Bellville South police station exhibit store.[19] So yet another of the guns meant to be safeguarded by cops[20] had ended up back on the street and in a gang hotspot.

Early in October 2017, Houssain Taleb was taken into custody for allegedly planning to kill a club owner – a witness in several cases against TSG. By this stage 'the Moroccan', who had previously been linked to the Beeka group, and then the Lifman and Naude group, was allegedly affiliated with the so-called Modack group in that he was a director of TSG. If this were true, it meant he'd weathered three transitions of underworld power in Cape Town.

Taleb had, apparently, cleaned up his act and then succumbed once again to the lure of the underworld several times over the years. For example, by 2012, when he was working for SPS, while acknowledging that violence had been an element of the work he'd done for Cyril Beeka at the end of the 1990s, he appeared to be a changed man who distanced himself from bad situations. He was running a gym out of his Milnerton home and training many students from disadvantaged backgrounds for free; he'd worked as a security consultant to politicians, and cooperated with authorities to help rid Long Street of a scourge of pickpockets.[21] 'That was the past. That time I go home and I can't sleep. I didn't like what I was seeing. Now I go home and sleep,' he said then.[22]

Fast-forward five years, however, and police were crawling all over Taleb's home, at one stage even reportedly hitting him in the face with a rifle butt and breaking his nose.[23] The allegation was that Taleb had contracted two individuals to carry out a hit on a club owner, providing them with firearms and a photograph of the person to be killed, plus information about the car he would be in. For this, they would each be paid R10 000. The duo had, however, been stopped and searched by cops, and the firearms and rounds of ammunition discovered. When questioned by the police, they fingered 'Houssain Moroccan, the kickboxer',[24] and police officers allegedly discovered two replica firearms as well as a police badge during the search of Taleb's home.

Policeman Edward Edwardes, who investigated the murder-plot matter, said informers had told him that Taleb, in his role in TSG, was 'the one that must collect protection money at the establishments under his so-called command.'[25] Edwardes provided chilling insight into how cutthroat the nightclub-security arena apparently was, referring to a potentially fatal catch-22 situation in which if Taleb tried to leave TSG, he would end up being killed.

It was later claimed that, as with Cronje's cocaine arrest, the Taleb murder-plot saga was a setup orchestrated by rival underworld figures, and that the two men also accused in the murder plot had been expressly tasked with making Taleb look guilty.[26] The case against Taleb was later withdrawn.

The university town of Stellenbosch was the next crime scene, and the venue was the town's branch of the cocktail bar/restaurant Cubana. In the early hours of Saturday 14 October Nicole Muller, a mother of two young boys, was shot dead, as was one Donovan Jacobs,[27] who sources claim was a 28s gang member and the target of the attack. Jacobs had been shot while fleeing his killers, and Muller, who was at Cubana celebrating a friend's birthday, had just been in the wrong place at the wrong time.

There were several claimed theories about this shooting, with sources with ties to policing saying that it was linked to retaliation for the attack on Jerome Booysen, others saying that Jacobs had found himself on the wrong side of the Mobsters and was therefore eliminated, and another claiming that the shooting was a result of fighting over drug turf between the 27s and 28s. Later, fingers started pointing to links in a massive perlemoen-smuggling case.

Describing the spate of shootings that had been tearing up Cape Town since the start of the fresh club-security turf war to this point, a police investigator said, 'It's all related to the nightclub industry and nightclub scene... It's all related. It's like tentacles going everywhere.'[28]

A few days later, on the morning of 18 October 2017, it became a case of third time lucky – or unlucky – for Jerome Booysen. This time he was targeted in a shooting at Cape Town International Airport, a national keypoint.[29] Five of 23 bullets struck Jerome, putting him in hospital for a week.

Claims then surfaced, by figures in the underworld, that the very next evening two men, one of them disguised as a woman, apparently tried to make their way into the Cape Town hospital in which Jerome Booysen was being treated.[30] It's claimed that a team of men linked to Nafiz Modack were stationed at the hospital – including, apparently, Colin Booysen, who had temporarily forgotten his fallout with his brother in the face of Jerome's serious injuries – and that they somehow identified one of the two men, whom they intercepted and slapped around.[31] Some believed this man had been after Colin, not Jerome.

Fabian Cupido, suspected by the state to be a 27s gang member, was arrested outside the hospital on the evening of the apparent attempted attack on Jerome (or Colin) Booysen but this was coincidental, and police didn't link Cupido to the potential attack; Cupido was allegedly found there with the keys to a stolen car.[32]

Three months after the Steroid King was killed there was a massive breakthrough in the murder case. In November 2017 brothers Matthew Broderick Breet and Sheldon Jaret Breet, originally from Johannesburg and who the state suspected had ties to members of the 27s gang, were arrested. The brothers had, according to the state, been Brian Wainstein's bodyguards.

Shortly afterwards, the Hawks made the alarming announcement that the brothers were likely to face extra charges because during their investigations they'd uncovered a cache of weapons, including 3 000 rounds of ammunition, four firearms and four grenades, plus two military hand radios, which were being kept in a storage facility in Kraaifontein allegedly belonging to one of the Breet brothers.[33]

A shocking revelation that emerged during the Breet brothers' (unsuccessful) bail application was that Sheldon Breet had been a police informant – Crime Intelligence had paid him R120 000 for information – and had also allegedly been involved in crimes including the illegal steroid business, drug dealing, the rhino-horn trade and possibly money laundering.[34] He moved in the same circles as Mark Lifman, Andre Naude, Marwaan 'Dinky' Desai (who'd been murdered in mid-2017) and Ralph Stanfield (who'd been wounded in a drive-by shooting in Johannesburg in mid-2017).[35]

The other Breet brother, Matthew, said that before his arrest for the Wainstein killing, he'd been running a private security company and conceded that it wasn't properly registered; he was also implicated in a case of illegal possession of firearms linked by cops 'to a plot to perpetrate violence in the ongoing conflict between organised crime players in the club security industry'[36] and had been charged with manufacturing an explosive device which he'd placed under someone's vehicle. (Months before the Breets' arrest, on the night of 9 April when a group had planned to converge on clubs in the city centre in an act that police thwarted, a cellphone belonging to Matthew Breet had been found in an abandoned vehicle outside the McDonald's in Sea Point where the groups had gathered.)

Two other suspects, alleged 27s gang member Fabian Cupido (the same man arrested outside the hospital where Jerome Booysen was recovering after a shooting) and Cheslyn Adams, suspected of being a member of both the 27s and a street gang called the Spoilt Bratz, were also arrested for Wainstein's murder, late in 2017 and early 2018, respectively. Cupido and Adams were allegedly associated with Kishor 'Kamaal' Naidoo, the man the Hawks had identified as controlling the so-called Lifman group's finances.

When all four of Wainstein's murder accused appeared in the Wynberg Magistrate's Court in Cape Town for their unsuccessful bail application in 2018, security was extra tight, with members of the police's tactical response team, several clutching shotguns and with their faces masked to conceal their identities, stationed in the courtroom – there was a real threat that the four would be targeted and there was strong belief at the time that members of the 28s were gunning for them.

In December 2018 Matthew Breet pleaded guilty to killing Wainstein and was sentenced to twenty years in jail.[37] The other three accused, if they pleaded not guilty, were expected to go on trial in 2019.

Towards the end of 2017, Nafiz Modack, after allegedly causing major ructions in Johannesburg, was back shaking things up in Cape

Town. The Grand Africa Café and Beach was again in his sights, with police alleging that TSG had pushed for those running the establishment to hand over R150 000 as a 'service management fee' for an event they planned to manage there on 4 November. After much negotiation involving a meeting between the management of the Grand Africa Café, Modack, Jacques Cronje and Colin Booysen, a fee of R90 000 was eventually agreed to, and was later paid to TSG from the proceeds of the establishment's cash bar.[38] This meant that patrons buying drinks may have unwittingly channelled money to suspected extortionists.

TSG seemed to be highly operational in the city centre by this point – most clubs in Long, Loop and Bree streets in Cape Town's CBD were using its services. But police and Hawks officers found that many security guards operating in Long Street and the parallel Loop Street, both areas highly populated by residents and tourists, weren't registered with PSIRA.

Police officers were patrolling the Long Street party strip on the night of 11 November, when Captain Althea Jeftha noticed a group of suspicious-looking men, wearing thick jackets despite the warm weather (which could have been concealing bulletproof wear), walking towards the Iconic Lounge,[39] the entertainment venue owned by Mark Lifman.

The patrolling police officers also went into the Iconic Lounge, passing a few men dressed in black at the entrance – bouncers – but once inside they couldn't find the group of men who'd entered shortly before them. However, upstairs (accessed after a constable figured out how to tweak a fingerprint access-control panel on the lower floor), a group of men, including Colin Booysen and Grant Veroni, who was wearing a shirt with the letters TSG embroidered on it, were discovered in a flat. Officers asked the men if they were armed and Veroni said he was; his firearm was allegedly registered to Eagle VIP Security.

THE ENFORCERS

At 11:30pm on 26 November 2017, Cape Town's Bree Street became the scene of a heated underworld skirmish when about two dozen of Nafiz Modack's 'enforcers'[40] effectively closed it off. 'It looks like a stampede. They pull a guy out a club and beat him senseless,'[41] was how one cop described the clash.

CCTV footage of the incident showed several vehicles stopping in the middle of the road, which was lined with parked cars on either side so the arriving vehicles blocked it off completely. A fairly large group of men emerged from the vehicles and walked towards an establishment, where they gathered near the entrance.

All of a sudden, despite revellers walking about, the men all focused their attention on one man among them, and their actions became quick and jostling – this, according to the cop, was when the man was beaten up, although in the grainy CCTV footage this isn't clear.

The group of men then started moving away, leaving one man lying on the ground. As people began gathering to see what had happened, the men quickly climbed into the waiting vehicles, which were driven away. The incident, from the arrival of the cars to their departure, had lasted less than five minutes.

Another version[42] of what had happened was that six models had been inside an unnamed establishment in Bree Street as part of a promotional event there, and a man (whose identity wasn't revealed, but who was thought to be indirectly linked to the so-called Lifman group) had acted inappropriately towards them. The situation was sensitive and security at the establishment were apparently reluctant to act.

Modack apparently got wind of the situation via security-industry contacts and, along with about twenty other men, went to the scene. Some of these men became angry when the man accused of acting inappropriately mentioned his links to men they considered rivals, and a scuffle broke out. Modack, it was claimed, jumped in to stop the brawl and calm the situation. This version portrayed Modack as a mediator, not an instigator.[43]

The next skirmish involving the Modack group took place two days later in the winelands town of Worcester, about 100 kilometres from Cape Town, which despite its reputation for scenic beauty and outdoor activities also had profound problems with gangs.

On Tuesday 28 November a group of men rocked up in Worcester to try and collect a R22-million debt from a businessman. Residents somehow got involved and a fight broke out during which a vehicle was vandalised. Modack and twelve other men were arrested on charges of business robbery and malicious damage to property.[44] Curiously, Modack then phoned Western Cape Crime Intelligence head Mzwandile Tiyo[45] (it was not known if Tiyo answered the call); and, just as curiously, the thirteen men weren't kept in custody but were released on notice to appear in the local court.

Two weeks later the case was withdrawn.

At the start of December 2017, in the runup to Cape Town's always-busy holiday season, a bouncer at Cubana in Green Point, Pitchou Falanga, was fatally stabbed and a second man was wounded.[46]

Apparently, Modack and several others, including Jacques Cronje, had gone to Cubana that evening and insisted on being given a VIP table. None was available, and according to a police investigator, an argument erupted in the early hours of Sunday morning, during which Falanga and the second man were stabbed. Modack had then quickly left the scene and had allegedly soon afterwards relocated Falanga's suspected killer to Johannesburg.[47]

But the author had previously established that this particular attack may have had more to do with Congolese faction fighting than the security turf war. Many bouncers who work in Cape Town are Congolese, and pro- and anti-President Joseph Kabila factions existed within the local Congolese community. A Congolese musician, Fally Ipupa N'simba, who was viewed as pro-Kabila, had been in Cape Town that weekend, and tensions relating to Ipupa may have caused the Cubana scuffle.[48]

Around the same time a bizarre letter, supposedly from TSG, was sent out to establishment owners in the city centre. Thanking those running venues for making 2017 'a special year' and for their 'loyal support', the letter also informed recipients that they would be charged double for 'services rendered' over the festive season.[49]

Despite the tsunami of violence that had crashed down on Cape Town, TSG was, it seemed, ploughing ahead.

Police officers escort a handcuffed Nafiz Modack to a waiting van following his arrest on 15 December 2017 on an extortion charge in Cape Town. Picture: Caryn Dolley, News24

But then the underworld bubble was suddenly popped. On a stiflingly hot day in mid-December 2017 Nafiz Modack, Jacques Cronje, Colin Booysen and two other men, Carl Lakay and Ashley Fields, were arrested.[50] They were detained for alleged extortion for the incident at the Grand Africa Café in Cape Town nearly eight months earlier, at the beginning of April, when Carl Lakay had arrived there saying that TSG would be taking over security at the venue.

As Modack, his hands cuffed in front of him, was led to a waiting police van hours after his arrest, he said, 'General Vearey is corrupt and I'll sort it out.'[51] This off-the-cuff comment, implying that his arrest was a setup, turned out to be the tip of a massive iceberg of claims the high-ranking cop was to face in this matter.

Jeremy Vearey, who was heading up the Cape Town cluster of police stations at the time, said that it had been necessary to carry out the arrests because it was tourist season, and holidaymakers shouldn't have to go out and experience the city while keeping an eye out for stray flying bullets. He thanked business owners who'd had 'the guts' to report extortion and related problems to the police, and noted that there were also 'cowards' who hadn't come forward.[52]

Modack and his four co-accused, who were held at the notoriously overcrowded and unsanitary Pollsmoor Prison,[53] applied for bail. A bail application is usually a fairly cut-and-dried procedure but the Modack-and-co one turned out to be more like a full-blown trial, stretching from December 2017 to the end of February 2018 in the Cape Town Magistrate's Court. It drew extreme security measures, with repeated bag and body searches of attendees, and police officers (some in plain clothes and others in full uniform, including snug black bulletproof vests) monitoring the courtroom and the packed public gallery, and accompanying Vearey and the case's investigating officer, Lieutenant Colonel Charl Kinnear, to and from the court building.

Initially, Modack appeared somewhat docile and bored in the dock of the Cape Town Magistrate's Court, a far cry from his more familiar attitude of casual confidence, characteristically with a cigarette clutched in fingers bedecked with chunky diamond-studded rings, a cellphone to an ear and several brawny men flanking him. Later, though, while in the dock, he displayed some sass and possibly tried to make a point of sorts, wearing a blue jacket with the ANC logo on its front.

The application was attended daily by several members of the Booysen family who often whispered about police corruption set to be exposed in court.

Also in attendance for the first few days of the hearing were cops Jeremy Vearey, Peter Jacobs and Andre Lincoln, sitting squeezed together on a small wooden bench towards the front of the packed courtroom. It appeared that the three – the two apartheid-era convicted terrorists and the one who'd fought his way back into the police after being unceremoniously kicked out – were putting on a united front.

CHAPTER 9
The Eastern European connection

Nafiz Modack was a bully who believed he was totally above the law and who ruthlessly grabbed from others security operations at various entertainment venues. At least, this is the way the state, presenting its case in the bail application, portrayed him.

But Modack's defence team presented a very different view of their client. Aside from the fact that the Grand Africa Café was still using the services of TSG for security, Modack's lawyers produced two audio recordings in which the venue's brand manager Radley Dijkers could be heard saying that there was 'no intimidation or anything like that'.[1] While the state believed Modack had led Dijkers to say this, it was undoubtedly a blow to their case.

But it was Igor Russol's[2] version of Modack's actions that was by far the most sensational. Russol's take (conveyed in absentia and via investigating officer Lieutenant Colonel Charl Kinnear) was that while he (Russol) was in Ukraine in April 2017, Modack had called him to, among other things, convey the news that his attorney,

Noorudien Hassan, had been murdered in November the previous year. During this call Modack had asked Russol to return to South Africa to work for him because, according to Russol, Modack said he was taking over clubs from Mark Lifman, Andre Naude and Jerome Booysen. Modack paid for Russol's air travel from Ukraine to South Africa, and Russol stayed in a Plattekloof home belonging to Modack.[3]

Some time in the first half of 2017, according to Russol, he was invited to the One&Only hotel where a large group, including Colin Booysen and 'gangsters', had convened. During this meeting Modack allegedly told Russol that they planned to kill Lifman and Jerome Booysen if these two men made contact (it wasn't specified whether physical or otherwise) with Modack and his associates. Taken aback, Russol had apparently responded, 'This is not a jungle we're living in. You cannot go and shoot everybody.'[4]

Russol further claimed that a few weeks after he arrived back in South Africa, Modack asked him to set up a meeting with Lifman and Jerome Booysen, and according to Kinnear, Russol's version was that Modack wanted to pretend to make peace with the duo but would instead use the opportunity to kill them. 'After he owned everything, he'd kill Colin Booysen too,' Russol had claimed,[5] implying that Modack was so power hungry he was willing to kill off even his allies.

Russol made a slew of other allegations against Modack, including that he'd extorted R20 000 from some men who'd wanted to sell special 'diamond champagne' in local clubs, and that he'd also extorted large sums of cash 'from rich Jewish people in the greater Cape Town area'. He claimed that Jacques Cronje, having worked for Cyril Beeka years earlier and based on this experience, had advised Modack on whom to target.[6]

Russol had left Modack's employ at the end of May 2017, and by the end of December that year, according to Kinnear, was working for Lifman as the manager of the Iconic Lounge in Long Street.[7] Later it was pointed out by the defence that this could have provided Russol with a clear agenda from the start: that as an employee of Lifman's, he'd wanted to tarnish Modack by making wild allegations against him.

The state's case seemed to be floundering, and perhaps to boost it, it offered up a statement by a senior forensic fraud investigator who worked for Absa bank. It said that in September 2015, while the investigator was probing two vehicles on which the payments were in arrears, he and a colleague had gone to a home in Plattekloof where the vehicles were parked; there, they'd been harassed and intimidated by first a man in a Golf and then four men in a Mercedes without number plates; two of the men were apparently armed. The investigator claimed that the following month a man who'd identified himself as Modack had called him and threatened to sue him in his personal capacity for R100 million. Finally, the investigator said, he'd 'found that this man is well connected with high-profile SAPS role player [sic], including people that is [sic] awaiting trial and connected with the Russian mafia. Due to this, I felt that my life and my family's lives will be endangered, and these people are capable in [sic] anything.'[8]

Even being behind bars was no guarantee of safety, it seemed. In January 2018 Nafiz Modack's advocate told the court, 'There appears to be some form of conspiracy to do my client harm while he's in prison. His life is in danger.'[9] And in February Colin Booysen's attorney Bruce Hendricks alleged that his client had been threatened in Pollsmoor Prison by people who wanted him dead in an incident that he described as 'an unlawful attack on his life'.[10] (Correctional Services officials denied any attack had taken place.[11])

While Modack and his four co-accused were behind bars, the killings in Cape Town continued unabated, and on 16 February 2018 yet another murder rocked the club scene. That Friday, Hampshire 'Hempies' Brown,[12] who co-owned Club Wendy's in Eerste River, was shot while driving in the area.[13] He died later in hospital.

Club Wendy's seemed above board. A motivation for an application for the extension of liquor trading hours for the club dated October 2017 noted that it was a well-respected business and that police representatives often visited the venue, providing positive feedback and therefore giving it a respectable standing in the community.[14]

Brown's wife Wendy told a local tabloid that others were jealous of what she and her husband had built up, and that he'd been shot trying to protect her.[15]

In the same month, in another rattling allegation in the Modack-focused bail application, Charl Kinnear testified that information picked up by the Crime Intelligence unit and State Security Agency operatives was that Modack, while still in jail in February 2018, was plotting to have Jeremy Vearey, along with himself (Kinnear), and a third police officer, Captain Althea Jeftha, as well as the prosecutor on the case at the time, Esna Erasmus, murdered. Kinnear and Jeftha were at that stage working under a team headed by Vearey. Extra security was immediately arranged for those allegedly being targeted.

Modack, via his legal team, vehemently denied the murder-plot allegations, slating them as fake information. 'I simply could not conspire to commit any offence whatsoever. I have had no contact with anyone with whom to conspire. I am an ordinary businessman and not in a position to arrange a murder, or, for that matter, any other crime. The very idea is preposterous,' Modack said.[16]

In response to Kinnear stating how Modack moved around with several armed men and in a convoy of vehicles 'like only the president can',[17] Modack's advocate Edwin Grobler asked (presumably hypothetically), 'So if Mr Mark Lifman puts a hit on your head you won't find it unreasonable if a person walks around with bodyguards?' (Bear in mind that while it's not against the law to use bodyguards, this show of force may be used to instil fear in others.) Grobler also argued that Jeftha had previously told Modack that there was a R20-million hit out on him.[18]

If all the murder-plot claims were to be believed, then in one average-sized room inside the Cape Town Magistrate's Court during certain parts of Modack's bail application, six people were at risk of being assassinated!

Charl Kinnear had been vehemently against Modack and his co-accused being released from custody. Among his reasons was that 'I see the possibility exists more innocent people will get killed and injured.'[19] Be that as it may, the state failed to sufficiently back up its stance to keep them detained, and Modack and co were granted bail at the end of February 2018.

Barely a week later, on the evening of 8 March, unsubstantiated claims were made that one of Modack's vehicles was shot at in Plattekloof.[20] And not even two weeks later, on the evening of 23 March, three sources[21] insisted that Jerome Booysen had again been targeted in a shooting, this time in Mitchells Plain, but that he'd been in a bulletproof vehicle at the time and hadn't been wounded. Police confirmed that there'd been a shooting in the area but said that nobody had lodged a case with them.

The next day Jerome Booysen denied that he'd been shot at and said it was just 'people making stories'.[22]

Claims also surfaced that Jerome Booysen was shot at on the afternoon of 24 April while in a bulletproof vehicle and that he'd been unharmed.[23] Booysen dismissed this story too.[24]

Then, on 25 April 2018, a murder in Johannesburg lifted the lid on a hotbed of sensational underworld links involving men from

Eastern Europe. On that Wednesday, a man driving in Strijdom Park was pumped full of bullets at a traffic light in what turned out to be a killing with multiple international layers.[25]

The bullet-riddled body was that of Milan Djuricic, the Serbian who, along with Dobrosav Gavric (the man who'd been driving Cyril Beeka when Beeka was killed), had been convicted of the assassination of Serbian warlord Arkan.

It wasn't clear how Djuricic had ended up in South Africa and why he'd been murdered, but perhaps Arkan's allies had indeed caught up with him; or perhaps he'd got involved in dubious dealings in this country that had backfired, putting an end to his life. Whatever the reason, Djuricic's murder meant a Serbian intelligence operative had been killed in South Africa; and just eleven days later this would be mirrored when a South African intelligence operative was killed in Serbia.

On the afternoon of 6 May 2018 came the news that George 'The Butcher' Darmanović had been shot dead in Belgrade in an assassination that closed several portals through which information and claims were leaked and spread to South Africa. According to Serbian media, four gunshots were heard and Darmanović was wounded in the head. He died later in hospital.[26]

Darmanović's murder became part of what was developing into a spate of shootings in Serbia and South Africa in which Serbian men, some with similar backgrounds, were targeted – Gavric had been wounded, and Djuricic and Darmanović had been killed, and this list was to grow.

The links between these three men are interesting: the South African contract state-intelligence agent killed in Serbia, Darmanović, was linked to the assassinated South African bouncer-kingpin intelligence operative, Beeka, who was close to the Cape Town-based Serbian assassin, Gavric, who was convicted of murdering Europe's most feared warlord, and who was also connected to his Serbian co-convict, Djuricic, who was killed in Johannesburg.

Several tales about Darmanović snaked around intelligence circles following his assassination. Described by some as a genius and by others as a bullshitter, he was said to have an engaging and affable way about him. In South Africa he'd gained a reputation as a somewhat unpredictable blabbermouth, and around 2014 several of his associates suggested that he leave the country because he'd blown his cover as a contract intelligence agent.

Darmanović was said to have been among those who'd leaked discrediting claims that Glynnis Breytenbach, a former prosecutor with South Africa's National Prosecuting Authority who was pushing to have ex-Crime Intelligence head Richard Mdluli prosecuted for corruption, had been an agent of an Israeli intelligence unit.[27] Darmanović had also apparently peddled unfounded claims against a former Hawks head, Anwa Dramat, who'd been involved in probing Mdluli, as well as claims against Vearey, claiming that Vearey and Dramat had been involved in a perlemoen-smuggling operation with now-former Western Cape-based Crime Intelligence officer Paul Scheepers.[28]

In the case of Dramat, he, like Vearey, was a former umKhonto weSizwe member, and he'd gone through a similar experience to that of Andre Lincoln in the very early stages of democracy – Dramat had also been painted as a criminal and felt he was being targeted because of investigations he was conducting.

A January 2007 document by the now-defunct crime-fighting unit the Scorpions detailed some older claims against Dramat, including that he was protecting suspects in a perlemoen scheme from prosecution[29] but this particular claim didn't amount to anything.

Then in another more recent saga, in 2014, Dramat was suspended by the Police Minister at the time, Nathi Nhleko, for claims against him involving the illegal rendition of Zimbabwean suspects.[30]

Dramat wrote to Nhleko saying he'd been maliciously targeted because he was investigating dockets implicating influential individuals, including Jacob Zuma, in relation to Zuma's controversial KwaZulu-Natal residence Nkandla.[31]

In September 2018 the National Prosecuting Authority confirmed it had withdrawn charges, reportedly concocted by former Crime Intelligence head Richard Mdluli and involving the rendition of Zimbabwean suspects, against Dramat.[32] The several claims against Dramat, some emanating from Darmanović, therefore hadn't stuck.

Leaked police documents, the authenticity of which hasn't been confirmed, hinted at Darmanović having been a conduit of information used by high-level South African authorities; one such noted that Crime Intelligence in the Western Cape appreciated the 'support that is being received from the [State Security Agency] and especially Mr G Darmanović to this office'.[33] It said that Darmanović had helped in solving crimes including kidnapping, gang-related murders, business robbery and the illegal manufacturing of drugs.

While in Serbia, Darmanović had kept his finger on the pulse of South Africa's underbelly, sharing information about crimes and happenings with local policing agencies and, according to some who knew him, whoever else would engage with him, including political figures, underworld operatives and some journalists.[34]

In the months leading up to his murder, Darmanović had his sights set on Mark Lifman, who he purportedly believed was involved in crime. Darmanović had wanted to fly to South Africa to 'nail' him.[35] He was peddling claims that Jeremy Vearey was working with suspected underworld figures and believed that Vearey had signed up Lifman as an informant.[36]

Darmanović's allegations against Vearey meant that Darmanović, an intelligence agent contracted by the state, had been spreading serious claims against, among others, a top police officer, also an official of the state.

Darmanović had also peddled wild (and unverified) claims that Lifman had travelled to the UK in 2017 to have talks with a biker group there that was to amalgamate with a biker group in South Africa, who would all then take on gangsters in Cape Town, Johannesburg and KwaZulu-Natal. 'Lots of killings planned,' Darmanović had said.[37]

The day after Darmanović was shot, Vojin Stankovic, alleged to have been the head of the underworld in Krusevac in central Serbia, was murdered;[38] then, one month after Darmanović was killed, Vojin's father Dejan Stankovic was assassinated. It was suspected that Dejan Stankovic had been among those who'd played a role in Darmanović's killing.[39]

In June 2018 the Ministry of Internal Affairs in Belgrade announced that two suspects, both from Krusevac, had been arrested on suspicion that they may have been involved in the planning of Darmanović's murder. They had apparently worked with another person, with the initials DS, who was no longer alive[40] – this was a reference to Dejan Stankovic.

On 17 July 2018 Darko Kulic, a member of the paramilitary group the Serbian Guard, was killed in an action-packed shooting in the Johannesburg suburb of Randburg in broad daylight and in full view of motorists. Two suspects in a white Mercedes-Benz had fired shots at the BMW that Kulic was driving, killing him and wounding two others who were also in the vehicle. A charred assault rifle was later discovered in the burnt-out Mercedes in nearby veld.[41]

Meanwhile, in Cape Town, the attacks on Jerome Booysen were also turning out to be relentless. On 1 August 2018 there was a sixth attempt on his life, but this time the murderous plan totally backfired and one of the two gunmen was fatally wounded. The attempted assassination played out in a Spur restaurant, a franchise widely known for catering to families with children, in a mall in

Kuils River. Booysen was wounded in the left arm. A 9mm Barretta and five cartridges were found at the scene.[42]

It was suspected that the dead man was a member of the Hard Livings gang and had lived in Woodstock, a stronghold of the Young Gifted Sexy Bastards gang, which has links to the Hard Livings.

By this stage it was clear that Jerome Booysen was on a hitlist, and there were three main claimed theories pointing towards who wanted him dead. The first was that Rashied Staggie wanted to make his own inroads into the nightclub-security industry, and was trying to have Jerome Booysen taken out to clear a path to nightclub-security domination. The second theory was that angry 28s members were after him and that their anger stemmed from the murder of the Steroid King, Brian Wainstein. And the third theory was that corrupt cops or other state officials were the ones who had it in for Jerome Booysen – by this point claims had been made that Jeremy Vearey was among those on his payroll, and if Vearey (and perhaps other cops) were indeed corrupt and on Booysen's payroll, the cop could want the alleged gangster permanently silenced.

Just four days after Jerome Booysen was again targeted, another killing churned up deep underworld tensions. Late on the evening of Sunday 5 August 2018, word started spreading that Carl Lakay, one of Modack's four co-accused in the Cape Town extortion case, had been murdered – he was shot twice in the head while sitting in his car outside a house in Goodwood in Cape Town's northern suburbs.[43]

Lakay was assassinated less than three months before he was expected back in court alongside Modack and the others facing charges relating to extortion, and thus Lakay's voice, and his potential verbal testimony and provision of clues, was silenced. His involvement in the nightclub-security industry spanned a significant period – back in December 2010, when Jacques Cronje had been heading Pro Access, Lakay was one of three managers working for him.[44]

The day after Lakay's assassination Nafiz Modack said, 'Whoever did it got away, so we don't know who it was. Colin [Booysen] and I have beefed up security, seen and unseen. Our guys have assault rifles and everything. Whoever wants to come after us, they must come. We're ready for them.'[45]

Eighteen days after Lakay was murdered a brother of Ashley Fields, another of Modack's co-accused in the extortion case, was wounded in a shooting in the suburb of Salt River. The man had been in Fields's vehicle, a BMW, at the time he was shot and may have been targeted in a case of mistaken identity.[46]

The following month, as late afternoon segued into twilight on Monday 24 September 2018, a shooting rocked the Johannesburg suburb of Bedfordview, with gunmen, said by sources to have been on two motorbikes, shooting at a motorist in a deep-blue Porsche. George Mihaljevic, also known as Hollywood George for his looks and flashy lifestyle, and an associate of Radovan Krejčíř's, was dead.[47] Mihaljevic, a jetsetter from Serbia, had been on holiday in Johannesburg when he was gunned down.

Barely four days after Hollywood George was murdered, bullets flew in Cape Town again, this time in Belhar. Sources said an argument from weeks earlier had led to the shooting, in which Adrian Pietersen died.[48] According to his mother, Pietersen had initially worked for Colin Booysen: he'd left school round the age of 14 to allegedly sell drugs for him. But about a month before her son's murder, she claimed, there'd been a split in the Sexy Boys gang and her son had started smuggling drugs on his own, which had upset Booysen.[49] It was alleged that during an argument Pietersen had opened fire on Booysen and apparent bodyguards who were with Booysen, and that those under fire had then shot back.[50] Pietersen had been killed in the flurry of bullets.

Colin Booysen, already a convicted killer, and two of his

bodyguards were arrested and charged with Pietersen's murder. They planned to plead not guilty.[51]

There was a month's lull, followed by another horrific murder, when advocate Pete Mihalik was shot in the head in front of his children as he dropped his 8-year-old son at school in Green Point on the morning of 30 October 2018, nearly two years to the day after his colleague Noorudien Hassan had been killed. Mihalik died in his car – a single bullet hole was evident in the driver's window – and his son was wounded; his daughter was the only one not physically harmed during the attack.

Hours after Mihalik's murder, there were murmurings in the underworld about plans to avenge his killing. Two suspects were arrested the very next day – members of the new police anti-gang unit under Andre Lincoln had driven the investigation. A third suspect was arrested about a week later.

Mihalik had initially been on the defence team in Modack's extortion case, and the lawyer's murder greatly aggrieved Modack. 'All I want is justice and will not stop until I get it. What happened to Advocate Mihalik was pure evil, that [sic] children of his will forever remember this horrible day and it breaks my heart as they have no one else, what animals are these people. They think their money can help them get away with everything well not this time, [sic]' he said.[52]

In the months leading up to his murder, Mihalik had started hinting just how deeply underworld shenanigans cut, and how proxy wars and misinformation campaigns had for decades shaped this arena. 'Apartheid guys were the absolute masters ... if you control the ideology you control the money and power ... It's very sad that we haven't learnt the evil nature of such things. It leads to the most atrocious violence,' he'd said.[53]

In the months following his assassination, sources said Mihalik was probably killed by those wanting to silence him because he'd

The Eastern European connection

amassed shocking information that could incriminate police officers, past and present. This information could apparently have proved that they were colluding with underworld figures, but would have meant also exposing those figures, so Mihalik had had to be silenced.

Pete Mihalik, an advocate murdered in Cape Town at the end of October 2018, was laid to rest on 10 November 2018. Picture: Caryn Dolley

A family man when away from work, Mihalik had represented suspects across the board, regardless of which faction or grouping they may have been linked to, because he was trying to bring about peace.[54] But he did also seem to socialise with some of those he legally represented – he was one of the men outside Mavericks on the night of that fateful Modack property auction on 29 March 2017.

Among the many mourners at Mihalik's funeral was Colin Booysen, and among the pallbearers was Ralph Stanfield.[55] Security was exceptionally tight, with several burly broad-shouldered men stationed in and outside the church.

On the afternoon of Sunday 3 February 2019, Mark Lifman was at a golf tournament in the suburb of Bellville when a car pulled up and an occupant fired a single shot at him. The bullet struck the ground near Lifman's feet, and he wasn't wounded.

'[I] pulled my firearm and they sped off,' Lifman said.[56]

CHAPTER 10
Friends in high places

It's a common thread: the denial by those involved in shady dealings that they have any inside links with law enforcement. Mark Lifman, for instance, claimed that he'd only ever been close to one person in the police service, and that this person wasn't an influential or high-ranking officer.[1] This was despite the fact that throughout the Modack bail hearing in late 2017 and early 2018 it was implied, and sometimes said, that Modack and his co-accused Jacques Cronje and Ashley Fields believed that Mark Lifman was behind their arrests.

By the same token, Jerome Booysen denied not only having influence in the police but being involved in gangsterism at all. 'Where the people come on with this gangsterism and gangster stuff, they must come and prove it to me because maybe I don't have a lot of friends in the police and that's why they can point fingers because they [are] pointing the finger away from them [sic],' he said.[2]

The evidence and mounting suspicions, however, often seemed

to contradict this. For example, during what appeared to be a fair amount of police dirty laundry aired during the Modack bail application, a cop investigator claimed that Nafiz Modack had previously said that police major generals Mzwandile Tiyo and Patrick Mbotho (who in December 2018 was named the new head of the Hawks for the North West province) would sort out issues Modack had.[3]

Mbotho's name was to come up again in questionable circumstances, when Brigadier Sonja Harri, the Western Cape's highest-ranking female detective commander, and who was seen to have been aligned to Vearey, complained to senior officers, including Police Minister Bheki Cele, about alleged victimisation by Mbotho, who'd been her former boss. After Vearey was sidelined from his position in mid-2016, in September that year, 'General Mbotho adopted a hostile attitude towards me and my work. He treated me in an arbitrary, disrespectful and downright abusive manner,' she wrote in January 2019 to police officers including the national and provincial commissioners. It had become clear, she said, 'that I was in the crossfire of a broader campaign being waged between senior officers in the Western Cape. I was deemed to be aligned to a certain "camp" and victimised because of my perceived affiliation to that camp.'[4]

But many more suspicions surfaced of police officers having become irregularly involved in matters, including those surrounding Nafiz Modack and Mark Lifman. The confiscation of firearms from those linked to Eagle VIP Security and TSG was, for instance, tainted with claims of unusual cop meddling. Police had seized firearms from men linked to the private security companies on the evening of 21 April 2017. Mathys Visser of Eagle VIP then took the police to court to get the guns back; coincidentally, the evening before the order for these firearms to be returned was made, the author had spotted Nafiz Modack seated with Northern Cape police

Friends in high places

commissioner Risimati Shivuri in the One&Only hotel in Cape Town.

Lieutenant Colonel Charl Kinnear said that that same day (4 May) a colonel from the police's legal services department had contacted him saying that it would cost R22 000 to oppose the court application launched by Eagle VIP to have the firearms returned, and that the police wouldn't spend this. Kinnear claimed that it later emerged that the stance about not wanting to spend the R22 000 was that of the colonel in legal services alone, and had not been an official police one,[5] something he found strange.

During Modack's lengthy extortion-case bail application Kinnear had also testified that when he began investigating the extortion complaint involving the Grand Africa Café in Cape Town, he'd cautiously registered the matter in such a way that not just any cops

Lieutenant Colonel Charl Kinnear, who investigated an extortion case against Nafiz Modack, leaves the Cape Town Magistrate's Court under police guard on 28 December 2017. Picture: Caryn Dolley, News24

could access details of it because it was believed that some officers were involved in what had allegedly transpired.

Kinnear, who usually kept his emotions firmly under wraps and maintained a steadfast gaze, gritted his teeth once or twice while in the witness box and testifying, especially when referring to a phone conversation Modack had had with George Darmanović[6] in which Modack had claimed that he (Kinnear) and Jeremy Vearey were on the payroll of Mark Lifman and Jerome Booysen. Kinnear had pointed to Modack's dealings with Darmanović, saying that Modack's communication with the intelligence operative 'shows the relationship the accused has with people in South African government'.[7]

But Charl Kinnear's conduct also hinted at something possibly amiss. He had, in fact, previously been to a home linked to Jerome Booysen, as well as one linked to Mark Lifman. In the case of the former, Kinnear admitted that one of his children had been a friend of the Booysens' niece, and so he'd been to the niece's home on occasion to fetch his children, but he insisted that he himself wasn't a friend of the Booysen family.[8] It certainly didn't help Kinnear that the house was pointed to by an attorney as one where police had found a massive stash of drugs – mandrax tablets – in the time leading up to the extortion arrests towards the end of 2017. A law-enforcement officer employed by the City of Cape Town had been arrested in connection with this, further fuelling rumours of cops colluding with gangsters.[9]

In the case of Lifman, Kinnear conceded that he'd met the businessman three times, twice at his house, but that neither visit was social and both related to a criminal case.

Bruce Hendricks, the attorney representing Colin Booysen, didn't buy any of this, pointing out that no crime had taken place at Lifman's home, so there was no reason for Kinnear to have been there.[10] Hendricks confidently claimed that, in fact, Mark Lifman controlled certain police officers, backing this up with an example of three arrests of Grant Veroni, a director of TSG, on charges relating to firearms, the last of which, meant to have been carried out on 25 December 2017, Lifman curiously appeared to have known about. 'Mr Mark Lifman then told me on the phone he knows about the warrant of arrest members of the Cape Town Cluster Unit has for me. [sic] He informed me further that he can assist me with the case,' Veroni alleged in an affidavit.[11]

Veroni further claimed that Lifman had wanted him to provide evidence and make a statement against Colin Booysen and the other accused in the Modack-centred extortion case – this tied in with the suspicions of some of the accused in the case that Lifman had set up their arrests.

The argument in court was how Lifman, as alleged by Veroni, was a private citizen who somehow had inside information about the police's intentions relating to Veroni. 'Someone is pulling the strings here and it's clear [who] from the affidavit of Mr Veroni,' Hendricks said.[12]

Kinnear countered, 'Nothing stays a secret in South Africa anymore. Not even a top-secret operation.'[13]

Interestingly, however, the most telling sign that Lifman could possibly have had the law in his pocket was an absence: only members of the so-called Modack group were in the dock; only one side of the so-called bouncer wars, as detailed by police themselves, was before the court.

On 7 February 2018 Mark Lifman was taken into police custody after landing at Cape Town International Airport following some time abroad. He was charged with pointing a firearm at the March 2017 auction during which he'd clashed with Modack and his men. Modack was the complainant; he'd lodged the criminal complaint in January 2018, while he was still in Pollsmoor Prison before being released on bail.

Lifman's attorney William Booth cried foul: he pointed out that the arrest was illegal as there'd been no warrant to carry it out. Lifman was held in police custody for two days; then, shortly before his anticipated appearance in the Bellville Magistrate's Court, the case against him was suddenly withdrawn.

Andre Naude was present at the Bellville court on the day Lifman was meant to appear, along with several bulky private-security guards in uniform black vests and with black company cars. When word went out that Lifman would be freed, Naude briskly directed the security guards to park some of the vehicles directly in front of the court building. When Lifman finally emerged, it was with a clearly annoyed Booth, who told journalists that a group of police officers had acted on their own, skipping required checks and balances, to carry out the arrest.

Lifman took action against the police relating to his 'unlawful arrest' – in early 2019 he was in the process of suing them.[14]

While Lifman managed to avoid setting foot in a courtroom dock in 2018, Modack was slapped with criminal complaint after criminal complaint, and repeatedly arrested. In mid-January 2018, while he was still in jail and his prolonged extortion-case bail hearing was in progress, a prosecutor announced that the state was planning to charge him and Jacques Cronje for the murder of Pitchou Falanga, the bouncer killed at Cubana in Green Point six weeks earlier.

Also in January, Modack and a relative were arrested for car theft and appeared in the Goodwood Magistrate's Court.

Then, in February, also while still in custody, Modack and Cronje were charged with threatening and trying to extort the owner of The Grand in Rivonia, Johannesburg, in July 2017.

Surprisingly, on 9 February Modack and his relative were granted bail in the car theft case, and a month later the case was withdrawn.

The next domino to fall was the Johannesburg attempted-extortion case: after bail was granted to Modack and Cronje, that case was also withdrawn.

And finally, Modack and his four co-accused were granted bail in the complicated and sensational application that had played out over more than two months in the Cape Town Magistrate's Court.

Nafiz Modack's troubles were far from over, however. In early April 2018, when he and his co-accused appeared in the Cape Town Magistrate's Court for the extortion case against them to be transferred to the regional court where they were expected to go on trial, police officers temporarily seized two Mercedes-Benzes and a Land Rover as it was suspected the vehicles were fitted with 'illegal gadgets'.[15]

Then, in March, Jacques Cronje and three others were arrested after an incident at an eatery in the upmarket suburb of Constantia during which someone allegedly pulled a knife.[16]

In May 2018 it emerged that in the extortion case the state was also accusing Modack of having illegally intercepted cellphone communications in order to obstruct the administration of justice: an amended charge sheet noted that calls with a potential witness in the case had allegedly been intercepted without the witness's consent in writing.

The extortion-case trial against Nafiz Modack and his three surviving co-accused (Jacques Cronje, Colin Booysen and Ashley Fields; the fourth, Carl Lakay, had been murdered) resumed in April 2019.

Meanwhile, at the end of December 2018 another string of shocking claims, about underhanded smear-campaign tactics being carried out by dirty cops, suddenly surfaced, causing the dormant coals of underworld issues to reignite.

Lieutenant Colonel Charl Kinnear wrote a complaint to his

bosses claiming that six officers with ties to Crime Intelligence in the Western Cape were using state resources to tarnish his reputation, as well as those of his colleagues, including Jeremy Vearey, Peter Jacobs and Althea Jeftha.[17]

Among the serious claims Kinnear made was that one officer in particular was aligned to Nafiz Modack, and had acted inappropriately to try and see to it that certain actions were carried out to Modack's advantage; this included the February 2018 arrest of Mark Lifman.[18]

Kinnear's claims, paired with what had been aired during Modack's extortion-case bail application, seemed to divide the Western Cape's cops into two perceived factions: one allegedly backing Mark Lifman and the other allegedly backing Nafiz Modack.

Kinnear also alleged that four officers had 'approached various drug dealers and gangsters' that he and his colleagues had investigated in Mitchells Plain from 2007 'and requested that they make statements and lay charges against us for any type of wrongdoing in order to have us arrested and subsequently discharged from the South African Police Service.'[19] (This echoed what Vearey had insisted was the case in the smear-campaign-claims saga involving Dan Plato.)

Another claim Kinnear made was that Crime Intelligence officers were illegally intercepting his cellphone communications. 'It needs to be mentioned that since I arrested Nafiz Modack I started to hear noises on my cellular telephone lines whilst making telephone calls,' he wrote. 'At times I could and still can hear the people who is [sic] supposed to listen to my lines talk to each other in the background.'[20]

He claimed the same was happening to Lieutenant Colonel Clive Ontong – Ontong happened to be deeply involved in the Project Impi 'guns-to-gangs' court case focused on Irshaad Laher.

Above all, Kinnear claimed that the officers he'd singled out were wasting taxpayers' money to try and frame him and some of his colleagues for wrongdoings in which they had no involvement.

Kinnear said that in October 2018 an attorney had told him that he'd heard from a cop that Kinnear and Vearey faced arrest, and that this was to be carried out before or on Christmas – the year before, during the Modack-focused extortion bail application, there had indeed been whispering among cops that investigators could be arrested by colleagues who were falsifying charges against them. Kinnear wanted those colleagues he claimed were working against him and his cop allies to be arrested. 'I hereby urgently request … a full investigation … and want all members involved [to] be suspended, arrested and charged for the commission of Defeating the Ends of Justice and/or any other charges formulated by the Director of Public Prosecutions,' he wrote in his December 2018 letter.[21]

Kinnear's detailed complaint was taken very seriously, but so were counterclaims that were then made by the officers he'd singled out, and all this became the focus of a national police investigation, as well as an Ipid probe. Police and the police watchdog were therefore investigating Western Cape cops.

Vearey, never one to keep quiet, also spoke out about the situation and yet again, as had happened several times before in his career, he labelled what was happening a smear campaign, this time saying it was being orchestrated by Crime Intelligence officers. 'They have been running a special operation for the past few years on the instruction of a general,' he claimed. 'This operation has the express purpose of discrediting me by manufacturing false allegations in order to affect [sic] the arrest of myself… The current information is an extension of what I have referred to before … around the [Pierre] Wyngaard, Queeny and Pierre Theron rumours.'[22]

Vearey likened the situation to what had happened to Andre Lincoln in the 1990s, when colleagues had accused Lincoln of working with criminal suspects, accusations that had led to criminal charges and Lincoln's being forced from the police (against which he'd successfully appealed).

Vearey, like Lincoln had been, was insistent on proving he was being set up. 'It is my intention to demonstrate the pattern of racketeering and criminal conspiracy involving state officials in an attempt to defame and frame me,' he said.[23]

South Africa's Crime Intelligence head Peter Jacobs also weighed in on the matter, sending a memorandum to police bosses labelling the group of officers identified by Kinnear as a 'rogue team'.[24] This was the very label plastered on the team that Andre Lincoln had headed in the mid-1990s that had looked into underworld figures including Cyril Beeka.

Jacobs's view of the team of police officers in the Western Cape was deeply unsettling because if what he was saying was true, it meant a group of turncoat cops were working in the sensitive intelligence arena to strangle the critical work of colleagues, and that proper criminal investigations, which should have been the focus of police, could have fallen by the wayside and robbed complainants of justice.

Equally, however, if what Kinnear and Vearey claimed, and what Jacobs was saying, proved to be false, then they could be pointed to as rogue elements within the police.

Corrupt hands shaping the underworld purposefully keep it amorphous and ambiguous so that it can't be pinned down and so that the truth diffuses. They deliberately add to the murk – the notions of right and wrong, good and bad often seem to be highly polished surfaces reflecting each other, the virtuous painted as corrupt and the corrupt portrayed as virtuous.

Adding to this confusion is perception. It's undoubtedly one of the mechanisms used to intentionally pump smoke into mirrored underworld alleyways, and some intelligence operatives and proxies in this realm are masters at clandestinely constructing and tweaking situations, creating scenarios they want people to believe.

This results in much second-guessing and 'what ifs'. What if, for example, the state's portrayal of Mark Lifman as a slick white-collar criminal is a fabrication created by those wanting, for whatever reason, to see his downfall? What if the Nafiz Modack described by the police – a bullying criminal with bad intentions – isn't the true man at all? This would mean that certain police officers, purportedly intent on fighting corruption, are, in fact, the criminals, safe in the guise of their blue uniforms. But what if this is the very idea that devious proxies and operatives are intentionally planting?

Underhanded informants and rogue state elements play a role in shaping the country, in some cases even writing history before it happens, although this often only becomes apparent after irreparable damage is done. This is what Andre Lincoln consistently claimed had happened to him: he'd been found guilty of an array of criminal charges that he says had been fuelled by false information supplied by colleagues. It took him years to get his career back on track and still there are those who view him as a sly criminal.

The extortion-case trial against Modack and his co-accused resumed in April 2019, with Radley Dijkers, who'd been the Grand Africa Café's brand manager, making startling admissions including that he felt he'd been pressured to proceed with the matter by Captain Althea Jeftha, and that he'd met with Mark Lifman two days after Modack and his co-accused were arrested.[25]

CHAPTER 11
Legacy does not die

Attempts over decades to clamp down on the underworld have failed. This is at least partly because of recent, as well as historic, collusion within the state, with nightclub-security battles linked to police infighting.

The sheer scope and scale of the ever-expanding underworld, which flourishes thanks to consistent fertilisation with generous doses of corruption, has also made it impossible to snuff out.

And it's not just individual suspects and errant aspects of the state. It has become a burgeoning mass of legacies. The stubborn stains of apartheid, gangsterism of all kinds, including that manipulated by the state, self-enriching politicians, illicit trades, nightclub-security skirmishes and rogue cops – over the years all have merged to produce an underworld that's as deep as it is wide. With several offshoots now extending far across the country's borders, the underworld birthed in South Africa is no longer restricted to home soil; it's bolstered via other countries.

This is what law-abiding police officers are up against: a gargantuan, entwined, self-sustaining monster that can't be handcuffed, made to stand trial or cut down in size.

A former club owner who's been informally monitoring shifts in Western Cape nightclub security over the years has pointed a finger firmly at the National Party, saying mafia links and organised crime were nurtured under the apartheid regime. 'Every ounce of criminality that exists today existed then and was guided by the hand of the National Party,' he said.[1]

Organised crime, which generates masses of money, has indeed been either passed on or involuntarily inherited by South Africa's democratic government and the politicians who've come into power. It's how that organised crime is tackled that informs the stability and strength of the government.

But simply separating those with good intentions from those intentionally furthering crime isn't easy. This is because sticky dirt, whether expertly manufactured or in the form of an indiscretion from years ago, can be dug up and flung onto whoever is trying to clean up. Simply put, everyone has dirt (fake or real) on everyone else.

When the dirt is manufactured it means that apartheid-style strategies, especially cunning misinformation campaigns along the lines of Stratcom,[2] live on in South Africa, tripping up serious cop investigations intended to uncover government wrongdoing, as well as poisoning and fragmenting the police service and other state agencies.

South Africa's police officers under apartheid were tasked with concocting and carrying out atrocious crimes; for some of these public servants, the 'thin blue line' disappeared completely, and they became common criminals. After apartheid, some of those same officers found themselves working alongside ex-ANC intelligence operatives whose circles they'd previously infiltrated, and vice versa. This is the foundation on which today's police service was constructed and it has repeatedly revealed fundamental flaws.

Operation Intrigue of 1996 involved probing underworld figures with suspected links to government officials, but it was derailed because the ex-ANC intelligence operative heading up the project was accused by his colleagues of siding with suspects.

The government-mandated Operation Slasher of 2002 and Project Impi of 2013 led to claims being made against apartheid-era cops and looked into crimes committed under apartheid, as well as into later underworld happenings; both involved investigation by former ANC intelligence operatives, and both became muddied by controversy, revealing extreme friction within the police.

Claims of corruption within the cop service resurfaced during a key bail hearing in late 2017 and early 2018, with not just those talking for the accused pointing the finger at dirty officers but police investigators themselves hinting at suspicions of corruption within their own ranks. Similar striking suspicions among cops resurfaced in the Western Cape in late 2018 and early 2019.

These claims of regional malfeasance are a microcosm of a much more expansive situation in South Africa as a whole. Police corruption nationally is mature and streetwise, an entire new devious generation steeped in dishonesty. As then Ipid head Robert McBride said in Parliament in 2018, 'The biggest threat to national security is corruption in the SAPS.'[3]

Suspects in underworld cases, and police officers who've become crime suspects, often claim their arrests are fuelled by ulterior motives. And at times it does indeed appear that there's a higher-level fight playing out between police and other state officials, and that alleged underworld figures, while not necessarily innocent of all wrongdoing, have become pawns in this game.

It's often through court cases that cops try to air their views of colleagues or plant seeds of doubt about colleagues' true intentions, but it's also through these that incongruencies between government agencies – police, prosecuting powers, the justice system and the legal fraternity – are exposed.

The Cape Town Magistrate's Court has been something of a revolving door for suspects linked, via claims by police, to the underworld: Cyril Beeka, Nafiz Modack, Mark Lifman, Jacques Cronje, Igor Russol, Houssain Taleb, Dobrosav Gavric ... the list is a long one. These matters passing through the court are a narrow example of how South Africa's broader underworld has become a cycle.

A sentiment expressed by a police captain back in 1999, that it was 'difficult to prosecute' the leaders of underworld operations 'as the public fears them and are hesitant to cooperate, to act as witnesses, or to lay charges', is echoed to this day. 'Nightclub owners feel police can't protect them or compensate them for damage should they lay charges,' he said then.[4] In 2017 a police sergeant stated, 'People don't want to make cases. They are afraid ... We can't allow no law and order on the streets and in the clubs.'[5] In 2018 a Gauteng police detective noted that complainants 'fear for their lives'.[6]

Despite these similar sentiments expressed by police officers, the underworld, and the court cases it births, shows no sign of diminishing. Something somewhere is grossly amiss: either suspects are being falsely accused of crimes, or there are foul mechanisms in place to ensure legitimate court cases disintegrate.

By 2019 in South Africa, following the fall of the Zuma administration that buckled under the increasing weight of countless corruption claims, several high-level national commissions of inquiry were up and running to purportedly try and pinpoint who was responsible for revolting acts that had facilitated the ravaging and greed-fuelled looting of state resources. There was a commission looking into the affairs of SARS, one into the state's asset manager, the Public Investment Corporation, and another into the broader phenomenon of state capture.

But there was no commission analysing how residents of the country, and of the Western Cape in particular, had been put in the way of injury and even death by firearms meant to be safeguarded by the cops, but which had instead, according to key police investigators, resulted in widespread woundings and killings. There was no commission trying to identify dirty cops and in some cases private businessmen, who by corrupt acts and reputational damage to certain individuals have perpetuated a war often centred around nightclub security.

Failure to try and sift out the good from the bad, and leaving the situation unchecked, presents a dangerous double-edged problem: not just state security structures, but also aspects of private security, have folded inside out, and instead of providing a secure shield for citizens, are stripping them of protection and posing a direct threat to them. Scrape away the conjecture and political ploys, look beyond nightclub doorways, and the true cost of underworld power battles is revealed: the collateral and the intentional damage, the rising count of the murdered and maimed, the numbers of bodies penetrated by bullets or blades.

Clean cops, when they're not watching their backs for knives crooked colleagues could plunge into them, can only try to slow down the decades-long and increasing toll of killed and wounded. This is what law-abiding residents are unwittingly exposed to.

Those who selfishly think they stand to benefit from smoothing over an already flawed foundation on which self-enriching corruption can be solidly built, especially those within the state, should think about whose agendas they're truly furthering. For their actions, while now maybe more sophisticated, aren't novel, and are keeping South Africa spinning in a circle of crime that dates back decades and is simply increasing in circumference.

Nightclub-security power shoves, political skulduggery, gang clashes and cop infighting bleed into each other and have become cyclical and generational. The seeds sown in these arenas in Cape Town in the 1990s and further back are still sprouting, meaning corrupt and criminal activities taking root now will affect the city, and in turn the country, for decades to come.

This inescapable reality ensures that our beautiful South Africa has a promising future as a heavyweight in global organised crime.

Notes

OPENING QUOTE

1   Information contained in an affidavit by Hawks Lieutenant Colonel Peter Janse Viljoen dated 31 January 2018, signed in Bellville, and used by the state in an extortion-case bail application, case number 16/818/2017, against Nafiz Modack and four co-accused in the Cape Town Magistrate's Court.

CHAPTER 1   *Apartheid's bouncer blueprint*

1   Shaw, M and Haysom, S (2016), 'Organised Crime in Late Apartheid and the Transition to a New Criminal Order: The Rise and Fall of the Johannesburg "Bouncer Mafia"', *Journal of Southern African Studies*, 6 July http://globalinitiative.net/the-rise-and-fall-of-the-johannesburg-bouncer-mafia/ Accessed 12 February 2019.

2   Ibid.

3   ANC submission to a special Truth and Reconciliation Commission hearing on the role of business, 20 November 1997 http://www.artsrn.ualberta.ca/amcdouga/Hist446_2011/documents_anc_old_site/ANC%20Submission%20to%20the%20TRC%20on%20Role%20of%20Business_1997.pdf Accessed 19 February 2019.

4   Ibid.

5   Shaw, M and Haysom, S (2016), 'Organised Crime in Late Apartheid and the Transition to a New Criminal Order: The Rise and Fall of the Johannesburg "Bouncer Mafia"', *Journal of Southern African Studies*, 6 July http://globalinitiative.net/the-rise-and-fall-of-the-johannesburg-bouncer-mafia/ Accessed 12 February 2019.

6   The Truth and Reconciliation Commission was a body set up in South

Notes

Africa after apartheid was officially abolished in 1994. Intended to deal with injustices committed during that era, it was in this forum that horrific and ghastly accounts of what transpired under authoritarian rule were revealed.

7   Testimony of Ferdinand Barnard at TRC hearing on 27 September 2000: 'TRC Documents', SABC Truth Commission Special Report http://sabctrc.saha.org.za/documents/amntrans/cape_town/54494.htm Accessed 15 January 2019.
8   Ibid.
9   Ibid.
10   Testimony of Ferdinand Barnard during a TRC hearing on 28 September 2000, TRC transcript, 'On resumption 28 September 2000 – Day 17' http://www.justice.gov.za/trc/amntrans%5C2000/200928ct.htm Accessed 19 March 2019.
11   Testimony of Ferdinand Barnard at TRC hearing on 27 September 2000: 'TRC Documents', SABC Truth Commission Special Report http://sabctrc.saha.org.za/documents/amntrans/cape_town/54494.htm Accessed 15 January 2019.
12   Testimony of Ferdinand Barnard during a TRC hearing on 28 September 2000, TRC transcript, 'On resumption 28 September 2000 – Day 17' http://www.justice.gov.za/trc/amntrans%5C2000/200928ct.htm Accessed 19 March 2019.
13   Ibid.
14   Ibid.
15   The term 'state capture' was first used by the World Bank around 2000 to describe the situation in central Asian countries where small corrupt groups used their influence over government officials to strengthen their own economic positions. This systemic political corruption in which private interests significantly influence a state's decision-making processes to their own advantage became an issue in South Africa in 2016, with allegations of a potentially corrupt relationship between the wealthy Gupta family and the then South African President Jacob Zuma, his family and leading members of the ANC. The Gupta family had migrated from the Indian state of Uttar Pradesh to South Africa in 1993. Based in Saxonwold, Johannesburg, and Dubai in the United Arab Emirates, they owned a business empire spanning computer equipment, media and mining.
16   *Lincoln v Minister of Justice and Constitutional Development and Another* (17967/2012) [2017] ZAWCHC 108 (22 September 2017), Western Cape High Court, Cape Town, Southern African Legal Information Institute

http://www.saflii.org/za/cases/ZAWCHC/2017/108.html Accessed 16 January 2019.

17 After the end of apartheid, Nelson Mandela tasked the first national police commissioner of a democratic South Africa, George Fivaz, with overseeing the amalgamation and integration of all police and security structures in the country. Years later Fivaz said this had involved absorbing 11 policing agencies, including '30 000 illiterate policemen', into one organisation. See Krost, P (1999) 'Fivaz happy to step down', IOL, 29 October https://www.iol.co.za/news/south-africa/fivaz-happy-to-step-down-17821 Accessed 16 January 2019.

18 *Lincoln v Minister of Justice and Constitutional Development and Another* (17967/2012) [2017] ZAWCHC 108 (22 September 2017), Western Cape High Court, Cape Town, Southern African Legal Information Institute http://www.saflii.org/za/cases/ZAWCHC/2017/108.html Accessed 16 January 2019.

19 Ibid.

20 In 2009 Palazzolo was sentenced in absentia to nine years in jail by an Italian court but he managed to avoid prison until his past eventually caught up with him and he was arrested in Thailand in 2012.

21 Smith, P (1999) 'Nats were in bed with mafia boss', *Mail&Guardian*, 5 February https://mg.co.za/article/1999-02-05-nats-were-in-bed-with-mafia-boss Accessed 16 January 2019.

22 Anesi, C and Rubino, G (2015) 'Africa: is Cosa Nostra', Correctiv: Recherchen fur die Gesellschaft, 16 April https://correctiv.org/en/investigations/mafia-africa/articles/2015/04/16/africa-cosa-nostra/ Accessed 16 January 2019.

23 In 1994, in the country's first non-racial election, the Western Cape was one of two provinces that did not elect an ANC provincial government (the other being KwaZulu-Natal), when the National Party won 53% of the votes.

24 Judgment in application for absolution in *Lincoln v the Minister of Justice and Constitutional Development and Another* (17967/2012), Western Cape High Court, Cape Town, 25 April 2017, a copy of which was provided to the author by a source on 25 April 2017.

25 Ibid.

26 Dolley, C (2017) 'How Mandela cop infiltrated suspected crime bosses', News24, 13 March https://www.news24.com/SouthAfrica/News/how-mandela-cop-infiltrated-suspected-crime-bosses-20170313 Accessed 23 April 2019.

27 Brummer, S (1995) 'Battle for control of police union', *Mail&Guardian*, 17 February https://mg.co.za/article/1995-02-17-battle-for-control-of-police-union Accessed 20 January 2019.

28 South African Police Union website https://www.sapu.org.za/about Accessed 8 March 2019.

29 Interview on National Public Radio in the USA. See De Vos, G, Tsuda, T and Romanucci-Ross, L (eds) (2006) *Ethnic Identity Problems and Prospects for the Twenty-first Century*, AltaMira Press, Maryland, USA.

30 Letter from Andre Lincoln to, among others, George Fivaz and Sydney Mufamadi, dated 15 October 1996, detailing Lincoln's work conditions.

31 Staff reporter (1997) 'Fivaz takes on Mbeki police squad', *Mail&Guardian*, 1 October https://mg.co.za/article/1997-10-01-fivaz-takes-on-mbeki-police-squad Accessed 11 February 2019.

32 *Lincoln v Minister of Justice and Constitutional Development and Another* (17967/2012) [2017] ZAWCHC 108 (22 September 2017), Western Cape High Court, Cape Town, Southern African Legal Information Institute http://www.saflii.org/za/cases/ZAWCHC/2017/108.html Accessed 16 January 2019.

33 Ibid.

34 Ibid.

35 Ibid.

36 Ibid. Lincoln also alleged that a group of police officers, including Knipe, had in the mid-1980s tampered with crime scenes where apartheid activists had been killed in order to try and conceal government involvement, and particularly police and Security Branch involvement. Knipe denied this.

37 Weaver, T (2002) 'Showdown looms in Cape's spy vs spy cold war', *Cape Times*, 11 July https://www.iol.co.za/news/politics/showdown-looms-in-capes-spy-vs-spy-cold-war-89581 Accessed 19 February 2019.

38 Weaver, T (2002) 'Showdown looms in Cape's spy vs spy cold war', *Cape Times*, 11 July https://www.iol.co.za/news/politics/showdown-looms-in-capes-spy-vs-spy-cold-war-89581 Accessed 17 January 2019.

39 Weaver, T (2002) 'Top cop carpeted as apartheid cold war erupts', *Cape Times*, 30 July https://www.iol.co.za/news/south-africa/top-cop-carpeted-as-apartheid-cold-war-erupts-90631 Accessed 17 January 2019.

40 Etheridge, J (2017) 'Former police commissioner had "no grudges" against ex-Mandela cop', News24, 15 May https://www.news24.com/SouthAfrica/News/former-police-commissioner-had-no-grudges-against-ex-mandela-cop-20170515 Accessed 16 January 2019.

41 Dolley, C (2017) 'Threats and "lies" – the ex-Mandela cop's case', News24, 13 March https://www.news24.com/SouthAfrica/News/threats-and-lies-the-ex-mandela-cops-case-20170313 Accessed 16 January 2019.

42 *Lincoln v Minister of Justice and Constitutional Development and Another* (17967/2012) [2017] ZAWCHC 108 (22 September 2017), Western Cape High Court, Cape Town, Southern African Legal Information Institute http://www.saflii.org/za/cases/ZAWCHC/2017/108.html Accessed 16 January 2019.

43 Dolley, C (2017) 'State Security Agency boss interference in ex-Mandela cop case - more details emerge', News24, 22 March https://www.news24.com/SouthAfrica/News/state-security-agency-boss-interference-in-ex-mandela-cops-case-more-details-emerge-20170322 Accessed 16 January 2019; and *Lincoln v Minister of Justice and Constitutional Development and Another* (17967/2012) [2017] ZAWCHC 108 (22 September 2017), Western Cape High Court, Cape Town, Southern African Legal Information Institute http://www.saflii.org/za/cases/ZAWCHC/2017/108.html Accessed 16 January 2019.

44 News24 (2018) 'State Security Agency DG Arthur Fraser moved to Correctional Services', 17 April https://www.news24.com/SouthAfrica/News/state-security-agency-dg-arthur-fraser-moved-to-correctional-services-20180417 Accessed 16 January 2019; and Stone, S (2018) 'Dintwe can't be trusted with state secrets – Fraser', *City Press* on News24, 15 April https://www.news24.com/SouthAfrica/News/dintwe-cant-be-trusted-with-state-secrets-fraser-20180414 Accessed 16 January 2019.

45 Mlamla, S (2018) 'South African Policing Union claim Anti-Gang Unit is "illegal"', IOL, 22 November https://www.iol.co.za/capeargus/news/south-african-policing-union-claim-anti-gang-unit-is-illegal-18215700 Accessed 11 March 2019.

46 Thamm, M (2019) 'Caught in the Crossfire: Politicians leverage endemic Cape Flats gangland violence ahead of election,' *Daily Maverick*, 25 February https://www.dailymaverick.co.za/article/2019-02-25-caught-in-the-crossfire-politicians-leverage-endemic-cape-flats-gangland-violence-ahead-of-election/ Accessed 8 March 2019.

47 Judgment in *Lincoln v the State* (A872/2003), Western Cape High Court, Cape Town, 16 October 2009, in which Lincoln successfully appealed 17 convictions, a copy of which was provided to the author by a confidential source on 29 August 2018.

48 Dolley, C (2017) 'Mbalula warns crime intelligence over its own criminal elements', News24, 19 September https://www.news24.com/SouthAfrica/News/mbalula-warns-crime-intelligence-over-its-own-criminal-

elements-20170919 Accessed 15 January 2019; and Gerber, J (2018) 'Crime intelligence was infiltrated – police commissioner', News24, 22 August https://www.news24.com/SouthAfrica/News/crime-intelligence-was-infiltrated-police-commissioner-20180822 Accessed 15 January 2019.

49 Dolley, C (2019) 'Analysis: Spy watchdog pushes on with probes, despite "threats and intimidation"', amaBhungane, 18 January https://amabhungane.org/stories/analysis-spy-watchdog-pushes-on-with-probes-despite-threats-and-intimidation/ Accessed 21 February 2019.

50 Testimony by Lieutenant Colonel Charl Kinnear in the Cape Town Magistrate's Court on 3 January 2018 during an extortion-case bail application, case number 16/818/2017, launched by Nafiz Modack and four co-accused in the Cape Town Magistrate's Court.

51 Information contained in an affidavit by Hawks Lieutenant Colonel Peter Janse Viljoen dated 31 January 2018, signed in Bellville, and used by the state in an extortion-case bail application, case number 16/818/2017, against Nafiz Modack and four co-accused in the Cape Town Magistrate's Court.

52 Interview with Nafiz Modack in Green Point, 21 September 2017. Dolley, C (2017), 'EXCLUSIVE: People want me dead because of my security industry connections – underworld figure Modack', News24, 22 September, https://www.news24.com/SouthAfrica/News/exclusive-people-want-me-dead-because-of-my-security-industry-connections-underworld-figure-modack-20170922 Accessed 17 April 2019.

53 Ibid.

54 Information contained in an affidavit by Hawks Lieutenant Colonel Peter Janse Viljoen dated 31 January 2018, signed in Bellville, and used by the state in an extortion-case bail application, case number 16/818/2017, against Nafiz Modack and four co-accused in the Cape Town Magistrate's Court.

55 Information contained in an affidavit by Nafiz Modack date-stamped 12 February 2018 and submitted by Modack's defence in an extortion-case bail application, case number 16/818/2017, launched by Modack and four co-accused in the Cape Town Magistrate's Court.

CHAPTER 2 *Cyril Beeka's rise to bouncer-racket domination*

1 Interview with a source in Cape Town on 18 January 2018.

2 Interview with a source in Cape Town on 20 February 2018. Lonte, who was, according to the source, 'an actual psychopath who was fun to talk

to', had the dubious distinction of having introduced crack, a form of cocaine that can be smoked, to the Cape Flats.

3   Interview with a source in Cape Town on 18 January 2018.
4   Ibid.
5   Testimony of Dirk Coetzee at Truth and Reconciliation amnesty hearing in Durban on 5-7 November 1996 http://www.justice.gov.za/trc/amntrans/amntrans-pdfs/trc-amntrans-am1996-Durban-02.pdf Accessed 12 February 2019.
6   Interview with Major General Jeremy Vearey in Cape Town on 31 August 2018.
7   Interview with a source in Cape Town on 18 January 2018.
8   Ibid.
9   Letter from Andre Lincoln to the Deputy President, the Minister of Safety and Security and the Minister of Justice dated 7 October 1997 informing the recipients about Operation Intrigue and figures it had identified as suspects. In the same letter, Lincoln listed Dirk Coetzee as a National Intelligence Agency official and alleged he was a confirmed associate of Cosa Nostra, the Italian crime grouping of which Vito Palazzolo was also a very high-ranking member.
10 Interview with a confidential source in Cape Town on 20 February 2018.
11 Testimony of Lieutenant Colonel Charl Kinnear in the Cape Town Magistrate's Court on 3 January 2018 in the extortion-case bail application, case number 16/818/2017, launched by Nafiz Modack and four co-accused.
12 Mentioned by Chad Levendal, legal representative of Jacques Cronje, in the Cape Town Magistrate's Court on 1 February 2018 in the extortion-case bail application, case number 16/818/2017, launched by Nafiz Modack and four co-accused.
13 Testimony of Jacques Cronje in the Cape Town Regional Court on 21 April 2015 in the case of *State v Mark Lifman and Andre Naude*, case number 30/51/2012, who were charged with operating a bouncer company without being registered with the Private Security Regulatory Authority.
14 Members of Pro Access cc included Cyril Beeka, Jacques Cronje and one Patrick Plum, apparently a childhood connection of Beeka's and also a respected martial-arts fighter. Plum later died of a heart attack.
15 Testimony of Jacques Cronje in the Cape Town Regional Court on 21 April 2015 in the case of *State versus Mark Lifman and Andre Naude*, case number 30/51/2012, who were charged with operating a

bouncer company without being registered with the Private Security Regulatory Authority.

16 In 2004 Staggie was convicted for the theft of the weapons and sentenced to thirteen years in jail.

17 Vanessa Johnstone, V (2000) 'Staggie plotted Faure raid, says co-accused', IOL, 5 October https://www.iol.co.za/news/south-africa/staggie-plotted-faure-raid-says-co-accused-49776 Accessed 19 January 2019.

18 SAPA (2002) 'Pagad men acquitted in Staggie murder trial,' IOL, 6 March https://www.iol.co.za/news/south-africa/pagad-men-acquitted-in-staggie-murder-trial-82912 Accessed 8 March 2019.

19 Dixon, B, and Johns, L (2001) *Gangs, PAGAD and the State: Vigilantism and Revenge Violence in the Western Cape*, Centre for the Study of Violence and Reconciliation http://www.csvr.org.za/docs/gangs/gangspagadstate.pdf Accessed 19 February 2019.

20 Ibid. By 2019 Pagad was no longer considered an urban terror group.

21 Lovell, J (2000) 'Bombed Planet Hollywood for Sale', News24, 14 August https://www.news24.com/xArchive/Archive/Bombed-Planet-Hollywood-for-sale-20000814 Accessed 21 January 2019.

22 News24 (2000) 'Chronology of Cape Town bomb blasts', 9 September https://www.news24.com/SouthAfrica/Chronology-of-Cape-Town-blasts-20000829 Accessed 21 January 2019.

23 Abarder, G (2000) 'Pagad leader blames NIA for V&A bombs', IOL, 9 February https://www.iol.co.za/news/south-africa/pagad-leader-blames-nia-for-v-and-a-bombs-27754 Accessed 21 January 2019.

24 McBride, a former umKhonto weSizwe operative, was sentenced to death for the bombing of two Durban beachfront bars in 1986 in which three people were killed and 73 injured. He was later granted amnesty. See SAPA (1999) 'McGoo bomb meant for security personnel: TRC', 27 September http://www.justice.gov.za/trc/media%5C1999%5C9909/p9900927c.htm Accessed 21 January 2019.

25 Mthetheleli Mackay, M (2000) 'Escort "forgets" details in Beeka case', IOL, 28 January https://www.iol.co.za/news/south-africa/escort-forgets-details-in-beeka-case-26585 Accessed 21 January 2019.

26 Testimony of Jacques Cronje in the Cape Town Regional Court on 21 April 2015 in the case of *State v Mark Lifman and Andre Naude*, case number 30/51/2012, who were charged with operating a bouncer company without being registered with the Private Security Regulatory Authority.

27 Blignaut, C (1999) 'Night club security boss up for murder', IOL, 8 October https://www.iol.co.za/news/south-africa/night-club-security-boss-up-for-murder-15674 Accessed 21 January 2019.

28 Ibid.

29 Mthetheleli Mackay, M (1999) 'Beeka used Moroccans for attacks: Police', IOL, 7 October https://www.iol.co.za/news/south-africa/beeka-used-morrocans-for-attacks-police-15469 Accessed 21 January 2019.

30 Mthetheleli Mackay, M (1999) 'Court told of Beeka's underworld empire', IOL, 29 September https://www.iol.co.za/news/south-africa/court-told-of-beekas-underworld-empire-14418 Accessed 21 January 2019.

31 Ibid.

32 Testimony of Jacques Cronje in the Cape Town Regional Court on 21 April 2015 in the case of *State v Mark Lifman and Andre Naude*, case number 30/51/2012, who were charged with operating a bouncer company without being registered with the Private Security Regulatory Authority.

33 Geldenhuys, H, Meyer W and Powell, I (2012) 'Kebble killers get their guns back', IOL, 3 March https://www.iol.co.za/news/south-africa/kebble-killers-get-their-guns-back-1247861 Accessed 28 January 2019; and Sole, S, Dawes N and Brümmer, S (2006) 'Jackie Selebi's shady Kebble links', *Mail&Guardian*, 26 May https://mg.co.za/article/2006-05-26-jackie-selebis-shady-kebble-links Accessed 28 January 2019.

34 News24 (2010) 'Agliotti goes free', 25 November https://www.news24.com/southafrica/news/agliotti-goes-free-20101125 Accessed 19 February 2019.

35 Mhlungu, G (2014) 'The men who "got away" with murder', *City Press*, 16 November https://www.news24.com/Archives/City-Press/The-men-whogot-away-withmurder-20150429 Accessed 28 January 2019; and News24 (2010) 'Agliotti goes free', 25 November https://www.news24.com/southafrica/news/agliotti-goes-free-20101125 Accessed 28 January 2019. Schultz, Smith and McGurk re-enacted the shooting in the documentary *204: Getting Away with Murder*; the number 204 refers to a section of the Criminal Procedure Act that involves a person who may have committed a crime testifying against others who were involved in exchange for possible indemnity from prosecution.

36 Dolley, C (2012) 'Russian gangster tells of fight for Cape', *Cape Times*, 16 January https://www.iol.co.za/news/russian-gangster-tells-of-fight-for-cape-1213618 Accessed 15 January 2019.

37 Ibid.

38 Interview with Houssain Taleb in Cape Town on 28 January 2012; and

Dolley, C (2012) 'Band of brothers who patrol club scene', *Cape Times*, 30 January https://www.iol.co.za/news/south-africa/western-cape/band-ofbrothers-who-patrol-club-scene-1223533 Accessed 22 January 2019.

39 Affidavit of Houssain Taleb read out in the Cape Town Magistrate's Court on 19 December 2017 during a bail application. Taleb was charged with conspiracy to commit murder.

40 Ibid.

41 Personal communication with a confidential source in Cape Town on 20 February 2018.

42 Dolley, C (2012), '"Russian" linked to extortion racket,' *Cape* Times, 2 March https://www.iol.co.za/capetimes/russian-linked-to-extortion-racket-1247573 Accessed 1 March 2019. A report by the Hawks providing details about Igor Russol, charges he faced, his background and insight as to why officers did not want him to be granted bail in an extortion case, CAS 464/01/2012, said he first entered South Africa at the end of October 2002 and became a permanent resident in January 2011. Russol obtained four temporary work permits between 2003 and 2010, and the employer listed on these was Mark Lifman Properties.

43 Ni Ghiollanaraithe, F (2007) 'Mo Shaik's underworld links', IOL, 22 December https://www.iol.co.za/news/politics/mo-shaiks-underworld-links-383661 Accessed 21 January 2019.

44 Testimony of Hawks investigator Paul Hendrikse during a bail application focusing on Dobrosav Gavric on 10 January 2012 in the Cape Town Magistrate's Court.

45 Personal communication with a confidential source on 5 May 2018.

46 Phone conversations with several confidential sources in May 2018.

47 Testimony of Jacques Cronje in the Cape Town Regional Court on 21 April 2015 in case number 30/51/2012, *State v Andre Naude and Mark Lifman*, who were accused of running a private security company that was not registered with the Private Security Industry Regulatory Authority.

48 Ibid.

49 Ibid.

50 SAPA (2010) 'The life and times of Lolly Jackson', 4 May https://www.iol.co.za/news/south-africa/the-life-and-times-of-lolly-jackson-482648 Accessed 24 January 2019.

51 Evans, J (2015) 'Dying Louka spills the beans on Lolly Jackson murder,' News24, 21 April https://www.news24.com/SouthAfrica/News/Dying-Louka-spills-beans-on-Lolly-Jackson-murder-20150421 Accessed 24 January 2019.

52 Interview with confidential source in Cape Town on 18 January 2018.

53 Late in 2018 Krejčíř was incarcerated in South Africa and extradition proceedings to the Czech Republic begun, but his name was still being linked to allegations of underworld dealings, and even while behind bars he was making rattling claims against powerful figures in South Africa's political arena. A prison cell couldn't confine his reputation, nor could it silence him.

54 Testimony of Jacques Cronje in the Cape Town Regional Court on 21 April 2015 in case number 30/51/2012, *State v Andre Naude and Mark Lifman*, who were accused of running a private security company that was not registered with the Private Security Industry Regulatory Authority.

55 This Audi was sold, then repossessed and then, according to sources, somehow disappeared from the bank's car pound and ended up back with the friend from whom Cyril Beeka had borrowed it. Several sources claimed this friend was Nafiz Modack. The author once asked Modack via message if this car had ever belonged to him; his response via WhatsApp was 'no comment'.

56 Testimony of Hawks investigator Paul Hendrikse during a bail application focusing on Dobrosav Gavric, accused of cocaine possession and who faced possible extradition to Serbia, on 10 January 2012 in the Cape Town Magistrate's Court.

57 The identities of the two men suspected of being involved in the assassination are known to the authorities. According to various sources, after the shooting, the men on the bike also crashed; one man sustained injuries – a burn from the motorbike's exhaust – but got medical treatment without, it seems, drawing the scrutiny of police at that point. It's believed the motorbike was resprayed, covering any signs of a crash. Investigators following up on these claims were told that the motorbike in question had been at a rally at the time of the murder, but it turned out that the date of the rally didn't coincide with that of Cyril Beeka's assassination.

58 Testimony of Hawks investigator Paul Hendrikse during a bail application focusing on Dobrosav Gavric, accused of cocaine possession and who faced possible extradition to Serbia, on 10 January 2012 in the Cape Town Magistrate's Court.

59 Interview with Nafiz Modack in Cubana, Green Point, on 21 September 2017, in the author's capacity as a journalist.

60 Peters, M (2011) 'Beeka buried in grand style', IOL, 3 April https://www.iol.co.za/news/south-africa/western-cape/beeka-buried-in-grand-style-1051183 Accessed 21 January 2019.

Notes

61 Ndenze, B and SAPA (2011) 'ANC, Beeka link explained', *Cape Times*, 4 April 2011 https://www.iol.co.za/news/south-africa/western-cape/anc-beeka-link-explained-1051603 Accessed 21 January 2019.

62 SAPA (2011) 'State opposes Krejčíř Bail', IOL, 8 April https://www.iol.co.za/news/state-opposes-Krejcir-bail-1054054 Accessed 21 January 2019.

63 Interview with confidential source in Cape Town on 18 January 2018.

64 Ibid.

65 Ibid.

66 Dolley, C and Sole, S (2019) 'SAPS Wars, Part 2: It ain't over till the fat Czech sings', amaBhungane https://www.dailymaverick.co.za/article/2019-03-07-saps-wars-part-two-it-aint-over-till-the-fat-czech-sings/ Accessed 11 March 2019.

67 Affidavit by Radovan Krejčíř dated 12 July 2018 deposed at Leeuwkop Prison in Johannesburg. It's not clear exactly why Krejčíř deposed the affidavit, but he said he wanted Ipid to investigate what he claimed in it; and Mashego, J (2019), '"I paid Zuma R2.5 million for asylum" – Radovan Krejcír', *City Press*, 1 January https://city-press.news24.com/News/i-paid-zuma-r25-million-for-asylum-radovan-krejcir-20190114 Accessed 18 February 2019.

68 Dolley, C (2018) 'REVEALED: Murders expose links of Serbian warlord's assassins in SA', News24, 9 May https://www.news24.com/SouthAfrica/News/revealed-murders-expose-links-of-serbian-warlords-assassins-in-sa-20180509 Accessed 13 March 2019.

69 *Dobrosav Gavric v Refugee Status Determination Officer, Cape Town and Others* (3474/13) [2016], 6 April 2016, Southern African Legal Information Institute http://www.saflii.org/za/cases/ZAWCHC/2016/36.html Accessed 21 January 2019. In September 2018 Gavric's application for refugee status in South Africa was turned down by the Constitutional Court on the grounds that the murder for which he'd been found guilty in Serbia in 2006 was criminal, not political.

70 Affidavit by Dobrosav Gavric dated December 2011, outlining his background and how he'd ended up in South Africa; a confidential source provided the author with an unsigned copy.

71 Ibid.

72 Ibid.

73 *Dobrosav Gavric v Refugee Status Determination Officer, Cape Town and Others* (3474/13) [2016], 6 April 2016, Southern African Legal Information Institute http://www.saflii.org/za/cases/ZAWCHC/2016/36.html Accessed 21 January 2019.

74 Ibid.
75 Affidavit by Dobrosav Gavric dated December 2011, outlining his background and how he'd ended up in South Africa; a confidential source provided the author with an unsigned copy.
76 Ibid.
77 Ibid.
78 Ibid.
79 Ibid. During Gavric's first court appearance in November 2011, the investigator on the case told him that, thanks to a fingerprint match made by Interpol and the Serbian authorities, his real identity had been known by South African police since June 2011.
80 Affidavit by Dobrosav Gavric dated December 2011, outlining his background and how he'd ended up in South Africa; a confidential source provided the author with an unsigned copy.

CHAPTER 3 Enter by blood, exit by death

1 South African Police Service (SAPS) head of strategic management Major General Leon Rabie's address to Parliament on the police's rollout of an anti-gang strategy on 12 February 2019.
2 Parliamentary Monitoring Group (2001) 'Gangsterism in the Western Cape: Briefing by SAPS', 6 November https://pmg.org.za/committee-meeting/1033/ Accessed 26 January 2019.
3 Portfolio Committee on Police: Briefing by the Management of SAPS on the Anti-gang Strategy: Western Cape, KwaZulu-Natal and Eastern Cape, presented to Parliament on 23 August 2017.
4 Truth and Reconciliation Commission amnesty hearing (2000) 12 June http://www.justice.gov.za/trc/amntrans%5C2000/200612ct.htm Accessed 26 January 2019.
5 Truth Commission Special Report (undated) http://sabctrc.saha.org.za/reports/volume3/chapter5/subsection39.htm Accessed 26 January 2019. Dullah Omar became a minister in the democratic South African cabinet, from 1994 until his death in 2004.
6 Truth and Reconciliation Commission amnesty hearing (2000) 12 June http://www.justice.gov.za/trc/amntrans%5C2000/200612ct.htm Accessed 26 January 2019.
7 Truth and Reconciliation Commission amnesty hearing (2000) 4 October http://www.justice.gov.za/trc/amntrans%5C2000/201004ct.htm Accessed 26 January 2019.
8 Truth Commission Special Report (undated) http://sabctrc.saha.org.za/reports/volume3/chapter5/subsection39.htm Accessed 26 January 2019.

Notes

9   Carter, C and Merten, M (1998) 'Gangster's fast life, hard death', *Mail&Guardian*, 13 November https://mg.co.za/article/1998-11-13-gangsters-fast-life-hard-death Accessed 26 January 2019.

10 Figure from Census 2011 cited in the draft Manenberg Investment Framework dated 14 October 2015 http://vpuu.org.za/wp-content/uploads/2016/11/MANENBERG-PIF-REPORT-COMPRESSED.pdf Accessed 24 February 2019.

11 Figure from Census 2011 http://resource.capetown.gov.za/documentcentre/Documents/Maps%20and%20statistics/2011_Census_CT_Suburb_Manenberg_Profile.pdf Accessed 24 February 2019.

12 *State v Nizaam Jordaan and Others*, Case No CC20/2017 (2018) http://www.saflii.org/za/cases/ZAWCHC/2018/10.pdf Accessed 26 January 2019.

13 Ibid.

14 Dolley, C (2015) 'Gangsters may have been hired', *Weekend Argus*, 14 June https://www.iol.co.za/news/south-africa/western-cape/gangsters-may-have-been-hired-1871412 Accessed 26 January 2019.

15 Zille, H (2015) 'The Puzzle of Gangs, Drugs, Police and Politics in the Western Cape', *Inside Government*, 15 October https://www.westerncape.gov.za/news/inside-government-puzzle-gangs-drugs-police-and-politics-wc Accessed 26 January 2019.

16 Information contained in an affidavit by Hawks Lieutenant Colonel Peter Janse Viljoen dated 31 January 2018 and signed in Bellville, used by the state in the extortion-case bail application, case number 16/818/2017, against Nafiz Modack and four co-accused in the Cape Town Magistrate's Court.

17 Dolley, C (2017) 'Gang, guns and rogue crime intelligence claims ruffle underworld', News24, 9 September https://www.news24.com/SouthAfrica/News/gang-guns-and-rogue-crime-intelligence-claims-ruffle-underworld-20170919 Accessed 15 January 2019.

18 Testimony of Hawks investigator Paul Hendrikse during a bail application focusing on Dobrosav Gavric, accused of cocaine possession and who also faced extradition to Serbia, on 10 January 2012 in the Cape Town Magistrate's Court.

19 Colin Booysen murdered a policeman in the 1990s and spent time in jail for this. See Evans, J (2018), '"He gave children guns" – new allegations emerge in Colin Booysen, bodyguards' bail application,' News24, 19 October https://www.news24.com/SouthAfrica/News/he-gave-children-guns-new-allegations-emerge-in-colin-booysen-bodyguards-bail-application-20181019 Accessed 8 March 2019.

20 Updated charge sheet from 2018 in *State v Ralph Stanfield and*

22 Others, an unsigned and undated copy of which was provided, at the author's request, via email on 2 May 2018 by the Western Cape National Prosecuting Authority.

21 A leaked National Prosecuting Authority document detailing the activities of the Mobsters. The date and other details that could have revealed the origin/creator of the document were removed by the confidential source who supplied it to the author in April 2016.

22 Dolley, C (2012) 'Suspected 28s boss wants to be a pastor', *Cape Times*, 14 September https://www.iol.co.za/news/suspected-28s-boss-wants-to-be-a-pastor-1383221 Accessed 28 January 2019. Thomas's entire face was covered in faint tattoos which included two swords on his forehead. He told the author he wanted to become a pastor.

23 PowerPoint presentation by the Western Cape National Prosecuting Authority about the George 'Geweld' Thomas case, a copy of which was obtained by the author via the Western Cape National Prosecuting Authority in April 2015 while Thomas was on trial in the Western Cape High Court for an array of crimes.

24 Dolley, C (2011) 'Six state witnesses slain', *Cape Times*, 12 May https://www.iol.co.za/news/six-state-witnesses-slain-1067865 Accessed 8 March 2019.

25 Kemp, Y (2004) 'Notorious Cape crime boss dies', IOL, 4 October https://www.iol.co.za/news/south-africa/notorious-cape-crime-boss-dies-223248 Accessed 26 January 2019.

26 Affidavit by Ralph Stanfield dated March 2016. Stanfield's legal representative at the time, Pete Mihalik, ensured the author was emailed a copy, which was not signed or stamped, on 19 April 2016, after she requested this.

27 Francke, R (2017) 'LOOK: Alleged gang kingpin dishes out money to community,' *Daily Voice*, 18 April https://www.iol.co.za/news/south-africa/western-cape/look-alleged-gang-kingpin-dishes-out-money-to-community-8703134 Accessed 26 February 2019.

28 *S v Booysen and Andere* (SS60/2002) [2003] ZAWCHC 32 (22 July 2003) Southern African Legal Information Institute http://www.saflii.org/za/cases/ZAWCHC/2003/32.html Accessed 26 January 2019 [author's translation].

29 Ibid.

30 A minor celebrity in his own right, Ernie Solomon is the subject of a feature film, *A Lucky Man*, about his life, and has dabbled in music, releasing CDs with titles relating to gang terminology.

31	*S v Booysen and Andere* (SS60/2002) [2003] ZAWCHC 32 (22 July 2003) Southern African Legal Information Institute http://www.saflii.org/za/cases/ZAWCHC/2003/32.html Accessed 26 January 2019.
32	Ibid.
33	These talks were backed by Western Cape politician Dan Plato, who became Cape Town mayor in 2018.
34	*S v Booysen and Andere* (SS60/2002) [2003] ZAWCHC 32 (22 July 2003) Southern African Legal Information Institute http://www.saflii.org/za/cases/ZAWCHC/2003/32.html Accessed 26 January 2019.
35	Personal communication with confidential source in Cape Town in January/February 2013. A source who was in contact with someone who visited a home belonging to Albern Martins in 2012 claimed that this person had seen stacks of cash piled up in a bathtub and covered with newspaper.
36	Dolley, C (2013) 'Enter by blood and exit by death', *Cape Times*, 20 May https://www.iol.co.za/capetimes/enter-by-blood-and-exit-by-death-1518722 Accessed 28 January 2019.
37	Ibid.
38	Report to the City of Cape Town subcouncil, listed as item number 07SUB12/01/17, relating to an application for a business licence for health and entertainment and for keeping or conducting a nightclub. An annexure of this is a police clearance certificate for Jerome Peter Booysen dated 30 December 2015.
39	Dolley, C (2018) 'Jerome "Donkie" Booysen – "Gangsterism is not the way to go"', News24, 1 June https://www.news24.com/SouthAfrica/News/exclusive-jerome-donkie-booysen-gangsterism-is-not-the-way-to-go-20180601 Accessed 26 January 2019.
40	Affidavit by Colin Booysen dated 6 February 2018 submitted by his defence attorney in an extortion-case bail application, case number 16/818/2017, launched by Nafiz Modack and four co-accused in the Cape Town Magistrate's Court.
41	Testimony by Colonel Charl Kinnear in the Cape Town Magistrate's Court on 2 January 2018 in an extortion-case bail application, case number 16/818/2017, launched by Nafiz Modack and four co-accused.
42	Affidavit by Colin Booysen dated 6 February 2018 submitted by his defence attorney in an extortion-case bail application, case number 16/818/2017, launched by Nafiz Modack and four co-accused in the Cape Town Magistrate's Court.
43	Information contained in an affidavit by Hawks Lieutenant Colonel Peter

Janse Viljoen dated 31 January 2018 and signed in Bellville, used by the state in an extortion-case bail application, case number 16/818/2017, against Nafiz Modack and four co-accused in the Cape Town Magistrate's Court.

44 Dolley, C (2016) 'Why was gang boss at tyre shop attack site?', *Weekend Argus*, 15 May https://www.iol.co.za/news/why-was-gang-boss-at-tyre-shop-attack-site-2021799 Accessed 23 January 2019; and February, S (2016) 'Cops hunt men who petrol bombed tyre shop', *Daily Voice*, 11 May https://www.iol.co.za/news/cops-hunt-men-who-petrol-bombed-tyre-shop-2020483 Accessed 23 January 2019.

45 *S v Booysen and Andere* (SS60/2002) [2003] ZAWCHC 32 (22 July 2003) Southern African Legal Information Institute http://www.saflii.org/za/cases/ZAWCHC/2003/32.html Accessed 26 January 2019.

46 Jeremy Vearey has said this in the author's presence, including in February 2018 in Cape Town.

47 ANC Western Cape (2016) 'ANC Western Cape Press Release on the ongoing attacks on police general Jeremy Vearey,' 28 April. This email was sent to a media mailing list and was forwarded to the author by a colleague.

CHAPTER 4 *Where the dog lies buried*

1 Jeremy Vearey's career history is outlined in an affidavit dated 3 October 2016 and signed in Cape Town, which he used in a Labour Court case in a matter in which he took on police bosses and colleagues because he believed he had been unfairly transferred within the Western Cape police in June 2016.

2 Kaplan, M (2001) *Engaging the Enemy*, documentary made by Rapid Blue for the Institute for Justice and Reconciliation https://www.youtube.com/watch?v=fd_4QVBSRlE&feature=youtu.be Accessed 19 February 2019.

3 Jeremy Vearey's career history is outlined in an affidavit dated 3 October 2016 and signed in Cape Town, which he used in a Labour Court case in a matter in which he took on police bosses and colleagues because he believed he had been unfairly transferred within the Western Cape police in June 2016.

4 IOL (2002) 'Iced gangbuster guns for "corrupt top brass"', 21 August https://www.iol.co.za/news/south-africa/iced-gangbuster-guns-for-corrupt-top-brass-91781 Accessed 17 January 2019.

5 Ibid.

6 Weaver, T (2002) 'Top cop carpeted as apartheid cold war erupts', *Cape Times*, 30 July https://www.iol.co.za/news/south-africa/top-cop-

carpeted-as-apartheid-cold-war-erupts-90631 Accessed 17 January 2019.

7 *Veary v Provincial Commissioner of Police and Others* (C900/02) [2002] ZALC 76; (2002) 23 ILJ 2330 (LC) (13 September 2002) Southern African Legal Information Institute http://www.saflii.org/za/cases/ZALC/2002/76.html Accessed 17 January 2019.

8 Weaver, T (2002) 'Showdown looms in Cape's spy vs spy cold war', *Cape Times*, 11 July https://www.iol.co.za/news/politics/showdown-looms-in-capes-spy-vs-spy-cold-war-89581 Accessed 19 February 2019.

9 Weaver, T (2002) 'Top cop carpeted as apartheid cold war erupts', *Cape Times*, 30 July https://www.iol.co.za/news/south-africa/top-cop-carpeted-as-apartheid-cold-war-erupts-90631 Accessed 17 January 2019.

10 Interview with Major General Jeremy Vearey in Cape Town on 31 August 2018.

11 Ibid.

12 *Lincoln v Minister of Justice and Constitutional Development and One Other* (17967/2012) [2017] ZAWCHC 108 (22 September 2017), Southern African Legal Information Institute http://www.saflii.org/za/cases/ZAWCHC/2017/108.html Accessed 11 February 2019.

13 *Veary v Provincial Commissioner of Police and Others* (C900/02) [2002] ZALC 76; (2002) 23 ILJ 2330 (LC) (13 September 2002), Southern African Legal Information Institute http://www.saflii.org/za/cases/ZALC/2002/76.html Accessed 17 January 2019.

14 Ibid.

15 News24 Archives (2003) 'Top cop disciplined', 28 January https://www.news24.com/SouthAfrica/News/Top-cop-disciplined-20030128 Accessed 30 January 2019.

16 In September 2018 Constable ML Eksteen was awarded an SAPS certificate of commendation for success in clamping down on gang violence in Manenberg, as well as for confiscating the most unlicensed firearms in the Western Cape between April 2018 and September 2018.

17 Williams, M (2014) 'Hitmen kill mom of anti-gang cop', IOL, 15 October https://www.iol.co.za/news/hitmen-kill-mom-of-anti-gang-cop-1765148 Accessed 19 January 2019.

18 De Wee, M (2016) '1 vuurwapen, 15 moorde,' Netwerk24, 15 July https://www.netwerk24.com/Nuus/Misdaad/een-vuurwapen-16-moorde-20160715 Accessed 19 January 2019. (This information was also relayed to the author by two other sources.) This same firearm was

suspected to have been used in the murder of Greg Goss Junior, the son of policeman Greg Goss.

19 Affidavit by Jeremy Vearey dated 3 October 2016 and signed in Cape Town, which he used in a Labour Court case in a matter in which he took on police bosses and colleagues because he believed he had been unfairly transferred within the Western Cape police in June 2016.

20 Testimony of Jeffery T Benzien at TRC hearing on 14 July 1997: 'TRC Documents', SABC Truth Commission Special Report http://sabctrc.saha.org.za/documents/amntrans/cape_town/54669.htm Accessed 17 January 2019.

21 Testimony of Peter Jacobs when questioning Jeffery T Benzien at TRC hearing on 14 July 1997: 'TRC Documents', SABC Truth Commission Special Report http://sabctrc.saha.org.za/documents/amntrans/cape_town/54669.htm Accessed 17 January 2019.

22 Dolley, C (2015) '"Police set up false licences"', *Weekend Argus*, 12 April https://www.iol.co.za/news/police-set-up-false-licences-1843856 Accessed 16 March 2019.

23 Affidavit by Jeremy Vearey dated 3 October 2016 and signed in Cape Town, which he used in a Labour Court case in a matter in which he took on police bosses and colleagues because he believed he had been unfairly transferred within the Western Cape police in June 2016.

24 Ibid.

25 ANC Western Cape (2016) 'ANC Western Cape Press Release on the ongoing attacks on police general Jeremy Vearey,' 28 April. This email was sent to a media mailing list and was forwarded to the author by a colleague.

26 Information contained in an affidavit by Jeremy Vearey dated 3 October 2016 and signed in Cape Town, which he used in a Labour Court case in a matter in which he took on police bosses and colleagues because he believed he had been unfairly transferred within the Western Cape police in June 2016.

27 Amended indictment, undated and unstamped, in the matter of *State v Irshaad Laher and Alan Robert Raves* signed by Shareen Riley, the Deputy Director of Public Prosecutions of the Division (Western Cape). A copy was provided to the author by a confidential source.

28 Thamm, M (2016) 'When Hell is not Hot Enough: A Top Cop who supplied weapons to country's gangsters and right wingers', *Daily Maverick*, 4 July https://www.dailymaverick.co.za/article/2016-07-04-when-hell-is-not-hot-enough-a-top-cop-who-supplied-weapons-to-countrys-gangsters-and-right-wingers/ Accessed 19 January 2019.

Notes

29 Amended indictment, undated and unstamped, in the matter of *State v Irshaad Laher and Alan Robert Raves* signed by Shareen Riley, the Deputy Director of Public Prosecutions of the Division (Western Cape). A copy was provided to the author by a confidential source.
30 Ibid.
31 The state's response to Irshaad Laher's request for further disclosure of information in the state's possession, dated 13 February 2018, in the case of *State v Irshaad Laher and Alan Robert Raves*, case number CC 29/2016.
32 Dolley, C (2016) 'Police escort for alleged gun runner', IOL, 23 July https://www.iol.co.za/news/police-escort-for-alleged-gun-runner-2048689 Accessed 19 January 2019.
33 WhatsApp message to the author from Pete Mihalik on 8 November 2016.
34 Malgas, N (2016) 'Pagad: death of prominent CT attorney "long overdue"' Eyewitness News, 8 November http://ewn.co.za/2016/11/08/pagad-death-of-prominent-ct-attorney-long-overdue Accessed 28 January 2019.
35 Court order in *State v Irshaad Laher and Alan Robert Raves*, case number CC 21/16, dated 19 May 2017, obtained in the Western Cape High Court by the state.
36 Email from Liddell, Weeber & Van der Merwe Incorporated to Advocate Christiaan de Jongh of the Director of Public Prosecutions in Cape Town, dated 26 February 2018.
37 Dolley, C (2017) '"Amateur" Crime Intelligence officers intentionally derailing high-level probes, claims top Cape cop', News24, 23 May https://www.news24.com/SouthAfrica/News/amateur-crime-intelligence-officers-intentionally-derailing-high-level-probes-claims-top-cape-cop-20170523 Accessed 28 January 2019.
38 Dolley, C (2017) '"Amateur" Crime Intelligence officers intentionally derailing high level probes, claims top Cape cop', News24, 23 May https://www.news24.com/SouthAfrica/News/amateur-crime-intelligence-officers-intentionally-derailing-high-level-probes-claims-top-cape-cop-20170523 Accessed 19 January 2019.
39 Red is widely said to be one of the most seasoned 27s gangsters in the Western Cape. In October 2009 @Red, whose real name is William Stevens, was wanted by police for allegedly shooting dead a wheelchair-bound crime fighter in the suburb of Mitchells Plain. See Warner, J (2009) '@Red at large', IOL, 27 October https://www.iol.co.za/news/south-africa/red-at-large-462860 Accessed 28 January 2019.
40 Lieutenant Colonel Charl Kinnear testified about a call between Nafiz Modack and state security operative and known double agent George

Darmanović, in which Modack allegedly made claims about Jeremy Vearey having been involved in Noorudien Hassan's murder. Kinnear testified to this in the Cape Town Magistrate's Court on 3 January 2018 in an extortion-case bail application, case number 16/818/2017, launched by Nafiz Modack and four co-accused. Further details about the call were provided to the author by two confidential sources on 3 January 2018.

41 Affidavit by Jeremy Vearey dated 3 October 2016 and signed in Cape Town, which he used in a Labour Court case in a matter in which he took on police bosses and colleagues because he believed he had been unfairly transferred within the Western Cape police in June 2016.

42 Ibid.

43 Letter from Western Cape Director of Public Prosecutions to provincial police commissioner Khombinkosi Jula dated 18 August 2016.

44 Ibid.

45 Sworn statement by Clive Joseph Ontong dated 23 September 2016 and signed in Cape Town, and used in the Cape Town Labour Court case launched by Jeremy Vearey and Peter Jacobs following their transfers within the Western Cape police in June 2016, to try and have their transfers reversed.

46 Affidavit by Peter Jacobs dated 4 October 2016 and signed in Cape Town, which he used in a Labour Court case in Cape Town, in a matter in which he took on police bosses and colleagues because he believed he had been unfairly transferred within the Western Cape police in June 2016.

47 Ibid.

48 Ibid.

49 In March 2019 it emerged that a tender for the building of houses in Valhalla Park had been awarded to a company of which Nicole Stanfield was a director. See Cruywagen, V (2019) 'Alleged gang boss's wife awarded lucrative City of Cape Town tender', *Cape Argus*, 14 March https://www.iol.co.za/capeargus/news/alleged-gang-bosss-wife-awarded-lucrative-city-of-cape-town-tender-19875973 Accessed 14 March 2019.

50 Dolley, C (2014) 'Police gave guns to gangs', *Weekend Argus*, 28 September https://www.iol.co.za/news/police-gave-guns-to-gangs-1756940 Accessed 28 January 2019.

51 Affidavit by Ralph Stanfield dated March 2016. Stanfield's legal representative at the time, Pete Mihalik, ensured the author was emailed a copy, which was not signed nor stamped, on 19 April 2016 after she requested this.

Notes

52 Ibid.
53 Ibid.
54 Ibid.
55 This firearm was also suspected to have been used in the shooting of police officer Lutfie Eksteen's mother in Manenberg in October 2014. De Wee, M (2016), '1 vuurwapen, 15 moorde', Netwerk24, 15 July https://www.netwerk24.com/Nuus/Misdaad/een-vuurwapen-16-moorde-20160715 Accessed 28 February 2019.
56 Serra, G (2016) 'Top cop: Police failed my dead son', IOL, 22 February https://www.iol.co.za/news/top-cop-police-failed-my-dead-son-1987898 Accessed 26 January 2019.
57 SA Government (2016) 'MEC Dan Plato condemns DoJ's criminal charges threat against SAPS cluster head', 15 August https://www.gov.za/speeches/mec-dan-plato-condemns-doj's-criminal-charges-threat-against-saps-cluster-head-15-aug-2016 Accessed 19 March 2019.
58 Affidavit by Peter Jacobs dated 4 October 2016 and signed in Cape Town, which he used in a Labour Court case in Cape Town in a matter in which he took on police bosses and colleagues because he believed he had been unfairly transferred within the Western Cape police in June 2016.
59 Affidavit made by Vytjie Mentor in Durbanville, Cape Town, on 9 May 2016.
60 Affidavit by Jeremy Vearey dated 3 October 2016 and signed in Cape Town, which he used in a Labour Court case in a matter in which he took on police bosses and colleagues because he believed he had been unfairly transferred within the Western Cape police in June 2016.
61 Prior to this, Major General Mzwandile Tiyo had already approached the Cape Town Labour Court as he felt that the Western Cape police commissioner Arno Lamoer was blocking him from becoming the province's Crime Intelligence head. Lamoer was eventually suspended in 2015, and in February 2018 was found guilty of corruption. He was sentenced to an effective six years in jail. Dolley, C (2015) '"I've been victimised for doing my job"', *Weekend Argus*, 3 May https://www.iol.co.za/news/ive-been-victimised-for-doing-my-job-1852851 Accessed 20 January 2019.
62 Affidavit by Peter Jacobs dated 4 October 2016 and signed in Cape Town, which he used in a Labour Court case in a matter in which he took on police bosses and colleagues because he believed he had been unfairly transferred within the Western Cape police in June 2016.
63 Dolley, C (2017) 'A criminal case, sexting saga and "compromised" cops - problems rocking the police', News24, 8 August https://www.news24.

64   com/SouthAfrica/News/a-criminal-case-sexting-saga-and-compromised-cops-problems-rocking-the-police-20170807 Accessed 20 January 2019.

64   Answering affidavit of Lieutenant-General Bonang Christina Mgwenya dated 7 February 2017 and signed in Mbombela in the Labour Court case involving Jeremy Vearey and Peter Jacobs.

65   Bateman, B (2018) 'Top cop seeks to quash complaints against new Crime Intel boss', Eyewitness News, 29 March https://ewn.co.za/2018/03/29/exclusive-top-cop-seeks-to-quash-complaints-against-new-crime-intel-boss Accessed 8 March 2019.

66   Answering affidavit of Lieutenant General Bonang Christina Mgwenya dated 7 February 2017 and signed in Mbombela in the Labour Court case involving Jeremy Vearey and Peter Jacobs.

67   Phahlane was arrested on 1 March 2019 in connection with tender rigging. He believed 'ulterior motives' linked to the non-renewal of the Ipid head's contract were behind his arrest. See Maphang, C (2019) 'Phahlane granted bail, lawyer argues arrest "nothing but a show for the media"', News24, 1 March https://www.news24.com/SouthAfrica/News/phahlane-granted-bail-lawyer-argues-arrest-nothing-but-a-show-for-the-media-20190301 Accessed 2 March 2019.

68   Answering affidavit of Lieutenant General Bonang Christina Mgwenya dated 7 February 2017 and signed in Mbombela in the Labour Court case involving Jeremy Vearey and Peter Jacobs.

69   Ibid.

70   A source provided the number for this case, CAS 204/03/2018. Responding to the author's formal request for information as a journalist, a police spokesperson said that the number related to an intimidation case registered on 14 March 2018, which had been closed because it was deemed unfounded, on 23 March 2018. It was later alleged by Lieutenant Colonel Charl Kinnear, in a complaint to his superiors dated 29 December 2018, that an inmate at Goodwood Prison claimed that a police officer, and others not identified, had wanted him to make an affidavit against Peter Jacobs and Jeremy Vearey about the theft of documents from the prisoner file of one Sylvano Hendricks. Hendricks, a transgender woman going by the name Queeny Madikizela-Malema, a self-proclaimed whistleblower, was once detained at Goodwood Prison and became central to claims that a smear campaign was being run against Vearey.

71   De Wee, M (2018) 'Klag van regsverydeling teen nuwe misdaadhoof', Netwerk24, 9 April https://www.netwerk24.com/Nuus/Algemeen/klag-van-regsverydeling-teen-nuwe-misdaadhoof-20180409 Accessed 20 January 2019.

72 Cele, B (2018) 'Peter Jacobs to head Crime Intelligence – Bheki Cele', Politicsweb, 29 March http://www.politicsweb.co.za/documents/peter-jacobs-to-head-crime-intelligence--bheki-cel Accessed 20 January 2019.

73 Updated charge sheet from 2018 in *State v Ralph Stanfield and 22 Others*, an unsigned and undated copy of which was provided, at the author's request, via email on 2 May 2018 by the Western Cape National Prosecuting Authority. Among the allegedly unlawfully possessed weapons and ammunition were a .22 rifle and a Glock pistol, and hollow-point rounds, which are intended to cause maximum damage by expanding on impact.

74 News24 (2018) 'WATCH: Cops arrested for allegedly taking bribe', 10 April https://www.news24.com/Video/SouthAfrica/News/watch-cops-arrested-for-allegedly-taking-bribe-20180410 Accessed 12 February 2019.

75 Appellant's notice of withdrawal of appeal in the matter *Minister of Police and six Others v Peter Jacobs, Jeremy Vearey and Another*, case CA19/2017, 27 February 2019.

CHAPTER 5 *Strength in numbers: amalgamation*

1 In December 2003, the year Naude took over the reins of Professional Protection Services, it emerged that both Professional Protection Services and Pro Access had apparently been signed up to provide security to the same establishment. Teams from both companies turned up and clashed but the situation was later defused. Interview with Andre Naude in Green Point on 20 January 2012.

2 Interview with Andre Naude in Green Point on 20 January 2012; and Dolley, C (2012), 'Plato tackles underworld figures', *Cape Times*, 23 January https://www.iol.co.za/capetimes/plato-tackles-underworld-figures-1218143 Accessed 19 March 2019.

3 Testimony of Jacques Cronje in the Cape Town Regional Court on 22 April 2015 in case number 30/51/2012, *State v Andre Naude and Mark Lifman*, who were accused of running a private security company that was not registered with the Private Security Industry Regulatory Authority.

4 Now known as the National Horseracing Authority of Southern Africa.

5 IOL (2001) 'Cape racehorse owner banned for life', 6 December https://www.iol.co.za/capeargus/sport/cape-racehorse-owner-banned-for-life-78043 Accessed 22 January 2019.

6 Breytenbach, K (2009) 'Businessman Lifman acquitted of sex charges', IOL, 29 September https://www.iol.co.za/news/south-africa/

businessman-lifman-acquitted-of-sex-charges-459931 Accessed 22 January 2019.

7   Testimony of Jacques Cronje in the Cape Town Regional Court on 22 April 2015 in case number 30/51/2012, *State v Andre Naude and Mark Lifman*, who were accused of running a private security company that was not registered with the Private Security Industry Regulatory Authority.

8   Ibid.

9   Testimony of Sergeant Edward Edwardes in the Cape Town Magistrate's Court on 19 December 2017 in a conspiracy-to-commit-murder case, which was in the bail-application phase, in which Houssain Taleb was the accused.

10 Testimony of Jacques Cronje in the Cape Town Regional Court on 22 April 2015 in case number 30/51/2012, *State v Andre Naude and Mark Lifman*, who were accused of running a private security company that was not registered with the Private Security Industry Regulatory Authority.

11 Dolley, C (2012) 'Band of brothers who patrol club scene', *Cape Times*, 30 January https://www.iol.co.za/news/south-africa/western-cape/band-of-brothers-who-patrol-club-scene-1223533 Accessed 22 January 2019.

12 Draft charge sheet against Mark Lifman, Andre Naude and Specialised Protection Services dated 2012 for allegedly running a private security company without being registered with the Private Security Regulatory Authority as required by law. A copy of the draft charge sheet was supplied to the author, at her request, by the Western Cape National Prosecuting Authority on 25 September 2012.

13 Correspondent (2018) 'Clifton beach row: New twist as controversial businessman Mark Lifman says PPA boss was his ultimate "yes" guy', News24, 30 December https://www.news24.com/SouthAfrica/News/clifton-beach-row-new-twist-as-controversial-businessman-mark-lifman-says-ppa-boss-was-his-ultimate-yes-guy-20181230 Accessed 21 February 2019.

14 Testimony of Jacques Cronje in the Cape Town Regional Court on 22 April 2015 in case number 30/51/2012, *State v Andre Naude and Mark Lifman*, who were accused of running a private security company that was not registered with the Private Security Industry Regulatory Authority.

15 Ibid.

16 Ibid.

17 Dolley, C (2015) 'Beeka man "felt threatened" by Lifman', *Weekend Argus*, 26 April https://www.iol.co.za/news/beeka-man-felt-threatened-by-lifman-1850651 Accessed 7 February 2019.

18 Meyer, W and Geldenhuys H (2012) 'Cronje bounces back with his story', IOL, 12 February https://www.iol.co.za/news/south-africa/western-cape/cronje-bounces-back-with-his-story-1237461 Accessed 6 April 2019.

19 Interview with Andre Naude in Green Point on 20 January 2012; and Dolley, C (2012), 'Plato tackles underworld figures', *Cape Times*, 23 January https://www.iol.co.za/capetimes/plato-tackles-underworldfigures-1218143 Accessed 19 March 2019.

20 Specialised Protection Services' code of conduct as supplied to the author by Andre Naude on 20 January 2012.

21 Dolley, C (2015) 'Dodgy dealings on "dodgy" Long Street', *Weekend Argus*, 27 June https://www.pressreader.com/south-africa/weekend-argus-saturday-edition/20150627/281724088201447 Accessed 15 February 2019.

22 Correspondent (2018) 'Clifton beach row: New twist as controversial businessman Mark Lifman says PPA boss was his ultimate "yes" guy', News24, 30 December https://www.news24.com/SouthAfrica/News/clifton-beach-row-new-twist-as-controversial-businessman-mark-lifman-says-ppa-boss-was-his-ultimate-yes-guy-20181230 Accessed 21 February 2019.

23 Ibid.

24 Towards the end of 2018 PPA Security became the centre of controversy when claims emerged that officers with the company had allegedly illegally removed visitors to Cape Town's popular Clifton Fourth Beach on the evening of 23 December 2018.

25 De Wee, M (2018) 'Klagte kom voor aandpiekniek op Kaapse strand', Netwerk24, 28 December https://www.netwerk24.com/Nuus/Algemeen/klagte-kom-voor-aandpiekniek-op-kaapse-strand-20181228 Accessed 21 February 2019.

26 Email dated 1 March 2013 from Western Cape National Prosecuting Authority spokesman Eric Ntabazalila. Albern Martins, along with four others, was charged in a case going back to 2005.

27 Geldenhuys, H (2013) 'Home of Sexy Boys "boss" shot at, petrol-bombed', *Weekend Argus*, 30 March https://www.iol.co.za/news/home-of-sexy-boys-boss-shot-at-petrol-bombed-1493721 Accessed 28 January 2019.

28 Dolley, C (2013) 'Organised crime behind latest hits', *Cape Times*, 15 May https://www.iol.co.za/capetimes/organised-crime-behind-latest-hits-1516188 Accessed 28 January 2019.

29   Lepule, T (2016) '28s made me kill Pastor Albern Martins', *Daily Voice*'s Facebook page, 15 March https://www.facebook.com/DailyVoiceSA/posts/1079391948792433:0 Accessed 28 January 2019.

30   Ibid.

31   *The Star* (2013) '007-style hit bid on Krejcir', 25 July https://www.iol.co.za/news/007-style-hit-bid-on-krejcir-1552337 Accessed 28 January 2019.

32   *Staggie v S* (38/10) [2011] ZASCA 88; 2012 (2) SACR 311 (SCA) (27 May 2011) Southern African Legal Information Institute http://www.saflii.org/za/cases/ZASCA/2011/88.html Accessed 28 January 2019.

33   Ibid.

34   Dolley, D (2013) 'Staggie rang to say sorry – victim's mom', IOL, 4 September https://www.iol.co.za/news/staggie-rang-to-say-sorry-victims-mom-1572678 Accessed 9 March 2019.

35   Baadjies, M (2013) 'Staggie rape victim is alive - mother', *Daily Voice*, 11 September https://www.iol.co.za/news/staggie-rape-victim-is-alive-mother-1576160 Accessed 28 January 2019.

36   In March 2014 Saliem John was sentenced to life in jail for crimes including three murders perpetrated in 2007 and an attempted murder in 2008.

37   Samodien, L (2013) 'Assassination attempt at Cape High Court', *Cape Times*, 10 October https://www.iol.co.za/news/assassination-attempt-at-cape-high-court-1589767 Accessed 22 February 2019.

38   Dolley, C (2013) 'Did Beeka link cost hitman his life?', *Cape Times*, 16 October https://www.iol.co.za/news/did-beeka-link-cost-hitman-his-life-1592942 Accessed 22 January 2019.

39   eNCA (2013) 'Bedfordview drive-by shooting victim identified', 12 October https://www.enca.com/south-africa/bedfordview-drive-shooting-victim-identified Accessed 10 March 2019.

40   *The Citizen* (2013) 'Krejcir whereabouts unknown after bomb blast – police', November 12 https://citizen.co.za/news/south-africa/84098/krejcir-whereabouts-unknown-bomb-blast-police/ Accessed 28 February 2019.

41   Founding affidavit of Mark Lifman dated 23 November 2016 and signed at the Sea Point police station, in the SARS matter in which he applied for a stay of proceedings, case numbers 13917/2016 and 14889/2015.

42   Delegation of authority with regard to the Tax Administration Act by SARS official Ivan Pillay signed on 10 April 2014.

43   Founding affidavit of Mark Lifman dated 23 November 2016 and signed at the Sea Point police station, in the SARS matter in which he applied

for a stay of proceedings, case numbers 13917/2016 and 14889/2015.

44 Draft charge sheet against Mark Lifman, Andre Naude and SPS dated 2012. Lifman and Naude were charged for allegedly running a private security company without being registered with the Private Security Regulatory Authority. A copy of the draft charge sheet was supplied to the author, at her request, by the Western Cape National Prosecuting Authority on 25 September 2012.

45 Legg, K (2014) 'Bellville bar fight spills into the street', *Cape Argus*, 16 October https://www.iol.co.za/news/bellville-bar-fight-spills-into-the-street-1760585 Accessed 8 February 2019.

46 Dolley, C (2014) 'I fired in self-defence, says suspect', *Weekend Argus*, 19 October https://www.iol.co.za/news/i-fired-in-self-defence-says-suspect-1767281 Accessed 22 January 2019.

47 Etheridge, J (2015) 'Beerhouse stabbing not meant to be fatal, police told', News24, 19 August https://www.news24.com/SouthAfrica/News/Beerhouse-stabbing-not-meant-to-be-fatal-police-told-20150819 Accessed 28 January 2019.

48 Testimony of Lieutenant Colonel Charl Kinnear in the Cape Town Magistrate's Court on 2 January 2018 in an extortion-case bail application, case number 16/818/2017, launched by Nafiz Modack and four co-accused.

49 Dolley, C (2015) 'Security bosses acquitted on 313 charges', *Weekend Argus*, 24 October https://www.iol.co.za/news/security-bosses-acquitted-on-313-charges-1935148 Accessed 22 January 2019.

50 Founding affidavit of Mark Lifman dated 23 November 2016 and signed at the Sea Point police station in the SARS matter in which he applied for a stay of proceedings, case numbers 13917/2016 and 14889/2015.

51 Court order dated 23 March 2010, obtained in the Western Cape High Court in case 3058/2009 launched by Irina Ulianitskaya against Mark Lifman and four other respondents in which she wanted partnerships between Yuri Ulianitski and the respondents declared to have existed. These partnerships were terminated on Ulianitski's death. The court ordered a liquidator to auction off, or privately sell, assets that fell under their partnership. The proceeds of the sale were to be split, in accordance with the court order, between Lifman and Irina Ulianitski.

52 The Lexus had initially belonged to Jerome Booysen; its personalised 'Percy 01' number plate was in reference to a Booysen brother killed in 1997 in a possible case of mistaken identity as it was believed another Booysen, Michael, had actually been the target. See Dolley, C (2016) 'Mark Lifman's cars auctioned to pay back Sars', IOL, 22 May

https://www.iol.co.za/news/mark-lifmans-cars-auctioned-to-pay-back-sars-2027660 Accessed 22 January 2019.

53 At that stage the author had been writing about gang violence and related incidents in Cape Town, and Colin Booysen, in explaining his wounding, casually mentioned to her that she should be careful because if a reporter caused tensions between gangs, a gang could turn on the reporter and not necessarily another gang.

54 Founding affidavit of Mark Lifman dated 23 November 2016 and signed at the Sea Point police station in the SARS matter in which he applied for a stay of proceedings, case numbers 13917/2016 and 14889/2015.

55 News24 (2017) '"Rogue unit" retraction: 5 questions answered', 18 September https://www.news24.com/Analysis/rogue-unit-retraction-5-questions-answered-20170918 Accessed 23 January 2019.

56 Founding affidavit of Mark Lifman dated 23 November 2016 and signed at the Sea Point police station in the SARS matter in which he applied for a stay of proceedings, case numbers 13917/2016 and 14889/2015.

57 Promotion of Access to Information Act (PAIA) request for information from a public body in the name of Mark Lifman submitted on 8 September 2016.

58 Sikhakhane, M (2014) 'Investigation Report: Conduct of Mr Johan Hendrikus van Loggerenberg, South African Revenue Service', 5 November http://www.sars.gov.za/AllDocs/Documents/Adhoc/Sikhakhane%20Report.pdf Accessed 23 January 2019.

59 Joubert, P (2014) 'Hawks boss link to Sexy Boys gang drug bust,' *Sunday Times*, 12 January https://www.pressreader.com/south-africa/sunday-times/20140112/281539403807138 Accessed 23 January 2019.

60 The author established the identity of this man, but he was never named officially in any court proceedings, and attempts by the author to contact him failed. The surname Choudhry was contained in an affidavit (in which it was spelled incorrectly as Choudry) and an attachment to the affidavit included his surname spelled incorrectly as Chaudhry. The affidavit was by Hawks Lieutenant Colonel Peter Janse Viljoen, dated 31 January 2018 and signed in Bellville, and which was used by the state in the extortion-case bail application, case number 16/818/2017, against Nafiz Modack and four co-accused in the Cape Town Magistrate's Court.

61 Evident on CCTV footage, seen by the author.

62 Testimony by Lieutenant Colonel Charl Kinnear in the Cape Town Magistrate's Court on 2 January 2018 in the extortion-case bail application, case number 16/818/2017, launched by Nafiz Modack and four co-accused.

63 Supplementary affidavit of Colin Booysen dated 12 February 2018 submitted by Booysen's defence attorney in the extortion-case bail application, case number 16/818/2017, launched by Nafiz Modack and four co-accused in the Cape Town Magistrate's Court.

64 In mid-October 2018, just more than two years after Craig Mathieson was killed, two suspects, Sillico Zainauet Oliphant and Moegamat Faizel Abrahams, were arrested for the murder. See Etheridge, J (2018), 'Pair arrested 2 years after murder of Sea Point hotel manager', News24, 23 October https://www.news24.com/SouthAfrica/News/pair-arrested-2-years-after-murder-of-sea-point-hotel-manager-20181023 Accessed 12 February 2019. The charges against them, according to an attorney involved in the case, were withdrawn in February 2019 as it was found there was no reasonable prospect of a successful prosecution.

65 Leaked National Prosecuting Authority document detailing the activities of the Mobsters. The date and other details that could reveal the origin/creator of the document were removed by the confidential source who supplied it.

66 Cellphone communication with a policeman in mid-March 2016.

67 National Prosecuting Authority memorandum (undated and unsigned) on Russel Jacobs and his co-accused relating to cases from 2008 in *State v Russel Jacobs and 15 Others*, a copy of which was supplied to the author by Western Cape National Prosecuting Aurthority spokesman Eric Ntabazalila on 25 January 2017 after the author requested from him details of the charges Jacobs had faced.

68 Ibid.

69 Ibid.

70 Personal communication; and Dolley, C (2017) 'Suspected perlemoen syndicate mastermind's murder sparks claims against police', News24, 27 January https://www.news24.com/SouthAfrica/News/suspected-perlemoen-syndicate-masterminds-murder-sparks-claims-against-police-20170127 Accessed 8 February 2019.

CHAPTER 6 *Money, murder, plots and politics*

1 Dolley, C (2012) 'Underworld bosses are drug kingpins', *Cape Times*, 13 February https://www.iol.co.za/news/underworld-bosses-are-drug-kings-plato-1233089 Accessed 18 January 2019; and interview with Dan Plato in Cape Town in February 2012.

2 amaBhungane reporters (2015) 'Zuma's "deal" with Cape gang bosses', *Mail&Guardian*, 20 November https://mg.co.za/article/2015-11-20-00-zumas-deal-with-cape-gang-bosses Accessed 24 February 2019.

3   Ibid.

4   Hosken, G (2003) 'Shooting sparks fears of KZN gang war', IOL, 25 April https://www.iol.co.za/news/south-africa/shooting-sparks-fears-of-kzn-gang-war-105436 Accessed 17 March 2019.

5   Several other sources have over the years insisted that the meeting in Cape Town between Zuma and the alleged gang bosses did indeed take place; the author has spoken to at least two sources who claim to have been in the meeting and others who say they were aware of the meeting. The reasons given for the meeting have, however, varied: one source (interviewed in Cape Town on 18 January 2018) referred to it as the beginning of the formation of a presidential task team of sorts for developing jobs and creating opportunities for skills development, and denied it had to do with a political ploy to have gangsters try and ensure the ANC took over the Western Cape.

6   During an interview with the author on 21 September 2017 in Cubana in Green Point, Nafiz Modack said that he knew Lloyd Hill, whom he had met through Cyril Beeka.

7   Interview with confidential source in Cape Town on 4 October 2017.

8   Personal communication with a confidential source in Cape Town on 27 March 2018.

9   Dolley, C (2018) 'Zuma's mystery meeting with South African spook murdered in Serbia', News24, 10 May https://www.news24.com/SouthAfrica/News/exclusive-zumas-mystery-meeting-with-south-african-spook-murdered-in-serbia-20180510 Accessed 9 March 2019.

10 Joubert, P (2014) 'Top Cape gangster gets VIP invite to Zuma birthday bash', *Sunday Times*, 27 April https://www.timeslive.co.za/sunday-times/lifestyle/2014-04-27-top-cape-gangster-gets-vip-invite-to-zuma-birthday-bash/ Accessed 17 January 2019.

11 Dolley, C (2012) 'Franciscus was in fear of his life – Plato dossier', *Cape Times*, 15 March https://www.iol.co.za/capetimes/franciscus-was-in-fear-of-his-life-plato-dossier-1257063 Accessed 18 January 2019; and interview with a confidential source in Cape Town in March 2012.

12 amaBhungane reporters (2015) 'Zuma's "deal" with Cape gang bosses', *Mail&Guardian*, 20 November https://mg.co.za/article/2015-11-20-00-zumas-deal-with-cape-gang-bosses Accessed 24 February 2019.

13 Dolley, C (2012) 'Franciscus was in fear of his life – Plato dossier', *Cape Times*, 15 March https://www.iol.co.za/capetimes/franciscus-was-in-fear-of-his-life-plato-dossier-1257063 Accessed 18 January 2019.

14 Ibid; the author's recollection of reading the contents of the Franciscus dossier; interview with a confidential source in Cape Town in March 2012;

and Bernardo, C (2016), 'Plato vs Vearey: ANC picks its side', Africa News Agency, 16 April https://www.iol.co.za/news/politics/plato-vs-vearey-anc-picks-its-side-2015446 Accessed 20 February 2019.

15 Dolley, C (2012) 'Franciscus was in fear of his life – Plato dossier', *Cape Times*, 15 March https://www.iol.co.za/capetimes/franciscus-was-in-fear-of-his-life-plato-dossier-1257063 Accessed 18 January 2019.

16 Jacobs, F (2016) 'Dan Plato has a smear campaign against Vearey – ANC W Cape', Politicsweb, 28 April https://www.politicsweb.co.za/politics/dan-plato-has-a-smear-campaign-against-vearey-anc- Accessed 5 February 2019.

17 Interview with a confidential source outside Cape Town on 6 February 2012.

18 Ibid.

19 Meyer, W (2012) 'The ANC is plotting with gang bosses', IOL, 26 March https://www.iol.co.za/news/anc-is-plotting-with-gang-bosses-1263619 Accessed 13 April 2018.

20 There was a fourth source, also linked to Dan Plato, who made serious and detailed claims about broader underworld dealings to the author in 2012, and while there may have been truth to these, he came across as so paranoid that he seemed imbalanced, and the author eventually cut all contact with him.

21 Meyer, W (2013) 'Plato source guided by angels', *Sunday Independent*, 3 August https://www.iol.co.za/sundayindependent/plato-source-guided-by-angels-1557093 Accessed 18 January 2019.

22 ANC Western Cape (2016) 'ANC Western Cape Press Release on the ongoing attacks on police general Jeremy Vearey,' 28 April, sent via email to a media mailing list and forwarded to the author by a colleague; and details of the affidavit were provided to the author by a confidential source in Cape Town in early 2013.

23 Dolley, C (2016) 'Voice clip reveals secret chat', IOL, 23 April https://www.iol.co.za/news/voice-clip-reveals-secret-chat-2013574 Accessed 18 January 2019.

24 Meyer, W (2013) 'Plato source guided by angels', *Sunday Independent*, 3 August https://www.iol.co.za/sundayindependent/plato-source-guided-by-angels-1557093 Accessed 18 January 2019.

25 Dolley, C (2016) 'Voice clip reveals secret chat', IOL, 23 April https://www.iol.co.za/news/voice-clip-reveals-secret-chat-2013574 Accessed 18 January 2019.

26 Affidavit by Pierre Theron made in George on 14 January 2013.

27 Ibid.

28 De Wee, M (2016) 'Geld was vir mediese sorg, nie inligting, sê Plato', Netwerk24, 3 May https://www.netwerk24.com/Nuus/Algemeen/geld-was-vir-mediese-sorg-nie-inligting-se-plato-20160503 Accessed 18 January 2019.

29 Myburgh, J (2010) 'The Smit murders: Re-examined', Politicsweb, 7 June https://www.politicsweb.co.za/news-and-analysis/the-smit-murders-reexamined Accessed 18 January 2019.

30 Western Cape Director of Public Prosecutions (2013) 'Director of Public Prosecutions declines to take steps on allegations referred by MEC Dan Plato', 30 July, press release issued to members of the media, including the author.

31 Eyewitness News (2013) 'Drug charges against Yester Garrido dropped', 9 February https://ewn.co.za/2013/02/09/NPA-drops-charges-against-Cuban-officer Accessed 9 March 2019.

32 Affidavit of Pierre Theron signed in Newtown, Johannesburg, on 27 October 2015.

33 Mashego, A (2106) 'Krejcír man's "payola" claim', *City Press*, 18 April https://city-press.news24.com/News/Krejcir-mans-payola-claim-20160416 Accessed 18 January 2019.

34 Sole, S and Evans, S (2016) 'amaBhungane: The Smuggler, The Spook and The Grabber', *Daily Maverick*, 27 August https://www.dailymaverick.co.za/article/2016-08-27-amabhungane-the-smuggler-the-spook-and-the-grabber/ Accessed 19 January 2019.

35 Affidavit of Paul Scheepers dated 13 October 2015 and signed in Cape Town in the case of *Eagle Eye Solution Technologies and Paul Scheepers v the Minister of Police and Two Others*.

36 Ibid.

37 Statement by warrant officer Shaun Kuter dated 27 July 2017 and signed in Bishop Lavis, made on the request of Paul Scheepers, relating to an application in the Western Cape High Court to have items seized from him by police, returned.

38 A stay of prosecution application brought by Paul Scheepers was expected to be heard in the Western Cape High Court towards the end of May 2019 and an outcome on this was expected to be announced towards the end of June.

39 Zille, H (2015) 'The Puzzle of Gangs, Drugs, Police and Politics in the Western Cape' *Inside Government*, 15 October https://www.westerncape.gov.za/news/inside-government-puzzle-gangs-drugs-police-and-politics-wc Accessed 19 January 2019.

40 Zille, H (2015) 'The "Unholy Triad" of Gangs, Cops and Elections in the

WC', *Inside Government*, 23 November https://www.westerncape.gov.za/news/inside-government-unholy-triad-gangs-cops-and-elections-wc Accessed 22 February 2019.

41 Dolley, C (2016) 'Cape "gang leader targeted tourists"', *Weekend Argus*, 17 April https://www.iol.co.za/news/cape-gang-leader-targeted-tourists-2010674 Accessed 11 February 2019.

42 Western Cape High Court judgment delivered on 17 May 2011 in *State v Willie Spannenberg*, South African Legal Information Institute http://www.saflii.org/za/cases/ZAWCHC/2011/429.html Accessed 11 February 2019.

43 Leaked National Prosecuting Authority document detailing the activities of the Mobsters. The date and other details that could reveal the origin/creator of the document were removed by the confidential source who supplied it.

44 Ibid.

45 Personal communication with a confidential source in March 2018 in Cape Town.

46 It was initially suspected that the Moses hit had been orchestrated and carried out by the Sexy Boys because, among other reasons, Mobsters members had knowingly encroached on Sexy Boys turf at a club in Bellville shortly before the killing.

47 Affidavit made by 'Queenie', whose real name was not included in it, on 26 February 2016 and stamped 'Department of Community Safety Western Cape 26 February Office of the Ombudsman'. The affidavit was purportedly made to provide details about the murder of Nathaniel Moses and contained several other claims, including that a South African Navy official was smuggling drugs and firearms out of South Africa for a gang boss, the firearms having been used in crimes in the Western Cape.

48 Dolley, C (2016) 'Pikoli's office drawn into Plato-Vearey row', *Weekend Argus*, 23 April https://www.iol.co.za/news/pikolis-office-drawn-into-plato-vearey-row-2013577 Accessed 9 March 2019.

49 Ibid.

50 In August 2018 Queeny named the author in a Facebook post in which she made wildly false and defamatory claims, including that the author had been paid '[R]48 000 to write' (although she didn't specify what) and claiming to have proof of this; she warned 'other jornos who took money I am coming for you' [sic]. Her post is available at https://www.facebook.com/search/top/?q=queeny%2048%20000&epa=SEARCH_BOX Accessed 9 February 2019.

51 Jali, TSB (2005) 'Spurious investigations', *Commission of Inquiry into alleged incidents of corruption, maladministration, violence or intimidation into the Department of Correctional Services* http://pmg-assets.s3-website-eu-west-1.amazonaws.com/docs/061016jalireport_0.pdf Accessed 18 January 2019.

52 Dolley, C (2016) 'Thuli's snitch threatened her predecessor', *Weekend Argus*, 21 May https://www.iol.co.za/news/thulis-snitch-threatened-her-predecessor-2024439 Accessed 18 January 2019.

53 ANC Western Cape (2016) 'ANC Western Cape Press Release on the ongoing attacks on police general Jeremy Vearey', 28 April, sent to a media mailing list and forwarded to the author by a colleague.

54 ANC Western Cape (2016) 'Criminal investigation opened into Dan Plato', Politicsweb, 18 May https://www.politicsweb.co.za/politics/criminal-investigation-opened-into-dan-plato--anc- Accessed 7 February 2019.

55 Western Cape Government (2016) 'Minister Plato welcomes ANC's interest in the rule of law', 18 May https://www.westerncape.gov.za/news/minister-plato-welcomes-anc%E2%80%99s-interest-rule-law Accessed 19 January 2019.

56 Affidavit by Jeremy Vearey, dated 3 October 2016 and signed in Cape Town, which he used in a Labour Court case in a matter in which he took on police bosses and colleagues because he believed he had been unfairly transferred within the Western Cape police in June 2016.

57 Lieutenant Colonel Charl Kinnear testified in the Cape Town Magistrate's Court on 23 January 2018 that there had been an instruction from police superiors that people be arrested for the Moses murder. He said Jeremy Vearey was not one of those to be arrested. Kinnear testified this in the extortion-case bail application, case number 16/818/2017, launched by Nafiz Modack and four co-accused.

58 Dolley, C (2017) 'Top Western Cape cop says police are framing him for murder', News24, 7 March https://www.news24.com/SouthAfrica/News/top-western-cape-cop-says-police-are-framing-him-for-murder-20170307 Accessed 19 January 2019.

CHAPTER 7 Modack makes his move

1 Dolley, C (2017) 'Gang bosses exploit private security loophole to "legally intimidate" rivals – sources', News24, 19 July https://www.news24.com/SouthAfrica/News/gang-bosses-exploit-private-security-loophole-to-legally-intimidate-rivals-sources-20170719 Accessed 25 January 2019.

2 Parliamentary Monitoring Group (2018) 'Private Security Industry Regulatory Authority (PSIRA) 2018/19 budget', 24 April https://pmg.org.za/

Notes

committee-meeting/26196/ Accessed 25 January 2019.

3   Parliamentary Monitoring Group (2018) 'PSIRA briefing', 20 March https://pmg.org.za/committee-meeting/26024/ Accessed 25 January 2019.

4   Presentation by PSIRA in Parliament to the Portfolio Committee on Police on 20 March 2018 by Manabela Chauke.

5   Testimony by Sergeant Edward Edwardes in the bail application of Grant Veroni on 30 November 2017 in the Cape Town Regional Court. Veroni faced a charge relating to an unlicensed firearm.

6   Chabalala, J (2017) 'Former business partner of Kebble shot dead', News24, 15 February https://www.news24.com/SouthAfrica/News/former-business-partner-of-kebble-killer-shot-dead-20170215 Accessed 28 January 2019.

7   Claims made by a confidential source on 21 November 2017.

8   Skhosana Maponyane Hall Phillips and Khumalo SA, trading as The Security Group Enterprises, based in Bellville in Cape Town. Directors of the company included Houssain Taleb, one Grant Veroni, and a niece of Jerome and Colin Booysen.

9   Information contained in an affidavit by Nafiz Modack, datestamped 12 February 2018 and submitted by Modack's defence in an extortion-case bail application, case number 16/818/2017, launched by Modack and four co-accused in the Cape Town Magistrate's Court.

10 Dolley, C (2017) '"Bogus" intelligence claims as underworld plot thickens', News24, 19 April https://www.news24.com/SouthAfrica/News/bogus-intelligence-claims-as-underworld-plot-thickens-20170419 Accessed 25 January 2019.

11 Testimony by Sergeant Edward Edwardes in the bail application of Grant Veroni on 30 November 2017 in the Cape Town Regional Court. Veroni faced a charge relating to an unlicensed firearm.

12 Information contained in an affidavit by Hawks Lieutenant Colonel Peter Janse Viljoen dated 31 January 2018 and signed in Bellville, used by the state in an extortion-case bail application, case number 16/818/2017, against Nafiz Modack and four co-accused in the Cape Town Magistrate's Court.

13 Email from Nafiz Modack dated 30 March 2017 in response to a query sent to him by the author in her capacity as a journalist.

14 On 30 March 2017 a photograph of flipflops was sent to the author via email from a sender who did not provide their name. The author, in her capacity as a journalist, sent Andre Naude the picture of the flipflops and asked if they were his and he denied it.

15   Email from Nafiz Modack dated 30 March 2017 in response to a query sent to him by the author in her capacity as a journalist.

16   The author interviewed Nafiz Modack in Green Point on 21 September 2017. The interview was conducted at Cubana, where the author had previously interviewed Andre Naude and Richard van Zyl in 2012. Several armed men, including Jacques Cronje, sat nearby for the 2017 interview, and the author was told that several more were stationed outside in the street. Modack chain-smoked and sipped on energy drinks and heavily sugared coffee; he interrupted the conversation several times to attend to one of three cellphones he carried. He pointed out that the author had chosen to sit in the seat Cyril Beeka had once favoured.

17   Interview with Nafiz Modack in Green Point on 21 September 2017, in the author's capacity as a journalist.

18   Information contained in an affidavit by Nafiz Modack, datestamped 12 February 2018, submitted by Modack's defence in an extortion-case bail application, case number 16/818/2017, launched by Modack and four co-accused in the Cape Town Magistrate's Court.

19   Ibid.

20   Ibid.

21   Interview with Nafiz Modack in Green Point on 21 September 2017, in the author's capacity as a journalist.

22   Video footage of what transpired outside Mavericks on the evening of 29 March 2017 was sent, via WhatsApp, to the author by an anonymous source on 30 March 2017.

23   Information contained in an affidavit by Hawks Lieutenant Colonel Peter Janse Viljoen dated 31 January 2018 and signed in Bellville, used by the state in an extortion-case bail application, case number 16/818/2017, against Nafiz Modack and four co-accused in the Cape Town Magistrate's Court.

24   Testimony by Lieutenant Colonel Charl Kinnear in the Cape Town Magistrate's Court in the extortion-case bail application, case number 16/818/2017, launched by Nafiz Modack and four co-accused.

25   Information contained in an affidavit by Hawks Lieutenant Colonel Peter Janse Viljoen dated 31 January 2018 and signed in Bellville, used by the state in an extortion-case bail application, case number 16/818/2017, against Nafiz Modack and four co-accused in the Cape Town Magistrate's Court.

26   Ibid.

27   Ibid. On the night of 31 March/morning of 1 April, the author received

several cellphone messages from an unfamiliar number. They read, 'thr gna be a war 2nyt in town with other gangs', stated that a club was going to be 'fucked up shortly' (at 1.06am), that a club had been smashed up (two hours later), and that the club had likely been trashed by 'the Moroccans'. The messages were accompanied by several photographs of men in what appeared, based on the lighting, to be nightclubs; Modack and Colin Booysen were in some of the images.

28 Decades before his murder, Shamiel Eyssen had been operating on the wrong side of the law and some of his criminal history is contained in a Supreme Court of Appeal judgment dating back to September 2008. The state alleged that Eyssen was the head of the Fancy Boys gang, which had operated out of a premises in Salt River, with members involved in mainly housebreakings and robberies across the Cape peninsula between 2001 and 2003. Eyssen was initially sentenced to an effective twenty years in jail, but through the appeals process this was whittled down to fifteen. See *Eyssen v S* (746/2007) [2008] ZASCA 97 (17 September 2008), Supreme Court of Appeal, Southern African Legal Information Institute http://www.saflii.org/za/cases/ZASCA/2008/97.html Accessed 12 February 2019.

29 Details provided by a confidential sources via WhatsApp on the day of and after Shamiel Eyssen's murder.

30 Testimony by Lieutenant Colonel Charl Kinnear in the Cape Town Magistrate's Court on 2 January 2018 in the extortion-case bail application, case number 16/818/2017, launched by Nafiz Modack and four co-accused.

31 Ibid.

32 Affidavit by Grant Veroni dated 29 November 2017, signed in Cape Town and submitted by his defence attorney in the Cape Town Regional Court during a successful bail application. Veroni had faced an unlicensed firearm charge.

33 Ibid.

34 Hyman, A (2018) '"I had no choice," says victim of Cape Town extortion racket', *TimesLive*, 12 November https://www.timeslive.co.za/news/south-africa/2018-11-12-i-had-no-choice-restaurant-protection-racket-victim-tells-court/ Accessed 10 March 2019.

35 Details about this incident, registered with the police as CAS171/08/2017, were provided to the author by a confidential source.

36 Pijoos, I (2017) 'Hawks nab suspect after guns, bullet proof jacket and blue light seized', News24, 22 August https://www.news24.com/

SouthAfrica/News/hawks-nab-suspect-after-guns-bullet-proof-jacket-and-blue-light-seized-20170822 Accessed 21 February 2019.

37   Affidavit by Hawks Lieutenant Colonel Peter Janse Viljoen, dated 31 January 2018 and signed in Bellville, used by the state in an extortion-case bail application, case number 16/818/2017, launched by Nafiz Modack and four co-accused in the Cape Town Magistrate's Court.

38   Dolley, C (2017) '"Innocent" patron caught up in suspected club turf shootout', News24, 20 April https://www.news24.com/SouthAfrica/News/innocent-patron-caught-up-in-club-shootout-20170420 Accessed 19 March 2019.

39   Affidavit by Hawks Lieutenant Colonel Peter Janse Viljoen dated 31 January 2018 and signed in Bellville, used by the state in an extortion-case bail application, case number 16/818/2017, launched by Nafiz Modack and four co-accused in the Cape Town Magistrate's Court.

40   Testimony by Sergeant Edward Edwardes in the bail application of Grant Veroni on 30 November 2017 in the Cape Town Regional Court. Veroni faced a charge relating to an unlicensed firearm.

41   Ibid.

42   Some sources told the author they believed certain police officers had no will to detain the three, as these individuals had been after Nafiz Modack or his associates who were not aligned to the officers.

43   Testimony by Sergeant Edward Edwardes in the bail application of Grant Veroni on 30 November 2017 in the Cape Town Regional Court. Veroni faced a charge relating to an unlicensed firearm.

44   Personal observation by author in Cape Town on 21 April 2017.

45   Interaction witnessed by the author outside the Cape Town Magistrate's Court on 13 November 2017.

46   Affidavit by Hawks Lieutenant Colonel Peter Janse Viljoen dated 31 January 2018 and signed in Bellville, used by the state in an extortion-case bail application, case number 16/818/2017, launched by Nafiz Modack and four co-accused in the Cape Town Magistrate's Court.

47   The name was changed to VIP24 Protection in July 2017.

48   Affidavit by Hawks Lieutenant Colonel Peter Janse Viljoen dated 31 January 2018 and signed in Bellville, used by the state in an extortion-case bail application, case number 16/818/2017, launched by Nafiz Modack and four co-accused in the Cape Town Magistrate's Court.

49   When the author interviewed Nafiz Modack in Green Point in September 2017, Mathys Visser had been one of several men who'd accompanied him.

50 Affidavit of Mathys Visser dated 3 May 2017 and signed in Cape Town in the case of *Eagle VIP Security (Pty) Ltd and Mathys Visser v the Provincial Commissioner of Police and Others* (7671/2017).

51 Ibid.

52 Ibid.

53 The City of Cape Town's valuation roll shows alongside the address of The Embassy that it belongs to Corpclo 701 CC https://web1.capetown.gov.za/web1/GV2015/Results?Search=ADD,101,CASTLE Accessed 5 February 2019. This close corporation is listed as one of Lifman's entities in a founding affidavit by Lifman dated 23 November 2016 and signed in Sea Point in case 228020/2016 in the matter between Mark Roy Lifman and the South African Revenue Service.

54 Affidavit by Hawks Lieutenant Colonel Peter Janse Viljoen dated 31 January 2018 and used by the state in an extortion-case bail application, case number 16/818/2017, against Nafiz Modack and four co-accused in the Cape Town Magistrate's Court.

55 Ibid.

56 Dolley, C (2017) '"Bogus" intelligence claims as underworld plot thickens', News24, 19 April https://www.news24.com/SouthAfrica/News/bogus-intelligence-claims-as-underworld-plot-thickens-20170419 Accessed 12 February 2019.

57 In March 2003, in what was said to be the third attempt on his life that year, McKenna was ambushed as he left a church in Ravensmead, in a retaliation shooting for the murders of two 28s gang bosses a week earlier; he was seriously injured but miraculously survived. In October that year McKenna, who was out on bail at the time – the charges against him included having an unlicensed firearm, resisting arrest, housebreaking, rape and assault – was arrested as part of a massive province-wide sweep to try and snuff out the operations of gang bosses. See Joseph, N (2003) 'Gang attack suspected drug dealer in church', IOL, 24 March https://www.iol.co.za/news/south-africa/gang-attack-suspected-drug-dealer-in-church-103241 Accessed 29 January 2019; and Aranes, J and Kemp, Y (2003) '"Gangsters will fall and they will fall hard"', IOL, 22 October https://www.iol.co.za/news/south-africa/gangsters-willfall-and-theyll-fall-hard-1152117 Accessed 29 January 2019. Rashied Staggie and Ernie 'Lastig' Solomon were arrested and charged with various crimes in the same sweep.

58 Personal communication, via message, with a confidential source on 30 and 31 April 2017.

59 Underworld and intelligence circles often overlap, as in this case: Russel

THE ENFORCERS

Christopher is the father of Marissa Christopher who at one stage was in a relationship with Radovan Krejčíř.

60 Testimony of Lieutenant Colonel Charl Kinnear in the Cape Town Magistrate's Court on 2 January 2018 in an extortion-case bail application, case number 16/818/2017, launched by Nafiz Modack and four co-accused in the Cape Town Magistrate's Court.

61 Ibid.

62 Ibid.

63 Using her cellphone, the author discreetly took some photographs. The next day, 5 May 2017, the author emailed Modack to enquire as to the reason for the meeting. He didn't answer the question but his response, with the ominous subject line 'WE HAVE EYES EVERY WHR', included a photograph of the author at the hotel the previous evening. The author asked Modack if this was a threat and he denied it, apologising if it had come across as such. Nonetheless, personal security guards were assigned to watch over the author for the next few days.

64 WhatsApp messages received by the author from an unidentified sender on 5 May 2017 between 8:45am and 9:37am. The sender purported to be from the new faction, the one linked to Nafiz Modack, taking over security.

65 This was the first of a series of increasingly brazen attacks on Booysen over the next few months. See Dolley, C (2018) 'Jerome "Donkie" Booysen – "Gangsterism is not the way to go"', News24, 1 June https://www.news24.com/SouthAfrica/News/exclusive-jerome-donkie-booysen-gangsterism-is-not-the-way-to-go-20180601 Accessed 29 January 2019.

66 Authorisation by Western Cape police commissioner Khombinkosi Jula dated 25 May 2017.

67 Affidavit by Hawks Lieutenant Colonel Peter Janse Viljoen dated 31 January 2018 and used by the state in an extortion-case bail application, case number 16/818/2017, launched by Nafiz Modack and four co-accused in the Cape Town Magistrate's Court.

68 Dolley, C (2017) 'Police with "machine guns, nyala" raid Booysen's home', News24, 2 June https://www.news24.com/SouthAfrica/News/police-with-machine-guns-nyala-raid-booysens-home-20170602 Accessed 24 January 2019.

69 Affidavit by Hawks Lieutenant Colonel Peter Janse Viljoen dated 31 January 2018 and used by the state in an extortion-case bail application, case number 16/818/2017, launched by Nafiz Modack and four co-accused in the Cape Town Magistrate's Court.

70 Details supplied by attorney Chad Levendal in the Cape Town

Notes

Magistrate's Court on 1 February 2018 during an extortion-case bail application, case number 16/818/2017, launched by Nafiz Modack and four co-accused.

71 Dolley, C (2017) 'Police make massive R500m cocaine bust in Overberg town', News24, 6 June https://www.news24.com/SouthAfrica/News/police-make-massive-r500m-cocaine-bust-in-overberg-town-20170622 Accessed 9 March 2019.

72 Bell Pottinger was a British PR company headquartered in London. During 2016/2017 it ran a 'dirty campaign' in South Africa, playing on racial animosity by creating fake news (among other tactics), in order to benefit its client Oakbay Investments, which was controlled by the Gupta family. The resulting scandal disgraced the firm and by September 2017 it had gone bankrupt.

73 Sources at the scene provided the author with details, via WhatsApp messages, of what allegedly happened; and testimony of Lieutenant Colonel Charl Kinnear in the Cape Town Magistrate's Court on 11 December 2017 during the extortion-case bail application, case number 16/818/2017, launched by Nafiz Modack and four co-accused.

74 Testimony of Lieutenant Colonel Charl Kinnear on 11 December 2017 during an extortion-case bail application, case number 16/818/2017, launched by Nafiz Modack and four co-accused in the Cape Town Magistrate's Court.

75 Affidavit of Colonel Jacques van Lill dated 27 July 2017 and signed in Cape Town, used in the Western Cape High Court to try and prevent from succeeding an application by Eagle VIP Security and Mathys Visser, to have it ordered that firearms seized by police be returned.

76 Ibid.

77 Ibid.

78 Dolley, C (2017) 'Guns seized in underworld clampdown on security company previously confiscated outside strip club', News24, 13 July https://www.news24.com/SouthAfrica/News/guns-seized-in-underworld-clampdown-on-security-company-previously-confiscated-outside-strip-club-20170713 Accessed 26 February 2019.

79 Affidavit of Colonel Jacques van Lill dated 27 July 2017 and signed in Cape Town, used in the Western Cape High Court to try and prevent from succeeding an application by Eagle VIP Security and Mathys Visser, to have it ordered that firearms seized by police be returned.

80 Affidavit of Lieutenant Colonel Michael Barkhuizen dated 7 July 2017 and signed in Bellville South, used in the Western Cape High Court, in Bellville CAS 07/2017, to try and prevent from succeeding an application

THE ENFORCERS

by TSG, to have it ordered that firearms seized by police be returned.

81   TSG's motivation, relating to the application for a licence to possess a firearm and ammunition, addressed to the Central Firearms Registry in Pretoria. The date is not clear on this document, handed up as part of the state's case to try and prevent TSG from having firearms seized by police returned to it.

82   Affidavit of Lieutenant Colonel Michael Barkhuizen dated 7 July 2017 and signed in Bellville South, used in the Western Cape High Court, in Bellville CAS 07/2017, to try and prevent from succeeding an application by TSG to have it ordered that firearms seized by police be returned.

83   Affidavit of Colonel Jacques van Lill dated 27 July 2017 and signed in Cape Town, used in the Western Cape High Court to try and prevent from succeeding an application by Eagle VIP Security and Mathys Visser to have it ordered that firearms seized by police be returned.

84   SMSs sent to the author from Nafiz Modack on 14 July 2017.

85   Ibid.

86   Ibid.

CHAPTER 8   *Dodging bullets in the City of Gold*

1   Statement by Warrant Officer Vincent Saunders of the Gauteng provincial investigation unit dated 22 January 2018 and signed in Cape Town, used by the state in the extortion-case bail application, case number 16/818/2017, against Nafiz Modack and four co-accused in the Cape Town Magistrate's Court.

2   Ibid.

3   Tandwa, L (2018) 'Suspected underworld kingpin Nafiz Modack gets R10k bail in Joburg nightclub case', News24, 26 February https://www.news24.com/SouthAfrica/News/suspected-underworld-kingpin-nafiz-modack-gets-r10k-bail-in-joburg-nightclub-case-20180226 Accessed 9 March 2019.

4   *Daily Voice* (2017) 'Alleged Cape gang boss hit 14 times in shooting in Joburg', 6 July https://www.iol.co.za/news/south-africa/western-cape/alleged-cape-gang-boss-hit-14-times-in-shooting-in-joburg-10164361 Accessed 20 February 2019; and personal communication with a confidential source on 6 July 2017.

5   *The Irish Times* (2007) 'Wicklow seller of illegal steroids is jailed', 21 July https://www.irishtimes.com/news/wicklow-seller-of-illegal-steroids-is-jailed-1.950727 Accessed 29 January 2019.

6   *Benjamin v Additional Magistrate Cape Town and Others* (14216/2013)

[2014] ZAWCHC 115 (1 August 2014) Southern African Legal Information Institute http://www.saflii.org/za/cases/ZAWCHC/2014/115.html Accessed 29 January 2019.

7   Testimony of Lieutenant Colonel Charl Kinnear in the Cape Town Magistrate's Court on 28 December 2017 in an extortion-case bail application, case number 16/818/2017, launched by Nafiz Modack and four co-accused in the Cape Town Magistrate's Court. However, in the same case and court on 14 February 2018, state prosecutor Esna Erasmus said these details should not have been brought up as these were irrelevant and without substance. See Dolley, C (2018) 'Testimony about advocate shouldn't have surfaced - Modack prosecutor', News24, 14 February https://www.news24.com/SouthAfrica/News/testimony-about-advocate-shouldnt-have-surfaced-modack-prosecutor-20180214 Accessed 22 February 2019.

8   WhatsApp messages received by the author from Pete Mihalik on 18 August 2017.

9   Argument by defence lawyer Rooshdeen Rudolph in the Cape Town Magistrate's Court on 2 February 2018 in the extortion-case bail application, case number 16/818/2017, launched by Nafiz Modack and four co-accused in the Cape Town Magistrate's Court, suggesting that the audio clip had been recorded hours before Brian Wainstein was murdered. However, the author is in receipt of information that the clip may actually have been recorded following the shooting of Ralph Stanfield, in a failed attempt to see if Mark Lifman knew details about, or would give his view on, this shooting if Wainstein brought up the incident; personal communication with the author via direct messaging on Twitter from an unknown source on 2 February 2018.

10 Audio recording played in the Cape Town Magistrate's Court on 2 February 2018 by lawyer for the defence Rooshdeen Rudolph in an extortion-case bail application, case number 16/818/2017, launched by Nafiz Modack and four co-accused. The origin of the recording, who recorded it and why it was recorded were not divulged in court.

11 Respondents' main heads of argument in the bail application of *Matthew Breet and Sheldon Breet v the State*, case number 4/1183/2017, in the Wynberg Magistrate's Court on 11 June 2018.

12 Dolley, C (2017) '"Underworld figures" clash in Emperors Palace casino', News24, 8 September https://www.news24.com/SouthAfrica/News/underworld-figures-clash-in-emperors-palace-casino-20170908 Accessed 24 January 2019.

13 SMS from Nafiz Modack in response to questions about the Emperors Palace incident on 14 September 2017; and Dolley, C (2017) '"Underworld

figures" clash in Emperors Palace casino', News24, 8 September https://www.news24.com/SouthAfrica/News/underworld-figures-clash-in-emperors-palace-casino-20170908 Accessed 20 February 2019.

14   WhatsApp message from Andre Naude on 8 September 2017.

15   Search warrant datestamped by police on 7 August 2017, signed illegibly, listing Andre Naude's address as the property to be searched. It's addressed to one Capt M Williams.

16   Dolley, C (2017) 'Mass suspensions and "truth" about missing police guns covered up – sources', News24, 21 September https://www.news24.com/SouthAfrica/News/mass-suspensions-and-truth-about-missing-police-guns-covered-up-sources-20170921 Accessed 21 February 2019.

17   De Villiers, J (2017) 'Stolen police guns will end up in the hands of gangsters', News24, 11 September https://www.news24.com/SouthAfrica/News/stolen-police-guns-will-end-up-in-the-hands-of-gangsters-mbalula-20170911 Accessed 29 January 2019.

18   A message detailing the shooting was sent to police as well as other individuals, including the author, via WhatsApp on 13 September 2017. The original sender of the message did not put their name on the message, the contents of which were confirmed by multiple sources.

19   'Investigations with regard to Mitchell's Plein and Bellville South missing firearms', delivered to Parliament on 14 November 2017 by acting national Hawks head Yolisa Matakata.

20   In June 2018 a police constable was arrested in connection with the firearms that were stolen from the Bellville South cops. See Pitt, C (2018) 'Bellville cop implicated in alleged theft of 18 guns, court set to hear details', News24, 20 June https://www.news24.com/SouthAfrica/News/bellville-cop-implicated-in-alleged-theft-of-18-guns-court-set-to-hear-details-20180620 Accessed 10 March 2019.

21   Affidavit of Houssain Taleb read out in the Cape Town Magistrate's Court on 19 December 2017 during a bail application. Taleb was charged with conspiracy to commit murder.

22   Dolley, C (2012) 'Band of brothers who patrol club scene', *Cape Times*, 30 January https://www.iol.co.za/news/south-africa/western-cape/band-of-brothers-who-patrol-club-scene-1223533 Accessed 22 January 2019.

23   Affidavit by Houssain Taleb read out in the Cape Town Magistrate's Court on 19 December 2017 in a conspiracy-to-commit-murder case, which was in the bail application phase, in which Taleb was the accused.

24   Testimony by Sergeant Edward Edwardes in the Cape Town Magistrate's Court on 19 December 2017 in a conspiracy-to-commit-murder case, which

was in the bail application phase, in which Houssain Taleb was the accused.

25 Testimony by Sergeant Edward Edwardes in the Cape Town Magistrate's Court on 19 December 2017 in a conspiracy-to-commit-murder case, which was in the bail application phase, in which Houssain Taleb was the accused.

26 Argument by attorney Bruce Hendricks in the Cape Town Magistrate's Court on 24 January 2018 in an extortion-case bail application, case number 16/818/2017, launched by Nafiz Modack and four co-accused in the Cape Town Magistrate's Court

27 Some claimed Jacobs was a reformed ex-convict. See Franck, R (2017) 'Family man killed in Stellies nightclub shooting "not a gangster"', *Daily Voice*, 17 October https://www.iol.co.za/news/south-africa/western-cape/family-man-killed-in-stellies-nightclub-shooting-not-a-gangster-11596929 Accessed 13 March 2019.

28 Testimony by Sergeant Edward Edwardes in the bail application of Grant Veroni on 30 November 2017 in the Cape Town Regional Court. Veroni faced a charge relating to an unlicensed firearm.

29 Dolley, C (2017) 'Cape Town airport shooting another attempted hit on suspected gang leader Jerome "Donkie" Booysen', News24, 18 October https://www.news24.com/SouthAfrica/News/cape-town-airport-shooting-another-attempted-hit-on-gang-leader-jerome-donkie-booysen-20171018 Accessed 11 February 2019.

30 Several confidential sources insisted to the author that the men had actually been after Colin Booysen.

31 Photographs were taken at the scene and a confidential source sent two of these to the author on the night of 19 October 2017. One showed a wig with straight locks splayed across a sterile white floor and spatters and smears of blood around it; another showed a man with a swollen nose and blood smeared across his face, sitting on a floor smeared with blood, and a woman's flat pump-style shoe on the floor next to him.

32 Staff reporter (2017) 'Hospital arrest not linked to "Donkie" shooting case', *Cape Times*, 24 October https://www.iol.co.za/capetimes/news/hospital-arrest-not-linked-to-donkie-shooting-case-11692033 Accessed 9 March 2019.

33 Ramovha, L (2017) 'Investigation and court update: Over 3000 rounds of assorted ammunition, grenades, firearms and military radios seized: Brian Wainstein alleged murder suspect nabbed', Western Cape Hawks, 28 November, press release emailed to members of the media.

34 Respondents' main heads of argument in the bail application of *Matthew Breet and Sheldon Breet v the State*, case number 4/1183/2017, in the

Wynberg Magistrate's Court on 11 June 2018.

35 Breytenbach, J (2018) 'Geen borgtog vir moord op koning van steroiede', Netwerk24, 12 July https://www.netwerk24.com/Nuus/Hof/geen-borgtog-vir-moord-op-koning-van-steroiede-20180712 Accessed 29 January 2019.

36 Respondents' main heads of argument in the bail application of *Matthew Breet and Sheldon Breet v the State*, case number 4/1183/2017, in the Wynberg Magistrate's Court on 11 June 2018.

37 Etheridge, J (2018) 'Man gets 20 years in jail after pleading guilty to "Steroid King" murder', News24, 5 December https://www.news24.com/SouthAfrica/News/man-gets-20-years-in-jail-after-pleading-guilty-to-steroid-king-murder-20181205 Accessed 8 February 2019. In April 2019 it emerged that Cheslyn Adams had been sentenced to an effective 25 years in jail, not just for Wainstein's killing but also for the Café Caprice shooting of April 2017.

38 Testimony of Lieutenant Colonel Charl Kinnear on 29 December 2017 in an extortion-case bail application, case number 16/818/2017, launched by Nafiz Modack and four co-accused in the Cape Town Magistrate's Court.

39 By May 2018 the Iconic Lounge no longer existed. Instead a new venue, Sneaker Cartel, a luxury takkie boutique with a bar, was launched at the start of May. Jerome Booysen's son Joel was directly involved in running Sneaker Cartel.

40 Testimony by Sergeant Edward Edwardes in the bail application of Grant Veroni on 30 November 2017 in the Cape Town Regional Court. Veroni faced a charge relating to an unlicensed firearm.

41 Ibid.

42 Information sent to the author by a source via WhatsApp on the afternoon of 30 November 2017, and corroborated by a second source.

43 Ibid.

44 Dolley, C (2017) 'Underworld figure Modack facing robbery and assault charges in "debt collection" debacle', News24, 29 November https://www.news24.com/SouthAfrica/News/underworld-figure-modack-facing-robbery-and-assault-charges-in-debt-collection-debacle-20171129 Accessed 24 January 2019.

45 Affidavit by Hawks Lieutenant Colonel Peter Janse Viljoen dated 31 January 2018 and signed in Bellville, used by the state in an extortion-case bail application, case number 16/818/2017, against Nafiz Modack and four co-accused in the Cape Town Magistrate's Court.

46 At least three sources alerted the author to this murder on the morning of 3 December 2017 and provided photographs of the scene.

47 Testimony of Lieutenant Colonel Charl Kinnear in the Cape Town Magistrate's Court on 3 January 2018 in an extortion-case bail application, case number 16/818/2017, launched by Modack and four co-accused in the Cape Town Magistrate's Court.

48 Dolley, C (2017) 'Violence in Cape Town as DRC factions fight over Kabila', News24, 4 December https://www.news24.com/SouthAfrica/News/violence-in-cape-town-as-factions-fight-over-drc-president-kabila-20171204 Accessed 25 January 2018.

49 Letter sent to club owners in Cape Town's city centre at the start of December 2017. The portion of the letter provided to the author by a confidential source didn't contain a date, nor the name of the person who sent it out, but several sources confirmed the letter was legitimate and was from TSG.

50 The arrests of Modack and his suspected henchmen didn't end underworld ructions in the Cape Town CBD. It was alleged by police that that very night, Mark Lifman's Iconic Lounge in Long Street was targeted by a group of men, but that a tipoff enabled management to act quickly and they locked the venue. The men then allegedly instead trashed a shop situated below it.

51 Personal communication with Nafiz Modack outside the Cape Town detective service's offices in Cape Town on 15 December 2017.

52 Comment by Major-General Jeremy Vearey outside the Cape Town Magistrate's Court on 18 December 2017.

53 Dolley, C (2015) 'Rats kill Pollsmoor prisoners', *Weekend Argus*, 19 September https://www.iol.co.za/news/rats-kill-pollsmoor-prisoners-1918458 Accessed 24 January 2019.

CHAPTER 9 *The Eastern European connection*

1 Recording of a cellphone conversation between Nafiz Modack and Radley Dijkers played by the defence in the Cape Town Magistrate's Court on 16 January 2018 in an extortion-case bail application, case number 16/818/2017, launched by Nafiz Modack and four co-accused.

2 In early 2012 Igor Russol was accused of extortion and intimidation, and among the claims against him was that he'd allegedly demanded R250 000 from a businessman or he would shut the business down. See Dolley, C (2012) '"Russian" linked to extortion racket', *Cape Times*, 2 March https://www.iol.co.za/capetimes/russian-linked-to-extortion-racket-1247573 Accessed 15 January 2019. Ultimately, Russol accepted a plea deal and was released from custody. This was mentioned by attorney Bruce Hendricks in the Cape Town Magistrate's Court on

THE ENFORCERS

      28 January 2017 in the extortion-case bail application, case number 16/818/2017, launched by Nafiz Modack and four co-accused.

3   Claims made by Igor Russol and conveyed by Lieutenant Colonel Charl Kinnear in the Cape Town Magistrate's Court on 3 January 2018 in an extortion-case bail application, case number 16/818/2017, launched by Nafiz Modack and four co-accused.

4   Ibid.

5   Ibid.

6   Ibid.

7   Lieutenant Colonel Charl Kinnear, without specifying a date, testified that someone had tried to shoot Russol inside the Iconic Lounge, above which Colin Booysen had a flat. Russol's version, as conveyed by Kinnear, was that a woman had walked into the club and because there were no women bouncers, only men, she wasn't searched. In this way she'd smuggled in a firearm and handed it to a man already inside, and this man had aimed the weapon at Russol, but Russol and others had tackled him and retrieved the firearm. Kinnear said this man was handed over to police, and he claimed that there were messages from Colin Booysen on a cellphone the man was found with, which said that the man 'must kill the Russian'.

8   Statement to police by Absa bank fraud investigator relating to an October 2015 matter. Some details, including the investigator's name, were redacted from this document by the state for security reasons. This statement was used by the state in an extortion-case bail application, case number 16/818/2017, launched by Nafiz Modack and four co-accused in the Cape Town Magistrate's Court.

9   Argument by Advocate Dirk Uijs in the Cape Town Magistrate's Court on 17 January 2018 in an extortion-case bail application, case number 16/818/2017, launched by Nafiz Modack and four co-accused in the Cape Town Magistrate's Court.

10   Message from attorney Bruce Hendricks on 22 February 2018 in response to a query.

11   Dolley, C (2018) 'EXCLUSIVE: Attempt to kill Jerome "Donkie" Booysen's brother in Pollsmoor Prison – attorney', News24, 22 February https://www.news24.com/SouthAfrica/News/exclusive-attempt-to-kill-jerome-donkie-booysens-brother-in-pollsmoor-prison-attorney-20180222 Accessed 11 February 2019.

12   Hampshire Brown was no stranger to allegations of underhand dealings – in October 2003 he'd been arrested on charges of selling liquor

	without a licence, assault, possession of dagga and reckless driving.
13	Jerome Booysen had gone to the scene of the shooting afterwards – a source sent the author a photograph of Booysen standing alongside others there.
14	Annexure to an application for extension of liquor trading hours of Club Wendy's dated October 2017. This annexure is part of a report to the City of Cape Town's subcouncil 22 and is listed as item number SUB20/11/2017.
15	February, S (2018) 'Hempie died saving my life', *Daily Voice*, 22 February https://www.dailyvoice.co.za/news/hempie-died-saving-my-life-13415178 Accessed 9 March 2019.
16	Affidavit by Nafiz Modack, datestamped 12 February 2018 and submitted by Modack's defence in an extortion-case bail application, case number 16/818/2017, launched by Modack and four co-accused in the Cape Town Magistrate's Court.
17	Testimony by Lieutenant Colonel Charl Kinnear in the Cape Town Magistrate's Court on 3 January 2018 during an extortion-case bail application, case number 16/818/2017, launched by Nafiz Modack and four co-accused in the Cape Town Magistrate's Court.
18	Argument by Advocate Edwin Grobler in the Cape Town Magistrate's Court on 16 January 2018 during an extortion-case bail application, case number 16/818/2017, launched by Nafiz Modack and four co-accused.
19	Testimony by Lieutenant Colonel Charl Kinnear in the Cape Town Magistrate's Court on 3 January 2018 during an extortion-case bail application, case number 16/818/2017, launched by Nafiz Modack and four co-accused.
20	SMS from unknown source on 8 March 2018.
21	Three sources sent WhatsApp messages to the author on 23 March 2018 saying Jerome Booysen had been shot at.
22	Personal communication (cellphone conversation) with Jerome Booysen on 24 March 2018.
23	A source sent a WhatsApp message to the author on 25 April 2017 claiming Booysen's vehicle was shot at.
24	Personal communication (cellphone conversation) with Jerome Booysen on 24 April 2018.
25	Dolley, C (2018) 'REVEALED: Murders expose links of Serbian warlord's assassins in SA', News24, 9 May https://www.news24.com/SouthAfrica/News/revealed-murders-expose-links-of-serbian-warlords-assassins-in-sa-20180509 Accessed 12 February 2019.

26 *Telegraf* (2018) 'Upucani Gorgija Gorg Darmanović preminuo u Zemunskoj bolnicia', 6 May http://www.telegraf.rs/vesti/hronika/2956374-upucani-gorgija-gorg-Darmanovićc-preminuo-u-bolnici Accessed 29 January 2019.

27 *City Press* (2014) 'How spy unit nailed Richard Mdluli "foes"', 10 August https://www.news24.com/Archives/City-Press/How-spy-unit-nailed-Richard-Mdluli-foes-20150430 Accessed 29 January 2019.

28 A confidential source supplied the author with messages from Darmanović to a third party on 6 May 2018.

29 Memorandum on a Scorpions letterhead headed 'Corruption SAPS members: Provincial undercover office', dated 19 January 2007.

30 Thamm, M (2018) 'NPA withdraws bogus charges against former Hawks head Anwa Dramat', *Daily Maverick*, 3 September https://www.dailymaverick.co.za/article/2018-09-03-npa-withdraws-bogus-charges-against-former-hawks-head-anwa-dramat/ Accessed 29 January 2019.

31 Ibid.

32 Ibid.

33 Document on an SAPS letterhead dated 8 July 2017, addressed to an operations director in the State Security Agency.

34 Several sources told the author this following George Darmanović's murder.

35 A confidential source supplied the author with messages from George Darmanović to a third party on 6 May 2018.

36 A cellphone message George Darmanović had sent to a contact of detailed allegations he'd made against (among others) Jeremy Vearey was forwarded to the author following his murder.

37 A confidential source supplied the author with messages from George Darmanović to a third party on 6 May 2018.

38 Dolley, C (2018) 'Serbian dentist's 2014 murder may be linked to SA spook's assassination', News24, 12 June https://www.news24.com/SouthAfrica/News/serbian-dentists-2014-murder-may-be-linked-to-sa-spooks-assassination-20180612 Accessed 29 January 2019.

39 Dolley, C (2018) 'BREAKTHROUGH: 2 arrested in connection with SA spook's murder in Serbia', News24, 11 June https://www.news24.com/SouthAfrica/News/breakthrough-2-arrested-in-connection-with-sa-spooks-murder-in-serbia-20180611 Accessed 12 February 2019.

40 Dolley, C (208) 'BREAKTHROUGH: 2 arrested in connection with SA spook's murder in Serbia', News24, 11 June https://www.news24.com/SouthAfrica/News/breakthrough-2-arrested-in-connection-with-sa-

spooks-murder-in-serbia-20180611 Accessed 29 January 2019.
41. Dolley, C (2018) 'Charred assault rifle found after murder of another Serbian man in Joburg', News24, 19 July https://www.news24.com/SouthAfrica/News/charred-assault-rifle-found-after-murder-of-another-serbian-man-in-joburg-20180719 Accessed 29 January 2019.
42. Personal communication with confidential sources on 1 August 2018.
43. Personal communication with confidential sources on the evening of 5 August 2018.
44. Testimony of Jacques Cronje in the Cape Town Regional Court on 21 April 2015 in the case of *State v Mark Lifman and Andre Naude*, case number 30/51/2012, who were charged with operating a bouncer company without being registered with the Private Security Regulatory Authority.
45. Hyman, A (2018) '"Our guys have assault rifles, we're ready for them" - Cape gang war intensifies after Lakay gunned down', *TimesLive*, 6 August https://www.timeslive.co.za/news/south-africa/2018-08-06-our-guys-have-assault-rifles-were-ready-for-them-cape-gang-war-intensifies-after-lakay-gunned-down/ Accessed 29 January 2019.
46. Personal communication with confidential sources on 24 September 2018.
47. Ibid.
48. Personal communication with confidential sources on 28 September 2018. A photograph was sent to the author showing Pietersen sitting on a bed holding parts of a firearm, allegedly an Uzi which was claimed to have been stolen from police in Gauteng.
49. Evans, J (2018) '"He gave children guns" – new allegations emerge in Colin Booysen, bodyguards' bail application', *News24*, 19 October https://www.news24.com/SouthAfrica/News/he-gave-children-guns-new-allegations-emerge-in-colin-booysen-bodyguards-bail-application-20181019 Accessed 18 March 2019.
50. Hyman, A (2018) 'Colin Booysen intimidation case scrapped as detective takes a bruising', *TimesLive*, 21 December https://www.timeslive.co.za/news/south-africa/2018-12-21-colin-booysen-intimidation-case-scrapped-as-detective-takes-a-bruising/ Accessed 18 March 2019.
51. Ibid.
52. WhatsApp message sent by Nafiz Modack to the author on 7 November 2018 and again on 6 December 2018.
53. WhatsApp message sent from Peter Mihalik to the author on 7 June 2018.
54. Ibid.
55. Alwyn Landman, the man Mark Lifman had invited to be involved in starting up a new security company after SPS was found to be operating

illegally (but who denied having been involved with Lifman), was also a pallbearer at Mihalik's funeral.

56 Phakgadi, P (2019) 'Controversial businessman Mark Lifman escapes alleged hit', News24, 4 February https://www.news24.com/SouthAfrica/News/controversial-businessman-mark-lifman-escapes-alleged-hit-20190204 Accessed 5 February 2019.

CHAPTER 10   *Friends in high places*

1 WhatsApp from Mark Lifman on 30 May 2018, in response to a question the author sent him about his possible connections to police officers.

2 Dolley, C (2018) 'Jerome "Donkie" Booysen – "Gangsterism is not the way to go"', News24, 1 June https://www.news24.com/SouthAfrica/News/exclusive-jerome-donkie-booysen-gangsterism-is-not-the-way-to-go-20180601 Accessed 25 January 2019.

3 In a recording of the 3 May 2017 meeting between Nafiz Modack, Jeremy Vearey and former State Security Agency official Russel Christopher, Modack had, according to Lieutenant Colonel Charl Kinnear, effectively claimed (using only their surnames) that police major generals Patrick Mbotho and Mzwandile Tiyo were looking out for him. Kinnear referred to the recording during the extortion-case bail application of Nafiz Modack and four co-accused that stretched from December 2017 to the end of February 2018 in the Cape Town Magistrate's Court.

4 A signed copy of her complaint, which was not dated and which did not say where it was made, was provided to the author by a source on 8 February 2019. See also Thamm, M (2019) 'Sexual offences unit head tells Cele of bullying and humiliation by senior officer', *Daily Maverick*, 7 February https://www.dailymaverick.co.za/article/2019-02-07-sexual-offences-unit-head-tells-cele-of-bullying-and-humiliation-by-senior-officer/ Accessed 24 February 2019.

5 Dolley, C (2018) 'REVEALED: Court hears identities of "high-ranking" cops allegedly working with underworld figure Modack', News24, 2 January https://www.news24.com/SouthAfrica/News/revealed-court-hears-identities-of-high-ranking-cops-allegedly-working-with-underworld-figure-modack-20180102 Accessed 24 February 2019.

6 Lieutenant Colonel Charl Kinnear testified about a recording of a cellphone conversation between Nafiz Modack and George Darmanović (it wasn't clear who recorded the conversation, or why and when it was recorded) in the Cape Town Magistrate's Court on 3 January 2018 in an extortion-case bail application, case number 16/818/2017, launched by Nafiz Modack and four co-accused.

Notes

7 Ibid.

8 Testimony of Lieutenant Colonel Charl Kinnear in the Cape Town Magistrate's Court on 1 February 2018 in an extortion-case bail application, case number 16/818/2017, launched by Nafiz Modack and four co-accused in the Cape Town Magistrate's Court. State prosecutor Esna Erasmus said a couple of weeks later (on 14 February) that the defence's bringing up of these details about Kinnear's son had been uncalled for. See Dolley, C (2018) 'Testimony about advocate shouldn't have surfaced - Modack prosecutor', News24, 14 February https://www.news24.com/SouthAfrica/News/testimony-about-advocate-shouldnt-have-surfaced-modack-prosecutor-20180214 Accessed 22 February 2019.

9 Dolley, C (2017) 'Hawks arrest Cape Town law enforcement officer with "gang-linked" mandrax', News24, 8 November https://www.news24.com/SouthAfrica/News/hawks-arrest-cape-town-law-enforcement-officer-found-with-gang-linked-mandrax-20171108 Accessed 28 February 2019.

10 Argument by attorney Bruce Hendricks in the Cape Town Magistrate's Court on 24 January 2018 in an extortion-case bail application, case number 16/818/2017, against Nafiz Modack and four co-accused.

11 Affidavit by Grant Veroni dated 12 January 2018 and stamped at the Goodwood police's community service centre. Veroni's affidavit outlined allegations that Mark Lifman knew about police matters (that Veroni was going to be arrested), and this affidavit was used in an extortion-case bail application, case number 16/818/2017, against Nafiz Modack and four co-accused.

12 Argument by attorney Bruce Hendricks in the Cape Town Magistrate's Court on 24 January 2018 in an extortion-case bail application, case number 16/818/2017, launched by Nafiz Modack and his four co-accused.

13 Testimony by Lieutenant Colonel Charl Kinnear in the Cape Town Magistrate's Court on 26 January 2018 during an extortion-case bail application, case number 16/818/2017, launched by Nafiz Modack and four co-accused in the Cape Town Magistrate's Court.

14 William Booth provided these details to the author, for an article she was writing for the amaBhungane Centre for Investigative Journalism, on 27 February 2019.

15 Etheridge, J (2018) 'Police search, seize fancy cars of Modack clan', News24, 5 April https://www.news24.com/SouthAfrica/News/police-search-seize-fancy-cars-of-modack-clan-20180405 Accessed 25 January 2019.

16 A source told the author about these arrests; the arrests were confirmed by police, and the author attended the first appearance of the accused in the Wynberg Magistrate's Court on 14 March 2018.

17 Letter dated 20 December 2018 from Lieutenant Colonel Charl Kinnear to several senior police officers, including Western Cape commissioner Khombinkosi Jula, detailing an array of claims against other police officers in the Western Cape.

18 Letter dated 20 December 2018 from Lieutenant Colonel Charl Kinnear to several senior police officers, including Western Cape commissioner Khombinkosi Jula, detailing an array of claims against other police officers in the Western Cape; and Dolley, C and Sole, S (2019) 'SAPS Wars Part 1: The blurry blue line between the cops and the Cape underworld', amaBhungane https://amabhungane.org/stories/saps-wars-part-1-the-blurry-blue-line-between-the-cops-and-the-cape-underworld/ Accessed 11 March 2019.

19 Ibid.

20 Letter dated 20 December 2018 from Lieutenant Colonel Charl Kinnear to several senior police officers, including Western Cape commissioner Khombinkosi Jula, detailing an array of claims against other police officers in the Western Cape.

21 Ibid.

22 Booysen, C (2019) 'Top cop Vearey slams "smear campaign" against him, other officers', *Cape Times*, 8 January https://www.iol.co.za/capetimes/news/top-cop-vearey-slams-smear-campaign-against-him-other-officers-18731911 Accessed 10 March 2019.

23 Ibid.

24 Letter dated 18 January 2019 from Lieutenant General Peter Jacobs to colleagues including national police commissioner Khehla Sitole in response to a complaint dated 20 December 2018 from Lieutenant Colonel Charl Kinnear detailing an array of claims against other police officers.

25 Testimony by Radley Dijkers in the Cape Town Regional Court on 16 April 2019 in the bail application case number 16/818/2017 launched by Nafiz Modack and four co-accused.

CHAPTER 11 *Legacy does not die*

1 Personal communication with a confidential source in Cape Town on 20 February 2018.

2 Stratcom was an apartheid propaganda operation run by the security police.

3 Merten, M (2018) 'Parliament: IPID says SAPS corruption is SA's biggest

national security threat', *Daily Maverick*, 29 March https://www.dailymaverick.co.za/article/2018-03-29-parliament-ipid-throws-shade-saying-saps-corruption-is-sas-biggest-national-security-threat/#.Wv6aWEiFPIU Accessed 30 January 2019.

4   Mthetheleli Mackay, M (1999) 'Beeka used Moroccans for attacks: Police', IOL, 7 October https://www.iol.co.za/news/south-africa/beeka-used-morrocans-for-attacks-police-15469 Accessed 30 January 2019.

5   Testimony by Sergeant Edward Edwardes in the Cape Town Regional Court on 1 December 2017 in the bail application of Grant Veroni on 30 November 2017.

6   Statement by Warrant Officer Vincent Saunders of the Gauteng provincial investigation unit, dated 22 January 2018 and signed in Cape Town, used by the state in the extortion-case bail application, case number 16/818/2017, against Nafiz Modack and four co-accused in the Cape Town Magistrate's Court.

Acknowledgements

Thank you, Mummy and Daddy (or, as others call them, Beverley and Larry Dolley), for putting me through school while I put you through my stubbornness, and for letting me pursue the journalism and writing path; and thank you, Michelle Dolley, for wisely not pursuing this path and thus allowing me to flop, belly first, into this unknown.

Larry C, you have unfalteringly backed me even when you had no reason to, dealing with the moods and exhaustion that emanated from this book and related work. Thank you for being there, for sticking by me and for accepting the very worst and best of me. I will strive to be the person you are to me.

Aunty Val, thank you for having Larry and not just Lance. Wise move. And Lance, thank you for being Larry's go-to person, even though you're a dog person.

Biddy, John (aka Mr Mouseling) and my three wonderful cousins, thank you for bringing much laughter to many a situation.

Miriam and Lauren, I wouldn't have got through this (and general life) without you; I might also have starved on certain days if it hadn't been for you two. This much is fact.

Allie, where do I start? So many thankyous to you, Allie.

Lynne and Daryl, Khulekani, Justin, you have buoyed me with your great personalities and weirdly wonderful humour.

The person with the ear (just the one; the other is, after all, ornamental), thank you for pointing out two paths.

Haloumi, my ginger boy, you're the greatest soul encased in a kitty shape and always make everything feel a little better.

To the person whose emoji smirk annoyed me terribly, thank you.

Yet another gratitude-filled thanks to the person who said 'never say never'.

To the security gents who monitored and looked after me, thank you, especially 'Bruce Willis', who cared beyond the necessary.

My colleagues in the newsrooms, both present and previous, thank you for being at my side and always encouraging me. Tony W and Sybs, you've helped me shape many an intro in many an article.

Ahmed, thank you for dealing, with such grace and apparent calm, with a part of my career and life I never want to relive. Adriaan, thank you for the push to get typing. Sam Sole and Stefaans, thank you for enabling me to experience another realm of journalism.

I've worked with and for amazingly strong women: Alide, Janet, Chiara, Di, Mel, Sam B, A'Eysha, Monica, Hanlie, Fatima, Michelle, Leila, Zara and Lizel S (to name a few), I will forever be grateful to you.

To the wonderful journalists and photographers with whom I've shared court benches and pavements, thank you for keeping it real when it's often surreal.

To the police officers, attorneys and advocates, prosecutors, spokespersons and businessmen, thank you for sharing your viewpoints with me, even when they were critical: I appreciate your trying to get me to see things from your perspective.

Acknowledgements

To the car guards around the Cape Town courts and the court orderlies, thank you for always having a quirky quip to brighten the day.

Jeremy Boraine of Jonathan Ball Publishers and Ester Levinrad, thank you for taking a chance on me. And thank you to Tracey Hawthorne, whose editing ironed out extremely tired and creased thoughts – what your notes and words have taught me is invaluable way beyond these pages.

Finally, thank you to everyone who gave of their time, no matter how little.

Index

Page numbers in *italics* refer to photographs.

26s gang 62, 101, 123, 144
27s gang 58, 68, 83, 136, 144, 147, 158–160
28s gang
  background of 59–63
  Mobsters faction 59, 122, 158
  nightclub-security industry 58, 158
  Project Impi 86, 88
  Sexy Boys gang and 61, 101
  suspected members of 68, 93, 103, 110–111, 115, 123, 152–153, 158, 160, 176
  turf lines 75

A

abalone poaching *see* perlemoen poaching
Absa bank 169
Adams, Cheslyn 160
African National Congress (ANC)
  anti-gang unit 26
  claims against 115–117
  DA and 26, 58, 116, 120, 122, 124–125
  intelligence operatives 15, 17, 24, 34, 70–74
  national key points 11
Agliotti, Glen 41
Alexander, Brian 64–65
America 153
American Secret Service 22
Americans gang 33, 56, 57
ANC *see* African National Congress
anti-gang unit, police 26–27, 178
apartheid, legacy of 10–21, 24–27, 72–74, 77, 122, 178, 192–194
Arkan *see* Raznatovic, Zeljko
auction of properties belonging to Nafiz Modack 1–3, 129–132, 153, 180, 185

B

Back Street Kids gang 61–63
Barkhuizen, Michael 149
Barnard, Ferdinand 'Ferdi' 12–16, 27
Barras, Raymond 'Razor' 128–129
Beeka, Cyril William Paul
  allegations of crime 39–40, 47
  background of 33–34
  Jacques Cronje and 44, 168
  death of 7, 48–50, 53, 96, 103
  funeral of 48
  Dobrosav Gavric and 52–53, 172
  Hard Livings gang 58
  Hemingways (club) 18
  'Lolly' Jackson and 45
  Nafiz Modack and 30
  Pro Access 36, 39–40, 95
  Pro Security 34–36
  at RAM Couriers 40
  Moe Shaik and 42–43
  Special Presidential Investigative Task Unit 20–21, 23
  Pierre Theron and 118
  Yuri Ulianitski and 42
  Waterfront bombings 39
Beerhouse 105–106
Belhar 61–62, 64, 68, 77, 112, 122, 156, 177
Belhar rugby club 65
Bellville South 61
Bellville South police station 155–156
Bishop Lavis 26–27, 60, 75, 77, 120, 134
Blue Downs 110, 122
bomb explosions 39
Bonteheuwel 132
Booth, William 46, 186
Booysen, Colin 66
  arrest of 165, 187
  attacks on 101

at auctions 108, 130
background of 66–67
Jerome Booysen and 67–68, 158–159
Desai killing 147
Kanyona killing 107
Mathieson killing 110
Pete Mihalik and 180
nightclub-security industry 7, 47, 59, 96–98, 130, 133–134, 161
Pietersen killing 177–178
Igor Russol and 168
Booysen, Jerome 'Donkie' 65
  attacks on 101, 144, 156, 158–159, 171, 175–176
  background of 65–66
  Cyril Beeka and 47–48
  Colin Booysen and 67–68
  Core 63
  denials of 181
  Noorudien Hassan and 82
  Charl Kinnear and 184
  Mark Lifman and 108–109
  nightclub-security industry 7, 47–48, 59, 97, 133–134, 158, 168
  Dan Plato and 112
  raid of house 145–146
  SARS and 104
  Sexy Boys gang 59, 65
Booysen, Llewellyn (Percy) 63
Booysen, Michael 63, 68
Booysen family 166
Bosnian Muslims 51
bouncers 7–8, 10–14
Brackenfell police station 149–150
Bree Street 11, 161–162
Breet, Matthew Broderick 136, 159–160
Breet, Sheldon Jaret 159
Breytenbach, Glynnis 173
Brown, Hampshire 'Hempies' 170
Brown, Wendy 170

C
cabinet reshuffle 92
Café Caprice, shooting at 137, 140
Cape Town central police station 11–12, 26–27
Cape Town International Airport, shooting at 158–159
Cape Town's central business district (CBD) 7, 11–12, 32–33, 58
Carnilinx 109
cars, stolen 122
CCB *see* Civil Cooperation Bureau
Cele, Bheki 92, 182
cellphone communications, intercepting of 187, 188
Central Firearms Registry, Pretoria 86, 93
Centre for the Study of Violence and Reconciliation 38
Charles, Morne 101
child victims 77
Choudhry, businessman known as 7, 109–110, 137
Christopher, Russel 142–143
cigarettes *see* tobacco industry
City Press 89
Civil Cooperation Bureau (CCB) 12–13, 33, 56
Club 31 138
Club Wendy's 170
cocaine 13, 50, 99, 116, 119, 146
Coco (nightclub) 144
'code' among gang members 67
Coetzee, Dirk 34, 35, 39
commissions of inquiry 195–196
Community Outreach (Core) 63, 100–101
Community Outreach II (Core II) 64
complicated nature of crime 8–9, 28–30, 191–193
Congolese community 163–164
contract killers 6, 55, 59, 154, 157
Core *see* Community Outreach
Core II *see* Community Outreach II
Cosa Nostra 18, 35
counterfeiting 22
court cases 195
Crime Intelligence 29, 82–83, 92–93, 106, 132, 136, 159, 170, 174, 188–189
Cronje, Jacques
  arrests of 37, 146, 165, 187

background of 36
bail hearing 181
Cyril Beeka and 35–36, 44, 168
charges against 186–187
nightclub-security industry 35–36, 43–44, 47, 95–99, 133–134, 139, 151–152, 161, 163
Saigon Bar incident 39–40
crystal methamphetamine (tik) 28
Cubana, Green Point 163, 186
Cubana, Stellenbosch 158
Culemborg 76
Cupido, Fabian 159, 160

D
DA *see* Democratic Alliance
Dalton, James 48
Darmanović, George 'The Butcher' 43, 114, 119, 172–175, 184
Davids, Igshaan 113
Davids, Leon 'Lyons' 96, 103
De Kock, Rodney 118
Democratic Alliance (DA) 26, 58, 113, 122
Department of Intelligence and Security 24, 71
Desai, Marwaan 'Dinky' 147, 159
Dijkers, Radley 135, 167
Directorate for Priority Crime Investigation *see* Hawks
Directorate of Covert Collection 12–13
District Six 56–57
Dixie Boys gang 56, 61–63
Djuricic, Milan 51, 172–173
dogs 34, 142
Dramat, Anwa 173–174
drug trafficking
cocaine 13, 50, 99, 116, 119, 146
crystal methamphetamine (tik) 28
gangsterism and 54, 144, 158
from India 63
in Johannesburg 10, 12
mandrax 60, 63, 184
Mobsters faction 122
police and 120–121
prostitution and 116

sniffer dogs 142
suspected persons involved with 33, 47, 159, 177
Villiersdorp farm 146–147
Dube, Brian 141

E
Eagle Eye Solutions Technology 120
Eagle VIP Security 139–140, 144, 148, 161, 182–183
Eastern Cape 55
Eastwoods Entertainment Lounge 105
Ebrahim, Abdus Salaam 38, 39, 80–81
Edwardes, Edward 128, 157
Eksteen, Lutfie 75
Electronic Communications Act 120
electronic gadgets 119–120, 187
Elsies River 70, 77, 87
Embassy, The (club) 108, 140–141
Emperors Palace Casino 154–155
Erasmus, Esna 170
Erasmus, Hennie 61–62
Eyssen, Shamiel 134

F
Falanga, Pitchou 163, 186
Fall, Muktar 40
Fancy Boys gang 134
Faure, police armoury in 37
fear 195
Fields, Ashley 106–107, 110, 165, 181, 187
Fields, Ashley, brother of 177
firearms
auction of properties belonging to Nafiz Modack 153
cache in Kraaifontein 159–160
Eagle VIP Security 139–140, 144, 148, 182–183
Faure armoury 37
legislation 85
licences 77, 86, 93, 128, 149
Makarov pistol 56
Mobsters faction 122
Project Impi 75–93, 155–156, 188
R5 rifles 155–156

TSG 139–140, 144, 148–149, 182–183
Firearms Control Act 147
Firm, The 62–63, 101
Fivaz, George 19, 21–22
Flash unit 147
forced removals 56–58
Franciscus, Jeffrey 114–116, 122
Fransman, Marius 115
Fraser, Arthur 25–26

G
gangsterism 6–7, 33, 37, 54–68, 75–93, 192–193
Gavric, Dobrosav 47–48, 50–53, 172–173
'Gifteds' *see* Young Gifted Sexy Bastards gang
Gold Father, The 49
Gordhan, Pravin 108
Gordon, Edward 'Peaches' 56
Goss, Greg, Junior 87–88
Goss, Gregory 87–88
'grabbers' 119–120
Grand, The (club) 151–152, 186
Grand Africa Café and Beach 100, 135, 161, 165, 167, 183–184
grenades 145, 159
Grobler, Edwin 170–171
Group Areas Act 56
guns *see* firearms
Gupta family 50, 89

H
handlers 19–20
Hardien, Isgak 56
Hard Livings gang 33, 57–58, 68, 82, 102, 106, 176
Harri, Sonja 182
Hassan, Noorudien 81–83, 109, 168
Hawks
    auction of properties belonging to Nafiz Modack 130
    Beeka's murder 42–43, 48
    head of 182
    Mentor's statement 89

nightclub-security industry 31, 58–59, 67, 107, 128, 133, 136–137, 139, 145, 147, 149
weapons cache 159
Western Cape Director of Public Prosecutions 118
Haysom, Simone 10, 12
Hells Angels biking group 48
Hemingways (club) 18
Hendricks, Bruce 169, 184–185
Hendricks, Sylvano (Queeny Madikizela-Malema) 123–124
Heroldt, Neville *see* Lonte, Jackie
Hill, Lloyd 113, 115
Hillbrow 10
hitmen *see* contract killers
Hong Laing Wu 40
horseracing 96
Hotel 303 109–110

I
Iconic Lounge 134, 161, 169
Idas, Jason 68
IMSI catcher 119–120
Independent Police Investigative Directorate (Ipid) 189
India 63
informants 8–9, 13, 30
inspectors 127–128
international mobile subscriber identity (IMSI) catcher 119–120
international reach of crime 55, 192–193
Ipid *see* Independent Police Investigative Directorate
Ipupa N'simba, Fally 164
Issa, Sam 104, 119
Italy 18

J
Jackson, Emmanuel 'Lolly' 44–45, 50, 152
Jacobs, Donovan 158
Jacobs, Peter 9, 16, 76–79, 84–86, 88–94, 91, 111, 166, 188, 190
Jacobs, Russel 110–111, 122
Janse Viljoen, Peter 30, 31, 133–134

261

Jeftha, Althea 139–140, 161, 170–171
Jockey Club of South Africa 96
Johannesburg 10, 12, 45, 101–102, 151–155
John, Saliem 103
Jordan, Pallo 18
Jula, Khombinkosi 84, 90, 140, 145

K
Kabila, Joseph 163–164
Kanyona, Joe Louis Kazadi 105–107
Kebble, Brett 12, 41, 128
Kinnear, Charl 165, 167–171, 183–185, *183*, 187–190
Knipe, Leonard 23
Koordom, McNolan 122
Kraaifontein, weapons cache found in 159
Krejčíř, Radovan 6, *44*, 45–47, 49–50, 102, 104, 117–119, 132, 152, 177
Kuils River 122, 176
Kulic, Darko 175
KwaZulu-Natal 55

L
Laher, Irshaad 'Hunter' 79–82, *81*, 84, 188
Lakay, Carl 135, 165, 176–177, 187
Landman, Alwyn 100
Lavender Hill 57, 64
legacies 192–197
Leisure and Lifestyle Security 135
Lentegeur police station 93
Levendal, Chad 146
Lifestyle Entertainment Services 100
Lifman, Mark Roy *46*
    arrest of 185–186, 188
    attacks on 180
    auction of properties belonging to Nafiz Modack 1–3, 129–131
    Cyril Beeka and 50
    George Darmanović and 174–175
    nightclub-security industry 7, 47, 59, 95–100, 107, 110, 133–134, 146–147, 168–169
    Dan Plato and 112
    police and 181–182, 184–185
    SARS and 104, 107–109
    Yuri Ulianitski and 42, 141
    Brian Wainstein and 153–154, 159
    at Zuma's birthday rally 114
'Lifman group' 67, 130, 133–134, 136–137, 140, 145, 160, 162
Lincoln, Andre 9, 16–27, *18*, 35, 72–74, 166, 178, 189–191
Loevenstein 67, 155
Long Street 5–6, 11, 106, 134, 161
Lonte, Jackie (Neville Heroldt) 33, 56
Loop Street 11, 144, 161
Louca, George 45

M
Mabasa, Joey 45
Macassar 122
Madikizela-Malema, Queeny (Sylvano Hendricks) 123–124
Madonsela, Thuli 124
Mail&Guardian 21
Major Offences Reaction Team 26–27
Malan, Magnus 12
Mandela, Nelson 19, 22–23, 71, 73, 113–114
mandrax 60, 63, 184
Manenberg 57–58, 75, 77, 102, 156
Marikana massacre 88
Marinus, Quinton 'Mr Big' 113
Martins, Albern 63, 64, 100–101
Mathieson, Craig 109–110
Mavericks 11, 132–133, 138–140, 144, 148, 180
Mazzotti, Adriano 109
Mbalula, Fikile 29, 92, 155
Mbeki, Thabo 19, 35, 113–114
Mbotho, Patrick 78, 142, 182
McBride, Robert 39, 194
McGurk, Nigel 41
McKenna, Mayon 141–142
Mdluli, Richard 173, 174
Mentor, Vytjie 88–92
Mgwenya, Bonang Christina 90
Mihalik, Pete *62*, 82, 133, 153, 178–180, *179*

Index

Mihaljevic, George (Hollywood George) 177
militarisation of security companies 10–11, 129–130
Miller, Andy 20–21
Milošević, Marko 51
Milošević, Slobodan 51
misinformation 178, 190–191, 193
Mitchells Plain 26–27, 61, 93, 155–156, 171
MK *see* umKhonto weSizwe
Mobsters (faction of 28s gang) 59, 122, 158
Modack, Nafiz 29, *131*
    arrests of 163, *164*, 165, 186–187
    auction of properties belonging to 1–3, 129–131, 185
    background of 132
    bail application 165–171, 177–178, 181–183, 187–188
    Cyril Beeka and 48–49
    nightclub-security industry 7, 30–31, 59, 67, 131–134, 137, 139, 142–144, 151–155, 158–165, 187
    raid of house 149–150
    Risimati Shivuri and 143–144, *143*, 182–183
    Jeremy Vearey and 83, 109, 165, 184
'Modack group' 133–134, 136, 139, 145, 156, 163, 185
Mohamed, Shaheem 147
Mokotedi, Prince 31
MoneyPoint 49
Montgomery, Percy 48
Moroccan men 35, 40, 97
Morreira, Jennifer 39
Moses, Nathaniel 122–123, 126
Motsuenyane Commission 73
movie industry 102
Muller, Nicole 158
Myburg, Ruben 40

N
Naidoo, Colonel 80
Naidoo, Kishor 'Kamaal' 67, 133–134, 160

National Intelligence Agency (now State Security Agency) 43, 74
National Intelligence Coordinating Committee 17
National Key Points Act 11
National Party 19, 193
National Prosecuting Authority 174
national security 11–14
Naude, Andre *98*
    attacks on 105, 152
    auction of properties belonging to Nafiz Modack 131
    nightclub-security industry 7, 47, 59, 95–97, 99–100, 107, 133–134, 168, 186
    raid of house 155
    SARS and 104
News24 website 91
Nhleko, Nathi 173–174
nightclub-security industry 5–6, 10–14, 58–59, 65, 95–100, 112–113, 133–134, 192–193, 196
Nkandla homestead 174
Nortje, Jan 'The Giant' 105
Ntlemeza, Berning 89
'Nuremberg' situation 73

O
Omar, Dullah 56
One&Only hotel 30–31, 143–144, *143*, 168, 183
Ontong, Clive 84–85, 188
Operation Combat 75, 149
Operation Honey Badger 109
Operation Intrigue 19–25, 194
Operation Slasher 71–75, 78, 194
Orrie, Haroon 82

P
Pagad *see* People Against Gangsterism and Drugs
Palazzolo, Vito Roberto 18–20, *20*, 23–25, 27, 30
Parliament 12, 55, 194
Parow 1–3, 129–131
Parow police station 150

263

People Against Gangsterism and Drugs
  (Pagad) 37–39, 56, 63, 80–82
perceptions 190–191
perlemoen (abalone) poaching 28,
  110–111, 158, 173
Phahlane, Khomotso 90
Phillips, Andrew 152
Phiyega, Riah 84, 88
'PI8' 27
Pietersen, Adrian 177
Pillay, Ivan 104
Pinelands 147
Planet Hollywood 39
Plato, Daniel 'Dan' 112–113, *114*,
  115–118, 123–126, 188
Plattekloof 132, 149–150, 168, 169
Plum, Patrick 40
police *see* South African Police Service
Police and Prisons Civil Rights Union
  79
politics 7, 8, 12, 15–18, 24–27, 56–58,
  88–91, 192–193
Pollsmoor Prison 165, 169
Potelwa, Novela 27
Potiska, Milosh 50
power dynamics 7–8
PPA Security 100
Prinsloo, Christiaan Lodewyk 79–80, 83,
  85, 90
prison system 64
private security industry 11, 127–128,
  196
see also nightclub-security industry
Private Security Industry Regulatory
  Authority (PSIRA) 36, 99, 127–128,
  148, 161
Pro Access 36, 39–40, 42, 43–44, 95–97
Professional Protection Services 95–97
Project Impi 76–82, 84–93, 126, 142,
  155, 188, 194
Project Ogies 111
Pro Security 34, 35
prostitution 13, 15, 27, 54
PSIRA *see* Private Security Industry
  Regulatory Authority
Public Protector 118, 124

Q
Queeny *see* Madikizela-Malema, Queeny

R
Ramaphosa, Cyril 26, 92
Ramatlakane, Leonard 74
RAM Couriers 40
Ravensmead 142, 144
Raves, Alan 79–81
Raznatovic, Zeljko (Arkan) 50–53, 172
Red (gang leader) 83
Reucker, Olaf 39
Richards, Frans 114
Richwood 129–130
Robben Island prison 70, 76
rogue units 21–22, 29, 93, 108–109, 141,
  190–191
Russol, Igor 'the other Russian' 41–42,
  146, 167–169

S
SADF *see* South African Defence Force
SA Hunters Association 79
Saigon Bar 39–40
Sailor, man known as 49
Salt River 38, 106, 177
SAP *see* South African Police
SAPS *see* South African Police Service
SARS *see* South African Revenue Service
Scheepers, Paul 119–121, 173
Schultz, Mikey 41
Scorpions 40, 173
Security Branch, SAP 17, 21, 24, 34, 43,
  72–74
Security Officers Board 36
Selebi, Jackie 41
Serbia 19, 49, 50–52, 172–175, 177
Sexwale, Tokyo, children of 36
sex workers *see* prostitution
Sexy Boys gang 58–59, 61–62, 65, 67–68,
  96–98, 101, 103, 112, 156, 177
Shaik, Moe 42–43
Shaw, Mark 10, 12
Shimmy Beach Club 100
Shivuri, Risimati 31, 143–144, *143*, 183
Sikhakhane Report 109

Index

Sitole, Khehla 29
Slasher unit 71–75, 78, 194
Smit, Jean-Cora 118
Smit, Robert 118
Smith, Faizel 'Kappie' 41, 128
'snitching' 67, 195
Solomon, Ernie 'Lastig' 63–64, 101
South African Defence Force (SADF) 11
South African Heritage Resource Agency 79
South African Police (SAP), Security Branch 17, 21, 24, 34, 43, 72–74
South African Police Service (SAPS)
   anti-gang unit 26–27, 178
   armoury in Faure 37
   Cape Town central police station 11–12, 26–27
   corruption in 7–8, 14, 113–114, 179, 181–191, 194–195
   friction in 15–18, 72–74, 76–78, 188, 193–194
   gangsterism and 55–57
   informants 102, 159
   national intervention unit 145
   nightclub-security industry 58–59, 133, 136, *138*, 139, 145–146, 149–150
   Project Impi 76–82, 84–93, 126, 142, 155, 188, 194
   Slasher unit 71–75, 78, 194
   special task force 145
   TSG 129–130
South African Police Union 20–21, 26
South African Revenue Service (SARS) 21–22, 104, 107–109
Special Branch *see* Security Branch, SAP
Specialised Protection Services (SPS) 36, 96–99, 105, 107, 127
Special Presidential Investigative Task Unit 19–25
Spoilt Bratz gang 160
SPS *see* Specialised Protection Services
Spur restaurant 175–176
Staggie, Rashaad 37–38
Staggie, Rashied 18, 20, 33, 37–38, *38*, 58, 63–64, 68, 102, 176

Stanfield, Colin 60–63, 68, 117
Stanfield, Francisca 86–87
Stanfield, Nicole 86–87
Stanfield, Ralph 6, 60–61, *62*, 68, 82, 86–88, 93, 152–153, 159, 180
Stankovic, Dejan 175
Stankovic, Vojin 175
state capture 16, 23, 89, 109
state informants *see* informants
state officials 8–9, 19, 117, 194–195
State Security Agency 141, 170
Stellenbosch 158
steroid trade, illegal 28, 116, 152–153, 159
Stratcom 193
Sunday Times 114

T

Taleb, Houssain (Houssain Moroccan) 20, 42, 97, 99, 105–106, 156–157
taxi industry 63, 66–67, 142
Teazers 44–45
Theron, Pierre (Jason) 117–119
The Security Group (TSG) 129–130, 135, 137, 139, 144, 147–149, 156–157, 161, 164–165, 167, 182–183
Thomas, George 'Geweld' 59–60, 111
tik (crystal methamphetamine) 28
Titus, Detective 87
Tiyo, Mzwandile 78, 89–90, 142, 163, 182
tobacco industry 28, 54, 109, 134
Truth and Reconciliation Commission 12–16, 27
TSG *see* The Security Group
turf lines 55, 58–59, 122, 133–134, 137, 158
26s gang 62, 101, 123, 144
27s gang 58, 68, 83, 136, 144, 147, 158–160
28s gang
   background of 59–63
   Mobsters faction 59, 122, 158
   nightclub-security industry 58, 158
   Project Impi 86, 88
   Sexy Boys gang and 61, 101

265

suspected members of 68, 93, 103, 110–111, 115, 123, 152–153, 158, 160, 176
turf lines 75

U
Ulianitski, Irina 41, 108, 141
Ulianitski, Yulia 41
Ulianitski, Yuri 'the Russian' 6, 20, 35, 41–42, 107, 141
umKhonto weSizwe (MK) 15–16, 17–18, 27, 48, 70, 76, 173
United States of America (USA) 22, 153
Unuvar, Bora 105
USA *see* United States of America

V
Valhalla Park 60–61, 103
Van Lill, Jacques 147–148
Van Zyl, Abram 'Slang' 55–56
Van Zyl, Richard 97, 100
Vearey, Jeremy Alan 70, *91*
    background of 69–71
    Cyril Beeka and 34
    claims against 9, 16, 69–70, 92, 111, 115–118, 121, 123–126, 176, 188–190
    George Darmanović and 173–174
    on friction in police 24
    gangsterism 68, 83, 102
    Nafiz Modack and 109, 142–143, 165–166, 170, 184
    Dan Plato and 113
    Project Impi 76–79, 84–85, 88–89, 92, 94, 126
    Slasher unit 71–74
    Ralph Stanfield and 87
    Mathys Visser and 140
vehicles, stolen 122
Venter, Neels 18
Veroni, Grant 135, 137, 148–149, 161, 185

Villiersdorp 146–147
violence 9, 14, 28–29, 40–41, 133, 196–197
Visser, Mathys 139–140, 182

W
Wainstein, Brian (Steroid King) 152–154, 159–160, 176
Waldeck, Ivan 63, 101
Walter, Belinda 109
Waterfront, bomb explosions in 39
weapons *see* firearms
Weaver, Tony 24
Webster, David 12
Wecco *see* Western Cape Community Outreach
Western Cape 55
Western Cape Community Outreach (Wecco) 64–65
Western Cape High Court 11–12
Wide Props *see* Pro Access
Williams, Deon 'Igor'/'Iger' 144
Woodstock 106, 134, 176
Worcester 163
Wyngaardt, Pierre Mark Anthony 117, 122, 125

Y
Yester Garrido, Nelson Pablo 118–119
Young Gifted Sexy Bastards gang 106, 110, 134, 176

Z
Zille, Helen 120, 121–122
Zimbabwean suspects, rendition of 173–174
Zouity, Hamid 39–40
Zuma, Duduzane 31, 50, 89, 113
Zuma, Jacob 22, 34, 42, 89, 92, 108, 113–115, 174

CPSIA information can be obtained
at www.ICGtesting.com
Printed in the USA
BVHW081317240619
551810BV00013B/916/P

9 781868 429202